Basics of . . .

Farming

Basics of . . .
Farming

An Introductory Course For Everyday People

CHARLES L. GOODRICH

Bureau of Plant Industry,
US Department of Agriculture

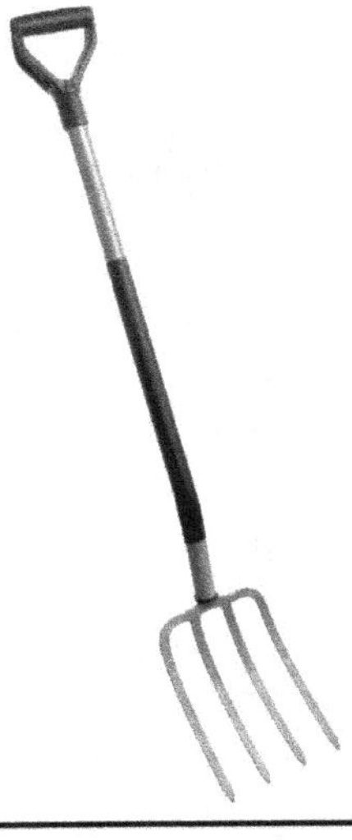

Basics of ...
A Basic Knowledge Imprint of
ABSOLUTELY AMAZING eBOOKS

ABSOLUTELY AMAZING eBOOKS

Published by Whiz Bang LLC, 926 Truman Avenue, Key West, Florida 33040, USA.

For information contact
Publisher@AbsolutelyAmazingEbooks.com

"Columella, the much traveled Spanish-Roman writer of the first century AD, said that for successful farming three things are essential: knowledge, capital, and love for the calling. This statement is just as true today as it was when written 1900 years ago by this early writer on European agriculture."

- *The Young Farmer: Some Things He Should Know*

Basics of . . .

Farming

The Farmer

PREFACE

The most successful farmers are those who work in harmony with the forces and laws of nature that control the growth and development of plants and animals. These men have gained their knowledge of those laws and forces by careful observation, experiment, and study.

This book is a result of the author's search for these facts and truths as a student and farmer, and his endeavor as a teacher to present them in a simple manner to others.

The object in presenting the book to the general public is the hope that it may be of assistance to farmers, students and teachers, in their search for the fundamental truths and principles of farming.

In the first part of the book an attempt has been made

to select the most important principles underlying all agriculture and to present them in the order of their importance, beginning with the most important.

A number of simple experiments have been introduced into the text in the belief that they will make the work more interesting to the general reader, and will aid the farm student in learning to make simple investigations for himself. The author recommends all who use the book to perform the experiments and to make the observations, and so come actively in touch with the work.

The observations begin on the farm. The author considers the plant the central and all-important factor on the farm. And the root is regarded as the most important part of the plant to itself, and consequently to the plant grower.

The general truths that state the conditions necessary for the growth and development of plant roots are regarded as the fundamental principles of all agriculture. These truths are as follows:

The roots of farm plants need for their best growth and development:

- A firm, mellow soil.
- A moist soil.
- A ventilated soil.
- A warm soil.
- A soil supplied with plant food.

The first two chapters lead the reader quickly through logical reasoning to these fundamental truths, on which the remainder of the work is based. A study of soils is made in connection with the root studies, as the two are so closely related.

After the study of roots and soils the other parts of the plant are considered in the order of their importance to the farmer or plant grower. The aim is always to get at the fundamental facts and principles underlying all agricultural and horticultural practice.

In the latter chapters the author takes up the discussion of certain farm operations and practices and their effects on these necessary conditions to root growth and development, and consequently the effect on the fertility of the soil.

The author extends gratitude to all who have in any way assisted in the preparation of this book, whether through advice, preparation of the text, preparation of the illustrations, or any other way in which he has received assistance.

- Charles L. Goodrich
Prince George County,
Maryland,

CONTENTS

PART II

Soil Fertility As Affected By Farm Operations And Farm Practices

THE FARM SCHEME

Farming is no pink tea. It is a serious business. After the young farmer has selected the farm he must develop his farm scheme. He must contemplate well and seriously the philosophy that underlies his plans. Unless he sees clearly what he is striving to attain and unless he understands the effect of his methods, he will fail in great measure to obtain his goal.

Satisfactory results in farming cannot be obtained as a general practice if the man is only interested in the results of a single year. It is not enough that a man shall grow a single large crop, but it is necessary that he continue to grow a satisfactory crop at least at regular intervals.

For example, a piece of land may be adapted to cabbage, celery, potatoes or hay. Assume for the moment it is adapted to cabbage and that by one or more seasons of preparation an enormous crop of cabbages may be secured. This fact is of little value unless sufficient quantity is raised and the process can be repeated annually. Cabbages cannot be grown again on this particular piece of land for from four to six years on account of club root. If the farmer does not have other areas that he can bring into cabbages year after year, for from three to five years, then he becomes a failure as a cabbage raiser.

There are two general questions at the basis of all farm schemes: (1) How to obtain a fairly uniform succession of cash products year after year, and (2) how to keep up or improve the fertility of the soil economically while doing so. In other words, how to keep the investment from decreasing while it is earning a satisfactory and fairly uniform income.

It is necessary, therefore, to consider what products are to be sold and what are simply subsidiary to the cash products. The cash products may, of course, be soil products or animal products, but more likely they will be both. When animals form a large part of the enterprise the cropping system must be carefully adjusted to meet the needs of these animals. Many apparently trivial details must be considered, as for example, whether the cropping system furnishes too little or too much feed or bedding for the livestock.

In considering profits the enterprise as a whole must be kept in view. For example, if a man is producing milk, it may be cheaper, so far as the production of milk is concerned, to allow the liquid excrement to run to waste rather than to arrange for sufficient bedding. If, however, by using an abundance of bedding and saving all the high-priced nitrogen and the larger part of the potash in the manure, he is able to raise twelve tons of silage in place of eight tons, or three tons of hay in place of two tons, his enterprise as a whole will be more profitable when he uses the extra amount of bedding, although so far as the production of a quart of milk is concerned the cost is increased.

Tradeoffs.

Assuming a given type of management, the question is, How much of the required nitrogen will be obtained from the legumes in the cropping system, how much from the manure, and how much must be purchased in commercial fertilizers?

There's more to farming than plowing a field.

- Thomas Forsyth Hunt

Part I

General Principles Underlying Plant Culture

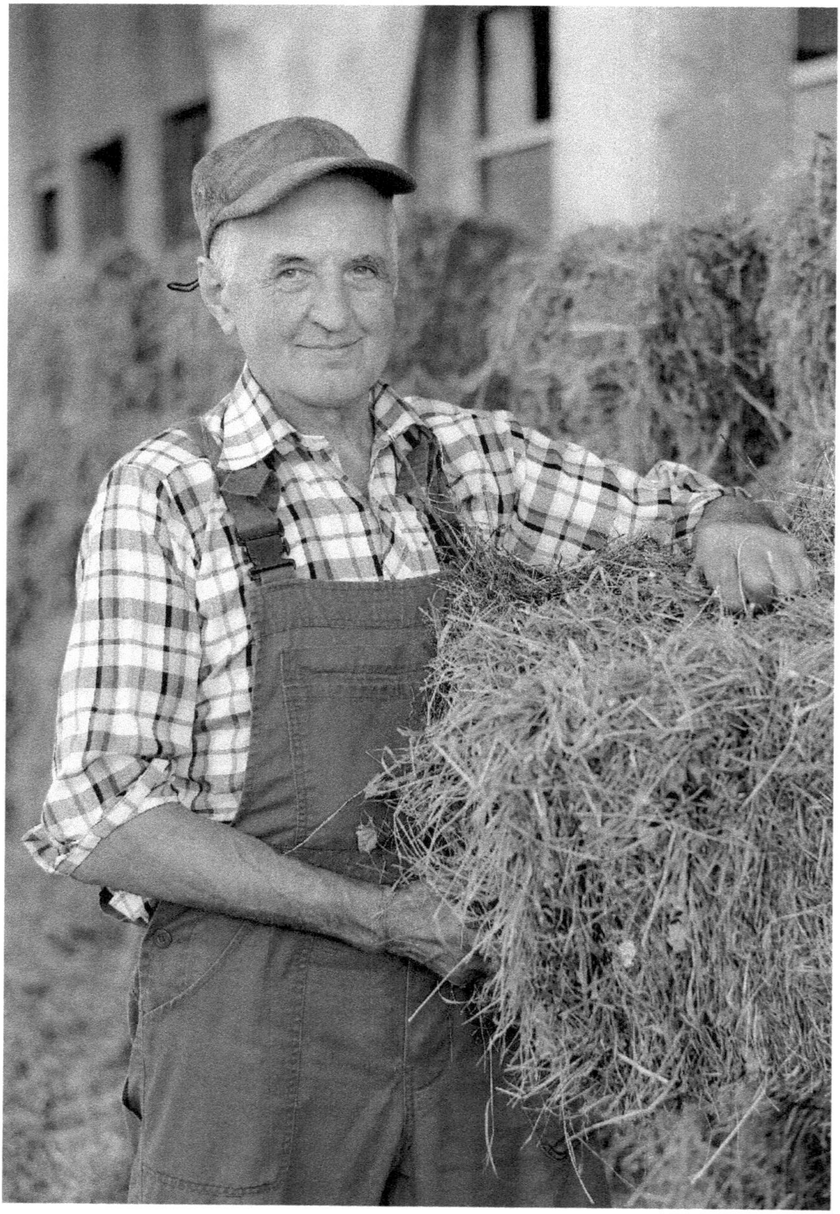

CHAPTER I

Introduction to Plants

Our object in reading and studying this book is to find out some facts that will help those of us who are thinking of going into farming and gardening as a business or recreation to start right, and will also help those of us that are already in the business to make our farms and gardens more productive.

In order to make the book of greatest value to you, I would urge you not only to read and study it, but also to make the excursions suggested and to perform the experiments. In other words, it will be of much greater value to you if you will make the observations and investigations and find out for yourselves the important facts and principles rather than simply take statements of the book unquestioned.

A very good time to begin this work is during the latter part of the summer, when the summer crops are ripening and the fall and winter crops are starting into growth. So suppose we begin our study with a visit to some farm in early September, to bring to mind the many things a farmer works with, the many things he has to think about and know about.

As we approach the farm we will probably see first the farmhouse surrounded by shade trees, perhaps elms or maples, with the barns and other buildings grouped nearby. As we pass up the front walk we notice more or less lawn of neatly clipped grass, with flower beds bordering the walk, or we may find a number of chickens occupying the front yard, and the flowerbeds, placed in red half-barrels, set upon short posts. In the flowerbeds we may find petunias, nasturtiums, geraniums, rose bushes and other flowering plants. Going around the house, we come upon the dairy, with its rack of cans and pans set out for the daily sunning and airing. Nearby is a well with its oaken bucket; at the barn we find the farmer, and he very kindly consents to go with us to answer questions. In the barn and sheds we find wagons, plows, harrows, seed drills, hoes, rakes, scythes and many other tools and machines. Passing on to the fields, we go through the vegetable garden, where are carrots, parsnips, cabbages, beets, celery, sage and many other vegetables and herbs.

On the right, we see a field of corn just ready to harvest, and beyond a field of potatoes. On the left is the orchard, and we are invited to refresh ourselves with juicy apples. In the field beyond the hired man is plowing with a fine team of horses. In the South we would find a field of cotton and one of sweet potatoes, and perhaps sugar cane or peanuts. We have not failed to notice the pigweeds in the cornfield nor the ragweed in the wheat stubble, and many other weeds and grasses in the fence corners.

Perhaps we meet the cows coming from pasture to the stable. All the way we have been trampling on something very important which we will notice on our way back. In this field we find a coarse sandy soil, in the next one a soil that is finer and stiffer. The plow is turning up a reddish soil. In the garden we find the soil quite dark in color.

But these are only a few of the things we have found. If you have used your notebook you will discover that you have long lists of objects which you have noticed, and these may be grouped under the following headings: Animals, Plants, Soils, Buildings, Tools, etc.

The farmer, then, in his work on the farm deals with certain agents, chief among which are Soils, Plants, Animals, Tools and Buildings. Other agents that assist or retard his work according to circumstances are the air, sunlight, heat, moisture, plant food, microscopic organisms called bacteria, etc. These agents are controlled in their relations to one another by certain forces that work according to certain laws and principles of nature. To work intelligently and to obtain the best results the farmer must become familiar with these agents and must work in harmony with the laws and principles that control them.

Let us take up the study of some of these groups of agents, beginning with the most important or central one on the farm.

Which do you think is the most important group? Some will say "tools." The majority will probably say, study the soil first, "because we must work the soil before we can grow good crops." Some few will mention "plants." This last is right. The farm animals are dependent on plants for food. We till or work the soil to produce plants. Plants are living, growing things, and certain requirements or conditions are necessary for their growth and development; we cannot intelligently prepare the soil for plant growth until we know something about the work of plants and the conditions they need to do their work well.

For our first study of plants let us get together a number of farm and garden plants. Say, we have a corn plant, cotton, beet, turnip, carrot, onion, potato, grass, geranium, marigold, pigweed, thistle, or other farm or garden plants. In each case get the entire plant, with as much root as possible. Do these plants in any way resemble one another? All are green, all have roots, all have stems and leaves, some of them have flowers, fruit, and seeds, and the others in time will produce them.

Why does the farmer raise these plants? For food for man and animals; for clothing; for ornamental purposes; for pleasure, etc.

Which part of any or all of these farm plants is of greatest importance to the plant itself?

I am sure that you will agree that the root is the part most important to the plant itself, for if any part of a plant be separated from the root, that part ceases growth and will soon die, unless it is able to put out new roots. But the root from which the plant was cut will generally send up new shoots, unless it has nearly completed its life work. When a slip or cutting is placed in water or in moist sand it makes a root before it continues much in growth. When a seed is planted its first effort is to send a rootlet down into the soil.

Experiment to see if this is true by planting slips of willow, or geranium, or by planting corn or beans in a glass tumbler of soil, or in a box having a glass side, placing the seeds close to the glass; then watch and see what the seed does. Figs. **2 and 3**.

Which of the parts of the plant is of greatest importance to the farmer or any plant grower, or to which part of a plant should the plant grower give his best attention?

Fig. 1. – SPECIMEN PLANTS FOR STUDY.

Fig. 2. The first effort of a sprouting seed is to send a root down into the soil.

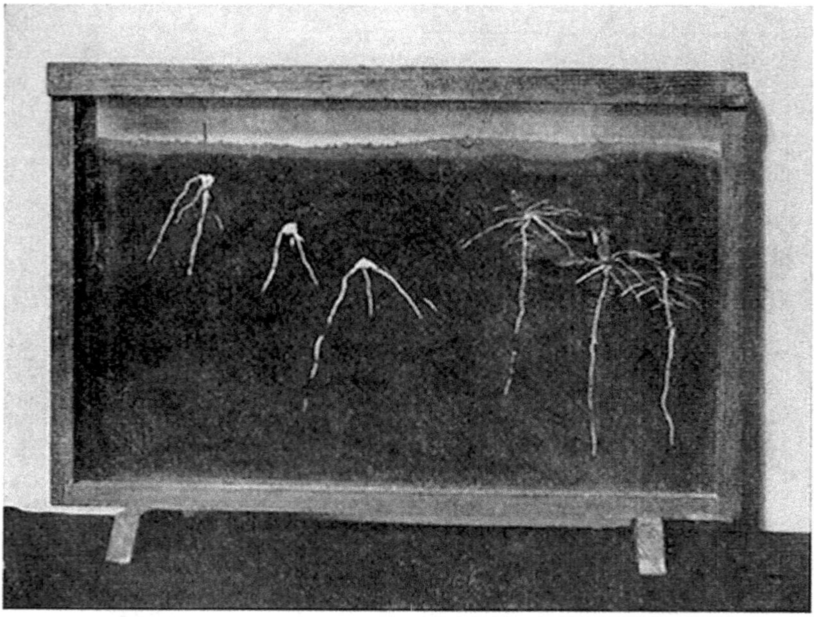

Fig. 3. Germinating seeds produce roots before they send a shoot up into the air.

You will probably mention different parts of the different plants in answering this question. For instance, some will say, "The seed is the most important part of the wheat plant to the farmer, for that is what the wheat is grown for." "The fruit is the most important part of the apple plant for the same reason." "The leaves and grain of the corn, the leaves of the cabbage, are the important parts of these plants and should have the best attention of the grower, because they are the parts for which he grows the plants." But you must remember that all of these parts are dependent on the root for life and growth, as was brought out in the answer to the last question, and that if the farmer or plant grower desires a fine crop of leaves, stems, flowers, fruit or seeds, he must give his very best attention to the root. Judging from the poor way in which many farmers and plant growers prepare the soil for the plants they raise, and the poor way they care for the soil during the growth of the plants, they evidently think least of, and give least attention to, the roots of the plants.

Then, in studying our plants, which part shall we study first? Why, the roots, of course: To find out what they do for the plant, how they do this work, and what conditions are necessary for them to grow and to do their work well.

CHAPTER II

Roots

Of what use are roots to plants, or, what work do they perform for the plants?

If the reader has ever tried to pull up weeds or other plants he will agree that one function of the roots of plants is to hold them firmly in place while they are growing.

Experiment – Pull two plants from the soil, shake them free of earth, and place the roots of one in water and expose the roots of the other to the air. Notice that the plant whose roots are exposed to the air soon wilts, while the one whose roots were placed in water keeps fresh.

You have noticed how a potted plant will wilt if the soil in the pot is allowed to become dry (see **Fig. 4**), or how the leaves of corn and other plants curl up and wither during long periods of dry weather. It is quite evident roots absorb moisture from the soil for the plant.

Experiment – Plant some seeds in tumblers or in boxes filled with sand and in others filled with good garden soil. Keep them well watered and watch their progress for a few weeks (see **Fig. 5**). The plants in the garden soil will grow larger than those in the sand. The roots must get food from the soil and those in the good garden soil get more than those in the poorer sand. Another important function of plant roots then is to take food from the soil for the plant.

You know how thick and fleshy the roots of radishes, beets and turnips are. Well, go into the garden and see if you can find a spring radish or an early turnip that has sent up a flower stalk, blossomed and produced seeds. If you are successful, cut the root in two and notice that instead of being hard and fleshy like the young radish or turnip, it has become hollow, or soft and spongy (see **Fig. 6**). Evidently the hard, fleshy young root was packed with food, which it afterwards gave up to produce flower stalk and seeds.

A fourth use of the root, then, is to store food for the future use of the plant.

Experiment – Plant a sweet potato or place it with the lower end in a tumbler of water and set it in a warm room. Observe it from day to day as it puts out new shoots bearing leaves and roots (see **Fig. 7**).

Break these off and plant them in soil and you have a number of new plants. If you can get the material, repeat this experiment with roots of horseradish, raspberry, blackberry or dahlia. From this we see that it is the work of some roots to produce new plants. This function of roots is made use of in propagating or obtaining new plants of the sweet potato, horseradish, blackberry, raspberry, dahlia and other plants.

We have now learned five important things that roots do for plants, namely:

Roots hold plants firmly in place.

They absorb water from the soil for the plants.

They absorb food from the soil for the plants.

Some roots store food for the future use of the plant.

Some roots produce new plants.

How do the roots do this work? To answer this question it will be necessary to study the habit of growth of the roots of our plants.

A. *B.*

Fig. 4. To show that plant-roots take water from the soil, the plants in *A* are suffering from thirst. *B* has sufficient water.

Fig. 5. To show that plant-roots take food from the soil. Both boxes were planted at the same time.

Fig. 6. A radish root, from which the stored food has been used to help produce a crop of seeds. □Notice the spindle shaded seed-vessels.

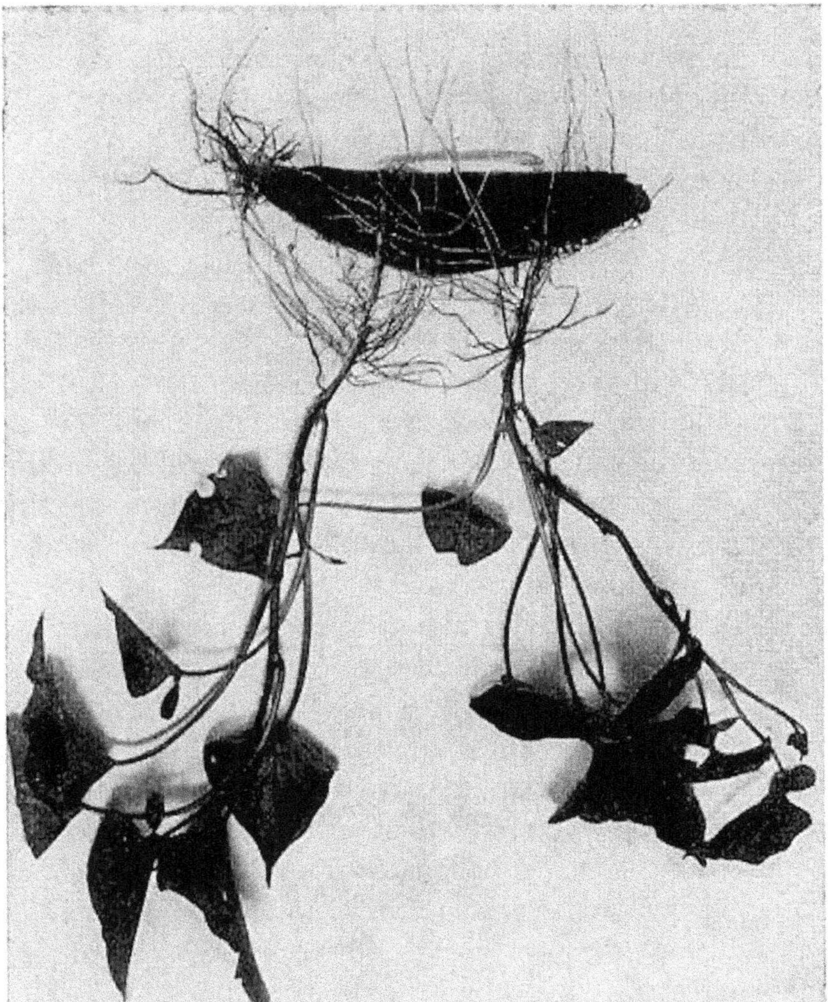

Fig. 7. A sweet-potato root producing new plants.

HABIT OF GROWTH OF ROOTS

The proper place to begin this study is in the field or garden. So we will make another excursion, and this time we will take with us a pickaxe or mattock, a shovel or two, a sharp stick, a quart or half-gallon pitcher, and several buckets of water. Arrived in the field, we will select a well-developed plant, say, of corn, potato or cotton.

Then we will dig a hole about six feet long, three feet wide, and five or six feet deep, close to the plant, letting one side come about four or five inches from the base of the plant. It will be well to have this hole run across the row rather than lengthwise with it.

Then with the pitcher pour water about the base of the plant and wash the soil away from the roots. Gently loosening the soil with the sharpened stick will hasten this work. In this way carefully expose the roots along the side of the hole, tracing them as far as possible laterally and as deep as possible, taking care to loosen them as little as possible from their natural position. (See **Figs. 8 and 9.**) Having exposed the roots of one kind of plant to a width and depth of five or six feet, expose the roots of six or eight plants of different kinds to a depth of about eighteen inches. As this may require more time than we can take for it in one day, it will be well to cover the exposed roots with some old burlaps or other material until we have them all ready, in order to keep them from drying and from injury.

When all is ready we will study the root system of each plant and answer these four questions:

In what part of the soil are most of the roots?

How deep do they penetrate the soil?

How near do they come to the surface of the soil?

How far do they reach out sidewise or laterally from the plant?

To the first question, "In what part of the soil are most

of the roots?" you will give the following answers: "In the upper layer." "In the surface soil." "In the softer soil." "In the darker soil." "In the plowed soil."

These are all correct, but the last is the important one. Most of the roots will be formed in that part of the soil that has been plowed or spaded.

The second question, "How deep do the roots penetrate the soil?" is easily answered. Roots will be found penetrating the soil to depths of from two to six feet or more. (See **Fig. 8.**) The author has traced the roots of cowpea and soy bean plants to depths of five and six feet, corn roots four and five feet, parsnips over six feet. The sweet-potato roots illustrated in Fig. 8 penetrated the soil to a depth of over five feet. The roots of alfalfa or lucerne have been traced to depths of from thirteen to sixteen feet or more.

How near to the surface of the soil do you find roots? Main side or lateral roots will be found within two or three inches of the surface, and little rootlets from these will be found reaching up as near the surface as there is a supply of moisture. After a continued period of wet weather, if the soil has not been disturbed, roots will be found coming to the very surface and even running along the top of the soil.

As to the fourth question, How far do roots reach out sidewise or laterally from the plant? you will find roots extending three, four, five and even six or more feet from the plant. They have numerous branches and rootlets, which fill all parts of the upper soil. Tree roots have been found thirty or forty feet in length.

We started on this observation lesson to find out something about the habit of growth of roots, so that we could tell how the roots do their work for the plant. But before going on with that question, let us stop right here and see whether we cannot find some very important lessons for the farmer and plant grower from what we have already seen. Is a knowledge of these facts we have learned about roots of any value to the farmer? Let us examine each case and see.

Of what value is it to the farmer to know that the larger part of the roots of farm plants develop in that part of the soil that has been plowed or spaded? It tells him that plowing tends to bring about the soil conditions that are favorable to the growth and development of roots. Therefore, the deeper he plows, the deeper is the body of the soil having conditions best suited for root growth, and the larger will be the crop which grows above the soil.

Of what value is it to the farmer to know that the roots of farm plants penetrate to depths of five or six feet in the soil? To answer this question it will be necessary for us to know something of the conditions necessary for root growth. So we will leave this till later.

Of what value is it to the farmer to know that many of the roots of his farm plants come very near the surface of the soil? It tells him that he should be careful in cultivating his crop to injure as few of these roots as possible. In some parts of the country, particularly in the South, the tool commonly used for field cultivation is a small plow. This is run alongside of the row, throwing the soil from the crop, and then again throwing the soil to the crop. Suppose we investigate, and see how this affects the roots of the crop.

Let us visit a field where some farmer is working a crop with a plow, or get him to do it, for the sake of the lesson. We will ask him to stop the plow somewhere opposite a plant, then we will dig a hole a little to one side of the plow and wash away the soil from over the plow (see **Fig. 10**), and see where the roots are. We will find that the plow-point runs under many strong-feeding lateral roots and tears them off, thus checking the feeding power of the plant, and consequently checking its growth. Now, if we can get a cultivator, we will have that run along the row and then wash away the loosened soil. It will be found that few, if any, of the main lateral roots have been injured.

Fig. 8. Sweet potato roots. The great mass of the roots is in

the plowed soil. Many of them reach out 5 to 7 feet from the plant. Some reach a depth of more than 5 feet, and others come to the very surface of the soil.

Fig. 9. Soybean roots showing location, extent and depth of root-growth.

Is it of any value to the farmer to know that roots extend laterally three to six feet and more on all sides of the plant, and that every part of the upper soil is filled with their branches and rootlets? This fact has a bearing on the application of manures and fertilizers. It tells the farmer that when he applies the manure and fertilizers to the soil he should mix the most of them thoroughly all through the soil, placing only a little directly in the row to start the young plant.

To find out how quickly the roots reach out into the soil, wash the soil away from some seedlings that have been growing only a few days, say, seven, ten and fifteen. (See **Fig. 11.**)

From our observations, then, we have learned the important lessons of deep, thorough plowing, careful shallow after-cultivation, and that fertilizers should be well mixed with the soil.

We are now ready to go back to our study of the habit of growth of roots, and can perhaps tell something of how the root does its work for the plant.

It is very easy to see how the roots hold the plant firmly in place, for they penetrate so thoroughly every part of the soil, and to such distances, that they hold with a grip that makes it impossible to remove the plant from the soil without tearing it free from the roots.

It is also on account of this very thorough reaching out through the soil that the roots are able to supply the plant with sufficient moisture and food.

We have doubtless observed that most of these roots are very slender and many very delicate. How did they manage to reach out into the soil so far from the plant? Or where does the root grow in length? To answer this question I will ask you to perform the following experiment:

Experiment – Place some kernels of corn or other large seeds on a plate between the folds of a piece of wet cloth. Cover with a pane of glass or another plate. Keep the cloth moist till the seeds sprout and the young plants have roots two or three inches long. Now have at hand a plate, two pieces of glass, 4 by 6 inches, a piece of white cloth about 4 by 8 inches, a spool of dark thread, and two burnt matches, or small slivers of wood.

A shallow tin pan may be used in place of the plate. Lay one pane of glass on the plate, letting one end rest in the bottom of the plate and the other on the opposite edge of the plate. At one end of the piece of cloth cut two slits on opposite sides about an inch down from the end and reaching nearly to the middle. Wet the cloth and spread it on the glass. Take one of the sprouted seeds, lay it on the cloth, tie pieces of thread around the main root at intervals of one-quarter inch from tip to seed. Tie carefully, so that the root will not be injured.

Place the second pane of glass over the roots, letting the edge come just below the seed, slipping in the slivers of wood to prevent the glass crushing the roots. Wrap the two flaps of the cloth about the seed. Pour some water in the plate and leave for development. (**Fig. 12.**) A day or two of waiting will show conclusively that the lengthening takes place at the tip only, or just back of the tip. Is this fact of any value to the farmer? Yes. The soft tender root tips will force their way through a mellow soil with greater ease and rapidity than through a hard soil, and the more rapid the root growth the more rapid the development of the plant. This teaches us again the lesson of deep, thorough breaking and pulverizing of the soil before the crop is planted.

We have learned that the roots grow out into the soil in search of moisture and food, which they absorb for the use of the plant. How does the root take in moisture and food? Many people think that there are little mouths at the tips of the roots, and that the food and moisture are taken in through them. This is not so, for examination with the most powerful microscopes fails to discover any such mouths.

Sprout seeds of radish, turnip or cabbage, or other seeds, on dark cloth, placed in plates and kept moist. Notice the fuzz or mass of root hairs near the ends of the tender roots of the seedlings (**Fig. 13**). Plant similar seed in sand or soil, and when they have started to grow pull them up and notice how difficult it is to remove all of the sand or dirt from the roots. This is because the delicate root hairs cling so closely to the soil grains. The root hairs are absorbing moisture laden with plant food from the surface of the soil particles. The root hairs are found only near the root tips.

As the root grows older, its surface becomes tougher and harder, and the hairs die, while new ones appear on the new growth just back of the root tips, which are constantly reaching out after moisture and food. The moisture gets into the root hairs by a process called osmosis. The following interesting experiment will give you an idea of this process or force of osmosis.

Experiment – Procure a wide-mouthed bottle, an egg, a glass tube about three inches long and a quarter-inch in diameter, a candle, and a piece of wire a little longer than the tube. Remove a part of the shell from the large end of the egg without breaking the skin beneath. This is easily done by gently tapping the shell with the handle of a pocketknife until it is full of small cracks, and then, with the blade of the knife, picking off the small pieces. In this way remove the shell from the space about the size of a nickel. Remove the shell from the small end of the egg over a space about as large as the end of the glass tube. Next, from the lower end of the candle cut a piece about one-half inch long. Bore a hole in this just the size of the glass tube. Now soften one end of the piece of candle with the hole in it and stick it on to the small end of the egg so that the hole in the candle comes over the hole in the egg. Heat the wire, and with it solder the piece of candle more firmly to the egg, making a watertight joint.

Fig. 10. A plow stopped in the furrow, to show what it does to the roots of plants when used for after-cultivation. Notice the point of the plow under the roots.

Fig. 11. A corn-plant ten days after planting the seed. To show how quickly the roots reach out into the soil. Some of the roots were over 18 inches long.

Place the glass tube in the hole in the piece of candle, pushing it down till it touches the egg. Then, with the heated wire, solder the tube firmly in place. Now run the wire down the tube and break the skin of the egg just under the end of the tube. Fill the bottle with water till it overflows, and set the egg on the bottle, the large end in contact with the water (**Fig. 14**). In an hour or so the contents of the egg will be seen rising in the glass tube. This happens because the water is making its way by osmosis into the egg through the skin, which has no openings, so far as can be discovered. If the bottle is kept supplied with water as fast as it is taken up by the egg, almost the entire contents of the egg will be forced out of the tube. In this way water in which plant food is dissolved enters the slender root hairs and rises through the plant.

Experiment – This process of osmosis may also be shown as follows (**Fig. 15**): Remove the shell from the large end of an egg without breaking the skin, break a hole in the small end of the egg and empty out the contents of the egg; rinse the shell with water. Fill a wide-mouthed bottle with water colored with a few drops of red ink. Fill the eggshell partly full of clear water and set it on the bottle of colored water. Colored water will gradually pass through the membrane of the egg and color the water in the shell.

Prepare another egg in the same way, but put colored water in the shell and clear water in the bottle. The colored water in the shell will pass through the skin and color the water in the bottle. Sugar or salt may be used in place of the red ink, and their presence after passing through the membrane may be detected by taste.

CONDITIONS NECESSARY FOR ROOT GROWTH

We have learned some of the things that the roots do for plants and a little about how the work is done. The next thing to find out is:

- What conditions are necessary for the root to do its work?
- We know that a part of the work of the root is to penetrate the soil and hold the plant firmly in place. Therefore, it needs a firm soil.
- We know that the part of the root that penetrates the soil is tender and easily injured. Therefore, for rapid growth the root needs a mellow soil.

- We know that part of the work of the root is to take moisture from the soil. Therefore, it needs a moist soil.
- We know that part of the work of the root is to take food from the soil. Therefore, it needs a soil well supplied with plant food.
- We know that roots stop their work in cold weather. Therefore, they need a warm soil.

Another condition needed by roots we will find out by experiment.

Experiment – Take two wide-mouthed clear glass bottles (**Fig. 16**); fill one nearly full of water from the well or hydrant; fill the other bottle nearly full of water that has been boiled and cooled; place in each bottle a slip or cutting of Wandering Jew (called also inch plant, or tradescantia, and spiderwort), or some other plant that roots readily in water.

Then pour on top of the boiled water about a quarter of an inch of oil – lard oil or cottonseed oil or salad oil. This is to prevent the absorption of air. In a few days roots will appear on the slip in the hydrant water, while only a very few short ones, if any, will appear in the boiled water, and they will soon cease growing.

Why is this?

To answer this question, try another experiment. Take two bottles, filled as before, one with hydrant water and the other with boiled water; drop into each a slip of glass or a spoon or piece of metal long enough so that one end will rest on the bottom and the other against the side of the bottle, and let stand for an hour or so (**Fig. 17**).

At the end of that time bubbles of air will be seen

collecting on the glass or spoon in the hydrant water, but none in the boiled water. This shows us that water contains more or less air, and that boiling the water drives this air out. The cutting in the boiled water did not produce roots because there was no air in it and the oil kept it from absorbing any.

Experiment – Into some tumblers of moist sand put cuttings of several kinds of plants that root readily (**Fig. 18**), geranium, tradescantia, begonia, etc. Put cuttings of same plants into tumblers filled with clay that has been wet and stirred very thoroughly, until it is about the consistency of cake batter. Keep the sand and puddled clay moist; do not allow the clay to crack, which it will do if it dries.

The cuttings in the sand will strike root and grow, while most, if not all, those in the clay will soon die. The reason for this is that the sand is well ventilated and there is sufficient air for root development, while the clay is very poorly ventilated, and there is not sufficient air for root growth.

These experiments show us that to develop and do their work roots need air or a well-ventilated soil.

We have found the conditions that are necessary for the growth and development of plant roots, namely:

- A firm, mellow soil.
- A moist soil.
- A soil supplied with available plant food.
- A warm soil.
- A ventilated soil.

These are the most important facts about plant growth

so far as the plant grower is concerned. In other words, these conditions that are necessary for root growth and development are the most important truths of agriculture, or they are the foundation truths or principles upon which all agriculture is based. Having found these conditions, the next most important step is to find out how to bring them about in the soil, or, if they already exist, how to keep them or to improve them. This brings us, then, to a study of soils.

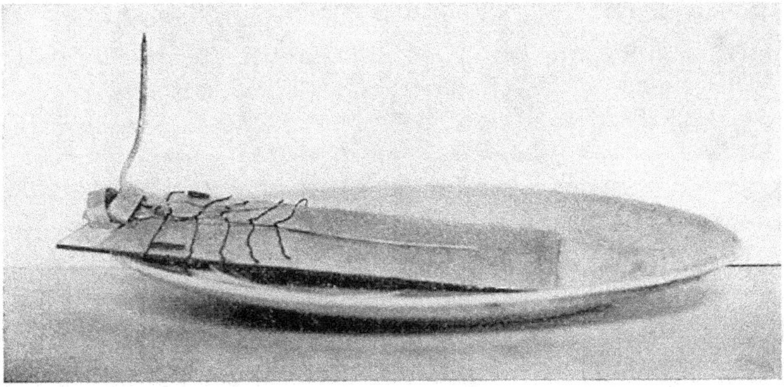

Fig. 12. To show where growth in length of the root takes place. Forty hours before the photograph was taken the tip of the root was 1/4 inch from the lowest thread. The glass cover was taken from this to get a good picture of the root.

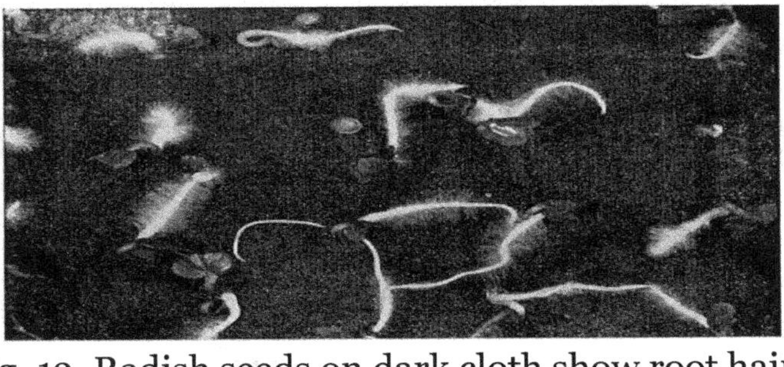

Fig. 13. Radish seeds on dark cloth show root hairs.

Fig. 14. To show how water gets into the roots of plants. Water passed up into the egg through the membrane and forced the contents up the tube until it began to overflow.

Fig. 15. To show osmosis.

CHAPTER III

Soils

The soil considered agriculturally, is that part of the earth's crust which is occupied by the roots of plants and from which they absorb food and moisture.

RELATION OF SOIL TO PLANTS

We have learned that plant roots penetrate the soil to hold the plant in a firm and stable position, to absorb moisture and with it plant food. We learned also that for roots to do these things well, the soil in which they grow must be mellow and firm, and must contain moisture and plant food, air must circulate in its pores and it must be warm.

How can we bring about these conditions? To answer this question intelligently it will be necessary for us to study the soil to find out something about its structure, its composition, its characteristics; also, how it was made and what forces or agencies were active in making it. Are these forces acting on the soil at the present time? Do they have any influence over the conditions that are favorable or unfavorable to plant growth? If so, can we control them in their action for the benefit or injury of plants?

We will begin this soil study with an excursion and a few experiments.

Go to the field. Examine the soil in the holes dug for the root lessons, noticing the difference between the upper or surface soil and the under or subsoil. Examine as many kinds of surface soils and subsoils as possible, also decayed leaf mold, the black soil of the woods, etc. If there are in the neighborhood any exposed embankments where a road has been cut through a hill, or where a river or the seawater has cut into a bank, visit them and examine the exposed soils.

Experiment – Place in separate pans, dishes, plates, boxes, or on boards, one or two pints each of sand, clay, decayed vegetable matter or leaf mold or woods soil, and garden soil. The soil should be fresh from the field. Examine the sand, clay and leaf mold, comparing them as to color; are they light or dark, are they moist or not? Test the soils for comparative size of particles by rubbing between the fingers (**Fig. 19**), noticing if they are coarse or fine, and for stickiness by squeezing in the hand and noting whether or not they easily crumble afterwards.

Experiment – Take samples, about a teaspoonful, of sand, clay and leaf mold. Dry them and then place each in an iron spoon or on a small coal shovel and heat in stove to redness. It will be found that the leaf mold will smoke and burn, and will diminish in amount, while the sand and clay will not.

Experiment – Take two wide-mouthed bottles; fill both nearly full of water. Into one put about a teaspoonful of clay and into the other the same amount of sand; shake both bottles thoroughly and set on table to settle (**Fig. 20**). It will be found that the sand settles very quickly and the clay very slowly.

As the result of our three experiments we will find something as follows:

- Sand is light in color, moist, coarse, not sticky, settles quickly in water, and will not burn.

- Clay is darker in color, moist, very fine, quite sticky, settles slowly in water, and will not burn.
- Leaf mold or humus is very dark in color, moist, very fine, slightly sticky, and burns when placed in the fire.

Experiment – We now have knowledge and means for making simple tests of soils. Repeat the last three experiments with the garden soil. We will find, perhaps, that it is dark in color and some of it burns away when placed in the fire, therefore it contains organic matter or decaying vegetable matter or humus, as it is called. This sample has perhaps fine particles and coarse particles; part of it will settle quickly in water while part settles very slowly, and it is sticky. Therefore we conclude that there are both clay and sand in it. If we shake a sample of it in a bottle of water and let it settle for several days, we can tell roughly from the layers of soil in the bottom of the bottle the relative amounts of sand and clay in the soil. Also if we weigh a sample before and after burning we can tell roughly the amount of organic matter in the soil. Test a number of soils and determine roughly the proportions of sand, clay and organic matter in them.

Experiment – Take the pans of soil used in our first soil experiment and separate the soils in the pans into two parts by a trench across the center on the pan. Now wet the soil in one side of the pan and stir it with a stick or a spoon, carefully smooth the surface of the soil in the other side of the pan and pour or sprinkle some water on it, but do not stir it. Set the pans aside till the soils are dry. This drying may take several days and in the meantime we will study the classification of soils.

CLASSIFICATION OF SOILS

Soil materials and soils are classified as follows:

Stones. – Coarse, irregular or rounded rock fragments or pieces of rock.

Gravel. – Coarse fragments and pebbles ranging in size from several inches in diameter down to 1/25 inch.

Sand. – Soil particles ranging from 1/25 of an inch down to 1/500 of an inch in diameter. Sand is divided into several grades or sizes.

Coarse sand 1/25 to 1/50 of an inch.

Medium sand 1/50 to 1/100 of an inch.

Fine sand 1/100 to 1/250 of an inch.

Very fine sand 1/250 to 1/500 of an inch.

These grades of sand correspond very nearly with the grains of granulated and soft sugar and fine table salt.

A. B.

Fig. 16. To show that roots need air. Bottle *A* was supplied with fresh water, and bottle *B* with water that had been boiled to drive the air out and then cooled.

Fig. 17. Bottle *A* contains fresh water, bottle *B* contains boiled water. Notice the air bubbles in bottle *A*.

Fig. 18. Tumblers *A* and *C* contained moist sand, *B* and *D* contained puddled clay. Cuttings in *B* and *D* died, because there was not sufficient ventilation in the clay for root-development.

Silt. – Fine soil particles ranging from 1/500 to 1/5000 of an inch in diameter. It feels very fine and smooth when rubbed between the fingers, especially when moist. A good illustration of silt is the silicon used for cleaning knives, a small amount of which can be obtained at most any grocery store. By rubbing some of this between the fingers, both dry and wet, one can get a fair idea of how a silty soil should feel. Silt when wet is sticky like clay.

Clay – The finest of rock particles, 1/5000 to 1/250000 of an inch in diameter, too small to imagine. Clay when wet is very soft, slippery and very sticky. Yellow ochre and whiting from the paint shop are good illustrations of clay.

Humus, or decaying vegetable and animal matter. This is dark brown or almost black in color – decaying leaves and woods soil are examples.

Soils composed of the above materials:

Sands or Sandy Soils – These soils are mixtures of the different grades of sand and small amounts of silt, clay and organic matter. They are light, loose and easy to work. They produce early crops, and are particularly adapted to early truck, fruit and bright tobacco, but are too light for general farm crops. To this class belongs the so-called Norfolk Sand. This is a coarse to medium, yellow or brown sand averaging about five-sixths sand and one-sixth silt and clay and is a typical early truck soil found all along the eastern coast of the United States.

"It is a mealy, porous, warm sand, well drained and easily cultivated. In regions where trucking forms an important part of agriculture, this soil is sought out as best adapted to the production of watermelons, cantaloupes, sweet potatoes, early Irish potatoes, strawberries, early tomatoes, early peas, peppers, egg plant, rhubarb and even cabbage and cauliflower, though the latter crops produce better yields on a heavier soil."

A very similar sand in the central part of the country is called Miami Sand and, on the Pacific Coast, Fresno Sand. These names are given to these type soils by the Bureau of Soils of the United States Department of Agriculture.

Loams or Loamy Soils, consist of mixtures of the sands, silt and clay with some organic matter.

The term loam is applied to a soil which, from its appearance in the field and the feeling when handled, appears to be about one-half sand and the other half silt and clay with more or less organic matter. These are naturally fine in texture and quite sticky when wet. They would be called clay by many on account of their stickiness. They are good soils for general farming and produce good grain, grass, corn, potatoes, cotton, vegetables, etc.

Sandy Loams, averaging about three-fifths sand and two-fifths silt and clay. These soils are tilled easily and are the lightest desirable soil for general farming. They are particularly adapted to corn and cotton and in some instances are used for small fruits and truck crops.

Silt Loam consists largely of silt with a small amount of sand, clay, and organic matter. These soils are some of the most difficult to till, but when well drained they are with careful management good general farming soils, producing good corn, wheat, oats, potatoes, alfalfa and fair cotton.

Clay Loams – These soils contain more clay than the silt loams. They are stiff, sticky soils, and some of them are difficult to till. They are generally considered the strongest soils for general farming. They are particularly adapted to wheat, hay, corn and grass.

Gravelly loams are from one-fourth to two-thirds coarse grained; the remaining fine soil may be sandy loam, silt or clay loam. They are adapted to various crops according to the character of the fine soil. Some of them are best planted to fruit and forest.

Stony Loam – Like the gravelly loam the stony loams are one-fourth to three-fourths sandy, silty or clay loam, the remainder being rock fragments of larger size than the gravel. These fragments are sometimes rough and irregular and sometimes rounded. The stones interfere seriously with tillage, and naturally the soils are best planted with forest or fruit.

Clay Soils – Clay soils are mixtures of sand, silt, clay and humus, the clay existing in quite large quantities, there being a greater preponderance of the clay characteristics than in the clay loams; they are very heavy, sticky, and difficult to manage. Some clay soils are not worth farming. Those that can be profitably tilled are adapted to wheat, corn, hay and pasture.

Adobe Soils – These are peculiar soils of the dry West. They are mixtures of clay, silt, some sand and large amounts of humus. Their peculiar characteristic is that they are very sticky when wet and bake very hard when dry and are, therefore, very difficult to manage, though they are generally very productive when they are moist enough to support crops.

Swamp Muck is a dark brown or black swamp soil consisting of large amounts of humus or decaying organic matter mixed with some fine sand and clay. It is found in low wet places.

Peat is also largely vegetable matter, consisting of tough roots, partially decayed leaves, moss, etc. It is quite dense and compact and in some regions is used for fuel.

HOW WERE SOILS MADE?

As a help in finding the answer to this question collect and examine a number of the following or similar specimens:

Brick – Take pieces of brick and rub them together. A fine powder or dust will be the result.

Stones – Rub together pieces of stone; the same result will follow, except that the dust will be finer and will be produced with greater difficulty because the stones are harder. Some stones will be found which will grind others without being much affected themselves.

Rock Salt or Cattle Salt – This is a soft rock, easily broken. Place on a slate or platter one or two pieces about the size of an egg or the size of your fist. Slowly drop water on them till it runs down and partly covers the slate, then set away till the water dries up. Fine particles of salt will be found on the slate wherever the water ran and dried. This is because the water dissolved some of the rock.

Lime Stone – This is harder. Crush two samples to a fine powder and place one in water and the other in vinegar. Water has apparently no effect on it, but small bubbles are seen to rise from the sample in vinegar. The vinegar which is a weak acid is slowly dissolving the rock. The chemists tell us water will also dissolve the limestone, but very slowly. There are large areas of soil that are the refuse from the dissolving of great masses of limestone.

We find that the rocks about us differ in hardness: they are ground to powder when rubbed together, some are easily dissolved in water; others are dissolved by weak acids.

Geologists tell us that the whole crust of the earth was at one time made up of rocks, part of which have been broken down into coarse and fine particles which form the gravel, sand and clay of our soils. The organic matter of our soils has been added by the decay of plants and animals. Several agencies have been active in this work of breaking down the rocks and making soils of them. If we look about we can perhaps see some of this work going on now.

Work of the Sun – Examine a crockery plate or dish that has been many times in and out of a hot oven, noticing the little cracks all over its surface. Most substances expand when they are heated and contract when they are cooled.

When the plate is placed in the oven the surface heats faster than the inner parts, and cools faster when taken out of the oven. The result is that there is unequal expansion and contraction in the plate and consequently tension or pulling of its parts against each other. The weaker part gives way and a crack appears. If hot water is put into a thick glass tumbler or bottle, the inner surface heats and expands faster than the outer parts and the result is tension and cracking. If cold water be poured on a warm bottle or piece of warm glass, it cracks, because there is unequal contraction.

In the early part of a bright sunny afternoon feel of the surface of exposed rocks, bricks, boards, or buildings on which the sun has been shining. Examine them in the same way early the next morning. You will find that the rocks are heated by the sun just as the plate was heated when put into the oven, and when the sun goes down the rocks cool again. This causes tension in the rocks and little cracks and checks appear in them just as in the heated plate, only more slowly.

This checking may also be brought about by a cool shower falling on the sun-heated rocks just as the cool water cracked the warm glass. Many rocks if examined closely will be found to be composed of several materials.

These materials do not expand and contract alike when heated and cooled and the tendency for them to check is greater even than that of the plate. This is the case with most rocks.

Work of Rain – Rain falling on the rocks may dissolve a part of them just as it dissolved the rock salt; or, working into the small cracks made by the sun, may wash out loosened particles; or during cold weather it may freeze in the cracks and by its expansion chip off small pieces; or, getting into large cracks and freezing, may split the rock just as freezing water splits the water pipes.

Work of Moving Water – Visit some neighboring beach or the banks of some rapid stream. See how the waves are rolling the sand and pebbles up and down the beach, grinding them together, rounding their corners and edges, throwing them up into sand beds, and carrying off the finer particles to deposit elsewhere. Now visit a quiet cove or inlet and see how the quiet water is laying down the fine particles, making a clay bed. Notice also how the water plants along the border are helping. They act as an immense strainer, collecting the suspended particles from the water, and with them and their bodies building beds of soil rich in organic matter or humus.

The sun, besides expanding and cracking the rocks by its heat, helps in another way to make soils. It warms the water that has been grinding soil on the beach or along the riverbanks and causes some of it to evaporate. This vapor rises, forms a cloud and floats away in the air. By and by the vapor forms into raindrops that may fall on the top of some mountain.

Fig. 19. – COMPARING SOILS.

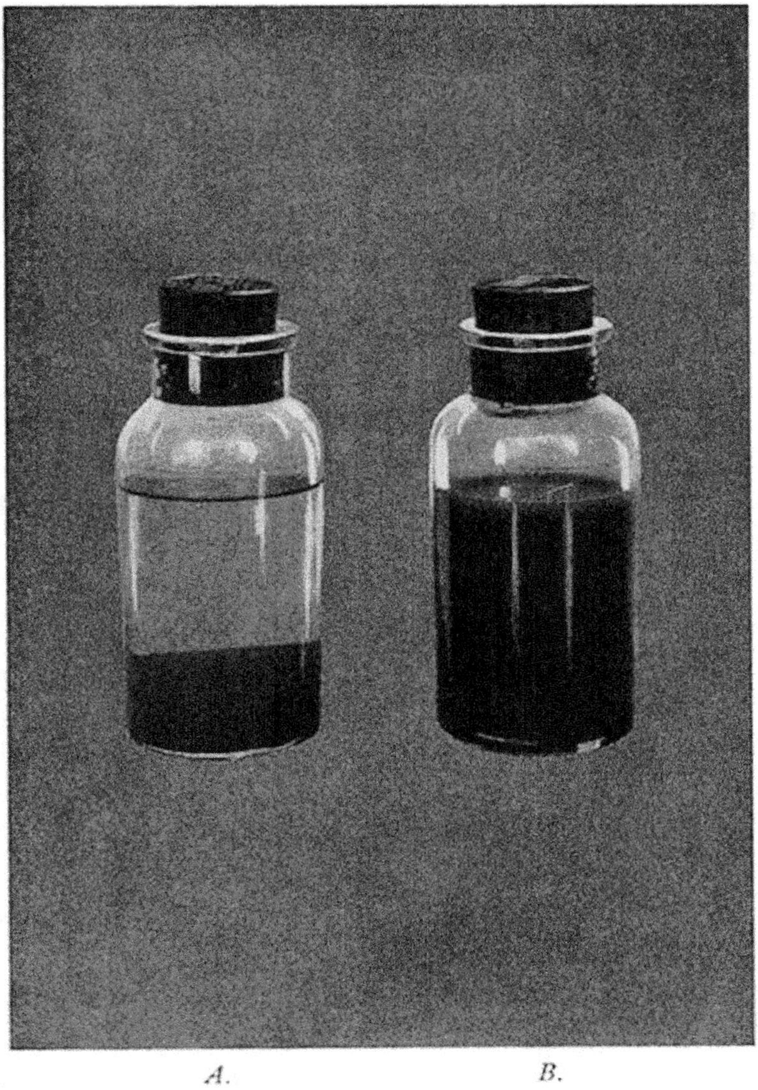

Fig. 20. – WATER TEST OF SOILS. Bottle *A* contains sand and water, bottle *B* clay and water. The sand settles quickly, the clay very slowly.

These raindrops may wash loosened particles from the surface or crevices of exposed rocks. These drops are joined by others until, by and by, they form a little stream, which carries its small burden of rock dust down the slope, now dropping some particles, now taking up others. Other little streams join this one until they form a brook which increases in size and power as it descends the mountainside. As it grows by the addition of other streams it picks up larger pieces, grinds them together, grinds at its banks and loads itself with rocks, pebbles, sand and clay. As the stream reaches the lower part of the mountain where the slope is less steep, it is checked in its course and the larger stones and pebbles are dropped while the sand and finer particles are carried on and deposited on the bottom of some broad quiet river farther down, and when the river overflows its banks, are distributed over the neighboring meadows, giving them a new coating of soil and often adding to their fertility. What a river does not leave along its course it carries out to sea to help build the sand bars and mud flats there. The raindrops have now gotten back to the beach where they take up again the work of grinding the soil.

The work of moving water can be seen in almost any road or cultivated field during or just after a rain, and particularly on the hillsides, where often the soil is loosened and carried from higher to lower parts, making barren sand and clay banks of fertile hillsides and destroying the fertility of the bottom lands below.

We have already noticed the work of freezing water in splitting small and large fragments from the rocks. Water moving over the surface of the earth in a solid form, or ice, was at an earlier period in the history of the earth one of the most powerful agencies in soil formation. Away up in Greenland and on the northern border of this continent the temperature is so low that most if not all of the moisture that falls on the earth falls as snow. This snow has piled up until it has become very deep and very heavy. The great weight has packed the bottom of this great snow bank to ice. On the mountains where the land was not level the masses of snow and ice, centuries ago, began to slide down the slopes and finally formed great rivers of solid water or moving ice.

The geologists tell us that at one time a great river of ice extended from the Arctic region as far south as central Pennsylvania and from New England to the Rocky Mountains. This vast river was very deep and very heavy and into its under surface were frozen sand, pebbles, larger stones and even great rocks. Thus it acted as a great rasp or file and did an immense amount of work grinding rocks and making soils. It ground down mountains and carried great beds of soil from one place to another. When this great ice river melted, it dropped its load of rocks and soils, and as a result we find in that region of the country great boulders and beds of sand and clay scattered over the land.

Work of the Air – The air has helped in the work of wearing down the rocks and making soils. If a piece of iron be exposed to moist air a part of the air unites with part of the iron and forms iron rust. In the same way when moist air comes in contact with some rocks part of the air unites with part of the rock and forms rock rust which crumbles off or is washed away by water. Thus the air helps to break down the rocks. Moving air or wind picks up dust particles and carries them from one field to another. On sandy beaches the wind often blows the sand along like snow and piles it into drifts. The entire surface of sandy regions is sometimes changed in this way. Sands blown from deserts sometimes bury forests which with their foliage sift the fatal winding sheet from the dust-laden winds.

The Work of Plants – Living plants sometimes send their roots into rock crevices; there they grow, expand, and split off rock fragments. Certain kinds of plants live on the surface of rocks. They feed on the rocks and when they die and decay they keep the surface of the rocks moist and also produce carbonic acid which dissolves the rocks slowly just as the vinegar dissolved the limestone in our experiment.

Dead decaying roots, stems, and leaves of plants form largely the organic matter of the soil. When organic matter has undergone a certain amount of decay it is called humus, and these soils are called organic soils or humus soils. The black soils of the woods, swamps and prairies, contain large amounts of humus.

Work of Animals – Earth worms and the larvae of insects which burrow in the soil eat soil particles that pass through their bodies and are partially dissolved. These particles are generally cast out on the surface of the soil. Thus these little animals help to move soil, to dissolve soil, and to open up passages for the entrance of air and rain.

SOIL TEXTURE

We have seen that the soil particles vary in size and that for the best development of the plant the particles of the soil must be so arranged that the delicate rootlets can readily push their way about in search of food, or, in other words, that the soil must have a certain texture. By the texture of the soil we mean the size of its particles and their relation to each other. The following terms are used in describing soil textures: Coarse, fine, open, close, loose, hard, stiff, compact, soft, mellow, porous, leachy, retentive, cloddy, lumpy, light, heavy. Which of these terms will apply to the texture of sand, which to clay, which to humus, which to the garden soil, which to a soil that plant roots can easily penetrate? We find then that texture of the soil depends largely on the relative amounts of sand, silt, clay and humus that it contains.

CHAPTER IV

Relation of Soils to Water

We learned in a previous paragraph that plant roots take moisture from the soil. What becomes of this moisture? We will answer this question with an experiment.

Experiment – Take a pot or tumbler in which a young plant is growing, also a piece of pasteboard large enough to cover the top of the pot or tumbler; cut a slit from the edge to the center of the board, then place it on top of the pot, letting the stem of the plant enter the slit. Now close the slit with wax or tallow, making it perfectly tight about the stem.

If the plant is not too large invert a tumbler over it (**Fig. 21**), letting the edge of the tumbler rest on the pasteboard; if a tumbler is not large enough use a glass jar. Place in a sunny window.

Moisture will be seen collecting on the inner surface of the glass. Where does this come from? It is absorbed from the soil by the roots of the plant and is sent with its load of dissolved plant food up through the stem to the leaves. There most of the moisture is passed from the leaves to the air and some of it is condensed on the side of the glass.

By experiments at the Cornell University Agricultural Experiment Station, Ithaca, N.Y., it has been found that during the growth of a sixty bushel crop of corn the plants pump from the soil by means of their roots, and send into the air through their leaves over nine hundred tons of water.

A twenty-five bushel crop of wheat uses over five hundred tons of water in the same way. This gives us some idea of the importance of water to the plant and the necessity of knowing something of the power of the soil to absorb and hold moisture for the use of the plant. Also the importance of knowing if we can in any way control or influence the water-holding power of the soil for the good of the plant.

SOURCES OF SOIL WATER

From what sources does the soil receive water? From the air above, in the form of rain, dew, hail and snow, falling on the surface, and from the lower soil. This water enters the soil more or less rapidly.

ATTITUDE OF THE SOILS TOWARDS WATER

Which soils have the greater power to take in the rain that falls on their surface?

Experiment – Take four student-lamp chimneys. (In case the chimneys cannot be found get some slender bottles like salad oil bottles or wine bottles and cut the bottoms off with a hot rod. While the rod is heating make a shallow notch in the glass with the wet corner of a file in the direction you wish to make the cut. When the rod is hot lay the end of it lengthwise on the notch. Very soon a little crack will be seen to start from the notch. Lead this crack around the bottle with the hot rod and the bottom of the bottle will drop off.) (**Fig. 23.**) Make a rack to hold them.

Fig. 21. To show what becomes of the water taken from the soil by roots. Moisture, sent up from the roots, has been given off by the leaves and has condensed on the glass.

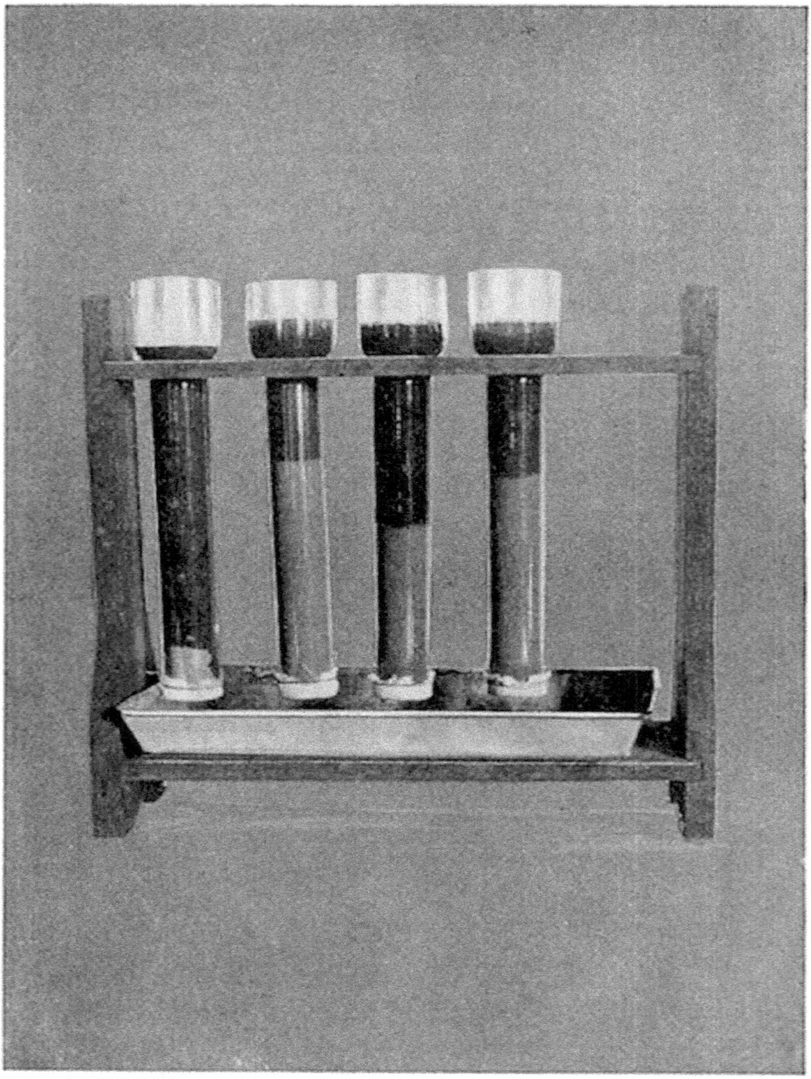

Fig. 22. – PERCOLATION EXPERIMENT. To show the relative powers of soils to take in water falling on the surface. *A*, sand; *B*, clay; *C*, humus; *D*, garden soil.

Tie a piece of cheesecloth or other thin cloth over the small ends of the chimneys. Then fill them nearly full respectively, of dry, sifted, coarse sand, clay, humus soil, and garden soil. Place them in the rack; place under them a pan or dish. Pour water in the upper ends of the tubes until it soaks through and drips from the lower end (**Fig. 22**).

Ordinary sunburner lamp chimneys may be used for the experiment by tying the cloth over the tops; then invert them, fill them with soil and set in plates or pans. The sand will take the water in and let it run through quickly; the clay is very slow to take it in and let it run through; the humus soil takes the water in quite readily. Repeat the experiment with one of the soils, packing the soil tightly in one tube and leaving it loose in another. The water will be found to penetrate the loose soil more rapidly than the packed soil. We see then that the power of the soil to take in rainfall depends on its texture or the size and compactness of the particles.

If the soil of our farm is largely clay, what happens to the rain that falls on it? The clay takes the water in so slowly that most of it runs off and is lost. Very likely it carries with it some of the surface soil that it has soaked and loosened, and thus leaves the farm washed and gullied.

What can we do for our clay soils to help them to absorb the rain more rapidly? For immediate results we can plow them and keep them loose and open with the tillage tools. For more permanent results we may mix sand with them, but sand is not always to be obtained and is expensive to haul. The best method is to mix organic matter with them by plowing in stable manures, or woods soil, or decayed leaves, or by growing crops and turning them under. The organic matter not only loosens the soil but also adds plant food to it, and during its decay produces carbonic acid which helps to dissolve the mineral matter and make available the plant food that is in it.

Clay soils can also be made loose and open by applying lime to them.

Experiment – Take two bottles or jars, put therein a few spoonsful of clay soil, fill with water, put a little lime in one of them, shake both and set them on the table. It will be noticed that the clay in the bottle containing lime settles in flakes or crumbs, and much faster than in the other bottle. In the same manner, lime applied to a field of clay has a tendency to collect the very fine particles of soil into flakes or crumbs and give it somewhat the open texture of a sandy soil. Lime is applied to soil for this purpose at the rate of twenty bushels per acre once in four or five years.

Which soils have the greater power to absorb or pump moisture from below?

Experiment – Use the same or a similar set of tubes as in the experiment illustrated in **Fig. 23**. Fill the tubes with the same kinds of dry sifted soils. Then pour water into the pan or dish beneath the tubes until it rises a quarter of an inch above the lower end of the tubes (**Fig. 24**). Watch the water rise in the soils. The water will be found to rise rapidly in the sand about two or three inches and then stop or continue very slowly a short distance further. In the clay it starts very slowly, but after several hours is finally carried to the top of the soil. The organic matter takes it up less rapidly than the sand, faster than the clay, and finally carries it to the top. By this and further experiments it will be found that the power of soils to take moisture from below depends on their texture or the size and closeness of their particles.

We found the sand pumped the water only a short distance and then stopped.

What can we do for our sandy soils to give them greater power to take moisture from below? For immediate results we can compact them by rolling or packing. This brings the particles closer together, makes the spaces between them smaller, and therefore allows the water to climb higher. For more lasting results we can fill them with organic matter in the shape of stable manures or crops turned under. Clay may be used, but is expensive to haul.

Which soils have greatest power to hold the water that enters them?

Experiment – Use the same or similar apparatus as for the last experiment. After placing the cloth caps over the ends of the tubes label and carefully weigh each one, keeping a record of each; then fill them with the dry soils and weigh again. Now place the tubes in the rack and pour water in the upper ends until the entire soil is wet; cover the tops and allow the surplus water to drain out; when the dripping stops, weigh the tubes again, and by subtraction find the amount of water held by the soil in each tube; compute the percentage. It will be found that the organic matter will hold a much larger percentage of water than the other soils; and the clay more than the sand. The tube of organic soil will actually hold a larger amount of water than the other tubes. (See also **Fig. 25.**)

In a previous experiment we noticed that the sand took in the water poured on its surface and let it run through very quickly. This is a fault of sandy soils.

What can we do for our sandy soils to help them to hold better the moisture that falls on them and tends to leach through them? For immediate effect we can close the pores somewhat by compacting the soil with the roller. For more lasting effects, we can fill them with organic matter.

Which soils will hold longest the water that they have absorbed? Or which soils will keep moist longest in dry weather?

Fig. 23. To show how bottles may be used in place of lamp chimneys shown in Figs 22 and 24.

Fig. 24. – CAPILLARITY OF SOILS. To show the relative powers of soils to take water from below.

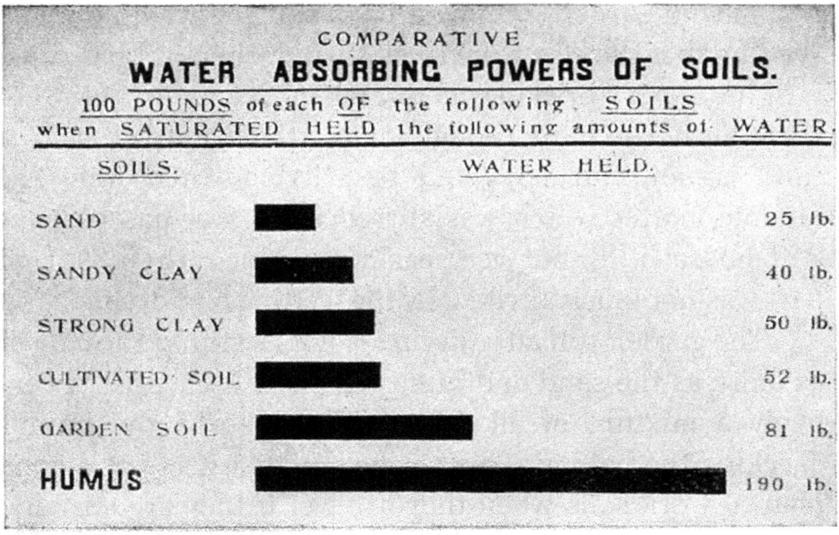

Fig. 25. – WATER-ABSORBING AND WATER-HOLDING POWERS OF SOILS.

Experiment – Fill a pan or bucket with moist sand, another with moist clay, and a third with moist organic matter; set them in the sun to dry and notice which dries last. The organic matter will be found to hold moisture much longer than the other soils. The power of the other soils to hold moisture through dry weather can be improved by mixing organic matter with them.

We find then that the power of soils to absorb and hold moisture depends on the amount of sand, clay, or humus that they contain, and the compactness of the particles. We see also how useful organic matter is in improving sandy and clayey soils.

THE EFFECT OF WORKING SOILS WHEN WET

By this time the soils we left in the pans, sand, clay, humus and garden soil, must be dry. If so, examine them. We find that the clay which was stirred when wet has dried into an almost bricklike mass, while that which was not stirred is not so hard, though it has a thick, hard crust. The sand is not much affected by stirring when wet. The organic matter which was stirred when wet has perhaps stiffened a little, but very easily crumbles; the unstirred part was not much affected by the wetting and drying.

The garden soil after drying is not as stiff as the clay or as loose as the sand and humus. This is because it is very likely a mixture of all three, the sand and the humus checking the baking. This teaches us that it is not a good plan to work soils when they are wet if they are stiff and sticky; and that our stiff clay soils can be kept from drying hard or baking by the use of organic matter. "And that's a witness" for organic matter.

The relation of the soil to moisture is very important, for moisture is one of the greatest factors if not the greatest in the growth of the crop.

The power to absorb or soak up moisture from any source is greatest in those soils whose particles are smaller and fit closer together.

It is for this reason that strong loams and clay soils absorb and hold three times as much water as sandy soils do, while peaty or humus soils absorb a still larger proportion.

The reason why crops burn up so quickly on sandy soils during dry seasons is because of their weak power to hold water.

The clay and humus soils carry crops through dry weather better because of their power to hold moisture and to absorb or soak up moisture from below. It is for this reason also that clay and peaty soils more often need draining than sandy soils.

When rain falls on a sandy soil it enters readily, but it is apt to pass rapidly down and be, to a great extent, lost in the subsoil, for the sand has not sufficient power to hold much of it.

When rain falls on a clay soil it enters less readily because of the closeness of the particles, and during long rains or heavy showers some of the water may run off the surface. If the surface has been recently broken and softened with the plow or cultivator the rain enters more readily. What does enter is held and is not allowed to run through as in the case of the sand.

Humus soil absorbs the rain as readily as the sand and holds it with a firmer grip than clay.

This fact gives us a hint as to how we may improve the sand and clay.

Organic matter mixed with these soils by applying manures or plowing under green crops will cause the sand to hold the rain better and the clay to absorb it more readily.

CHAPTER V

Forms of Soil Water

Water that comes to the soil and is absorbed exists in the soil principally in two forms: Free water and capillary water.

FREE WATER

Free water is that form of water which fills our wells, is found in the bottoms of holes dug in the ground during wet seasons and is often found standing on the surface of the soil after heavy or long continued rains. It is sometimes called ground water or standing water and flows under the influence of gravity.

Is free water good for the roots of farm plants? If we remember how the root takes its food and moisture, namely through the delicate root hairs; and also remember the experiment which showed us that roots need air, we can readily see that free water would give the root hairs enough moisture, but it would at the same time drown them by cutting off the air. Therefore free water is not directly useful to the roots of house plants or farm plants, excepting such as are naturally swamp plants, like rice, which grows part of the time with its roots covered with free water.

CAPILLARY WATER

If you will take a number of glass tubes of different sizes, the largest not more than one-fourth of an inch in diameter, and hold them with one end of each in water or

Fig. 26. – CAPILLARY TUBES. To show how water rises in small tubes or is drawn into small spaces.

Fig. 27. – CAPILLARY PLATE. Water is drawn to the highest point where the glass plates are closest together.

Fig. 28. A cone of soil to show capillarity. Water poured about the base of this cone of soil has been drawn by capillary force halfway to the top.

Fig. 29. Shows the relative amounts of film-moisture held by coarse and fine soils. The colored water in bottle *A* represents the amount of water required to cover the half-pound of pebbles in tumbler *B* with a film of moisture. The colored water in bottle *C* shows amount required to cover the soil grains in the half-pound of sand in tumbler *D*.

some colored liquid, you will notice that the water rises in the tubes (**Fig. 26**), and that it rises highest in the smallest tube. The force that causes the water to rise in these tubes is called the capillary force, from the old Latin word *capillum* (a hair), because it is most marked in hair-like tubes, the smaller the tube the higher the water will rise. The water that rises in the tubes is called capillary water.

Another method of illustrating capillary water is to tie or hold together two flat pieces of glass, keeping two of the edges close together and separating the opposite two about one-eighth of an inch with a sliver of wood. Then set them in a plate of water or colored liquid and notice how the water rises between the pieces of glass, rising higher the smaller the space (**Fig. 27**). It is the capillary force that causes water to rise in a piece of cloth or paper dipped in water. Take a plate and pour onto it a cone-shaped pile of dry sand or fine soil; then pour water around the base of the pile and note how the water is drawn up into the soil by capillary force (**Fig. 28**).

Capillary water is the other important form of water in the soil. This is moisture that is drawn by capillary force or soaks into the spaces between the soil particles and covers each particle with a thin film of moisture.

FILM WATER

Take a marble or a pebble, dip it into water and notice the thin layer or film of water that clings to it. This is a form of capillary water and is sometimes called film water or film moisture. Take a handful of soil that is moist but not wet, notice that it does not wet the hand, and yet there is moisture all through it; each particle is covered with a very thin film of water.

Now this film water is just the form of water that can supply the very slender root hairs without drowning them, that is, without keeping the air from them. And the plant grower should see to it that the roots of his plants are well supplied with film water and are not drowned by the presence of free water. Capillary water may sometimes completely fill the spaces between the soil particles; when this occurs the roots are drowned just as in the case of free water as we saw when cuttings were placed in the puddled clay (see **Fig. 18**). Free water is indirectly of use to the plant because it serves as a supply for capillary and film moisture.

Now I think we can answer the question which was asked when we were studying the habit of growth of roots but was left unanswered at the time. The question was this: Of what value is it to the farmer to know that roots enter the soil to a depth of three to six feet? We know that roots will not grow without air. We also know that if the soil is full of free water there is no air in it, and, therefore, roots of most plants will not grow in it. It is, therefore, of interest to the farmer to see that free water does not come within at least three or four feet of the surface of the soil so that the roots of his crops may have plenty of well ventilated soil in which to develop. If there is a tendency for free water to fill the soil a large part of the time, the farmer can get rid of it by draining the land. We get here a lesson for the grower of houseplants also. It is that we must be careful that the soil in the pots or boxes in which our plants are growing is always supplied with film water and not wet and soggy with free water. Water should not be left standing long in the saucer under the pot of a growing plant. It is best to water the pot from the top and let the surplus water drain into the saucer and then empty it out.

Which soils have the greatest capacity for film water?

Experiment – Place in a tumbler or bottle one-half pound of pebbles about the size of a pea or bean; pour a few drops of water on them and shake them; continue adding water and shaking them till every pebble is covered with a film of water; let any surplus water drain off. Then weigh again; the difference in the two weights will be approximately the weight of the film water that the pebbles can carry. Repeat this with sand and compare the two amounts of water. A striking illustration can be made by taking two slender bottles and placing in them amounts of colored water equal to the amounts of film water held by the pebbles and sand respectively. In the accompanying illustration (**Fig. 29**), *A* represents the amount of water that was found necessary to cover the pebbles in tumbler *B* with a film of moisture. *C* is the amount that was necessary to cover with a film the particles of sand in *D*. The finer soil has the greater area for film moisture. It has been estimated that the particles of a cubic foot of clay loam have a possible aggregate film surface of three-fourths of an acre.

CHAPTER VI

Loss of Soil Water

We noticed in previous paragraphs that soil might at times have too much water in it for proper ventilation and so check the growth of the roots of the plant. Now is it possible that soil water may be lost or wasted and if so can we check the loss?

In the experiment to find out how well the soils would take in the rainfall we noticed that the clay soil took in the water very slowly and that on a field of clay soil part of the rain water would be likely to run off over the surface and be lost. Free water may be lost then, by surface wash.

We noticed methods of checking this loss, namely, pulverizing the soil with the tillage tools and putting organic matter into it to make it absorb the rain more readily.

We noticed that water poured on the sand ran through it very quickly and was apt to be lost by leaching or percolation. This we found could be checked by rolling the soil and by putting organic matter into it to close the pores.

We learned that roots take water from the soil for the use of the plant and send it up to the leaves, which in turn send it out into the air, or transpire it, as this process is called. We learned also that the amount transpired is very great. Now water that is pumped up and transpired by the crops we are growing we consider properly used. But when weeds grow with the crop and pump and transpire water we consider this water as lost or wasted.

Water may be lost then by being pumped up and

transpired by weeds. And this is the way weeds do their greatest injury to crops during dry weather. The remedy is easily pointed out. Kill the weeds or do not let them get a start.

There is another way, which we are not apt to notice, by which water may be lost from the soil. When the soil in the pans in a previous experiment had been wet and set aside a few days it became very dry. How did the water get out of this soil? That at the surface of the soil evaporated or was changed into vapor and passed into the air. Then water from below the surface was pumped up by capillary force to take its place just as the water was pumped up in the tubes of soil. This in turn was evaporated and the process repeated till all of the water in the soil had passed into the air. Now this process is going on in the field whenever it is not raining or the ground is not frozen very hard.

Water then may be lost by evaporation.

How can we check this loss?

Suppose we try the experiment of covering the soil with some material that cannot pump water readily.

Experiment – Take four glass fruit jars, two-quart size, with straight sides. If you cannot get them with straight sides cut off the tops with a hot iron just below the shoulder; tin pails will do if the glass jars cannot be had. Fill these with moist soil from the field or garden, packing it till it is as hard as the unplowed or unspaded soil. Leave one of them in this condition; from two of them remove an inch or two of soil and replace it in the case of one with clean, dry, coarse sand, and in the case of the other with chaff or straw cut into half-inch lengths. Stir the soil in the fourth one to a depth of one inch, leaving it light and crumbly. Now weigh the jars and set them aside. Weigh each day for several days. The four jars illustrated in Fig. 30 were prepared in this way and allowed to stand seven days. In that time they lost the following amounts of water:

Amounts of water lost from jars of prepared soil in seven days. No. 1 packed soil – lost 5.5 oz. equal to about 75 tons per acre. No. 2 covered with straw – lost 2 oz. equal to about 27 tons per acre. No. 3 covered with dry sand – lost 0 oz. equal to about tons per acre. No. 4 covered with crumbled soil – lost 2.5 oz., equal to about 34 tons per acre.

Why did not 2, 3 and 4 lose as much water as No. 1?

The soil in jar No. 1 was packed and water was pumped to the surface by capillary force and was evaporated as fast as it came to the surface.

In No. 2 the water could rise rapidly until it reached the straw, then it was stopped almost entirely. But the straw being coarse, the air circulated in it more or less freely and there was a slow loss by evaporation. In jar No. 3 the water could rise only to the sand, which was so coarse that the water could not climb on it to the surface, and the air circulated in the sand so slowly that there was not sufficient evaporation to affect scales weighing to one-quarter ounce. No. 4 lost less than No. 1 because, as in the case of the sand, the water could not climb rapidly to the surface on the coarse crumbs of soil. The loss that did take place from No. 4 was what the air took from the loosely stirred soil on the surface with a very little from the lower soil. Simply stirring the surface of the sod in No. 4 reduced the loss of water to less than half the loss from the hard soil in No. 1.

This experiment gives us the clew to the method of checking loss of water from the soil by evaporation. It is to keep the water from climbing up to the surface, or check the power of the soil to pump the water to the surface by making it loose on top. This loose soil is called a soil mulch. Everything that we do to the soil that loosens and crumbles the surface tends to check the loss of water by evaporation from the soil below.

1 2 3 4

Fig. 30. – TO SHOW THE EFFECT OF A SOIL MULCH 1. Packed soil, lost in 7 days 5.5 ozs. water, equal to 75 tons per acre. 2. Packed soil, covered with straw, lost in 7 days 2 ozs. water, equal to 27 tons per acre. 3. Packed soil, covered with sand, lost in 7 days 0 ozs. water, equal to tons per acre. 4. Packed soil, covered with soil mulch, lost in 7 days 2.5 ozs. water, equal to 34 tons per acre.

CHAPTER VII

Soil Temperature

We learned that roots need heat for their growth and development. Now what is the relation of the different kinds of soil toward heat or what are their relative powers to absorb and hold heat?

Experiment – Some days before this experiment, spread on a dry floor about a half-bushel each of sand, clay and decayed leaf mold or black woods soil. Stir them occasionally till they are thoroughly dry. When they are dry place them separately in three boxes or large flowerpots and keep dry. In three similar boxes or pots place wet sand, wet clay, and wet humus. Place a thermometer in each of the soils, placing the bulb between one and two inches below the surface (**Fig. 31**). Then place the soils out of doors where the sun can shine on them and leave them several days. If a rain should come up protect the dry soils. Observe and make a record of the temperatures of each soil several times a day. Chart the average of several days' observations. Fig. 32 shows the averages of several days observations on a certain set of soils.

It will be noticed that the temperature of the soils increased until the early part of the afternoon and after that time they lost heat.

HOW SOILS ARE WARMED

Experiment – Hold your hand in bright sunlight or near a warm stove or radiator. Your hand is warmed by heat radiated from the sun or warm stove through the

Fig. 31 – SOIL TEMPERATURE EXPERIMENT.
Thermometer in pot of soil.

air to your body. In the same manner the rays of the sun heat the surface of the soil.

Experiment – Take the stove poker or any small iron rod and hold one end of it in the fire or hold one end of a piece of wire in a candle or lamp flame. The end of the rod or wire will quickly become very hot and heat will gradually be carried its entire length until it becomes too hot to hold. This carrying of the heat from particle to particle through the length of the rod is called heating by conduction. Now when the warm rays of the sun reach the soil, or a warm wind blows over it, the surface particles are warmed and then pass the heat on to the next ones below, and these in turn pass it to others and so on till the soil becomes heated to a considerable depth by conduction.

A clay soil will absorb heat by conduction faster than a

sandy soil because the particles of the clay lie so close together that the heat passes more readily from one to another than in the case of the coarser sand.

If the soil is open and porous, warm air and warm rains can enter readily and carry heat to the lower soil.

You have noticed how a pile of stable manure steams in cold weather. You doubtless know that manure from the horse stable is often used to furnish heat for hotbeds and for sweet potato beds.

Now the heat which warms the manure and sends the steam out of it, and warms the hotbed and sweet potato bed, is produced by the decaying or rotting of the manure. More or less heat is produced by the decay of all kinds of organic matter. So if the soil is well supplied with organic matter, the decay of this material will add somewhat to the warmth of the soil.

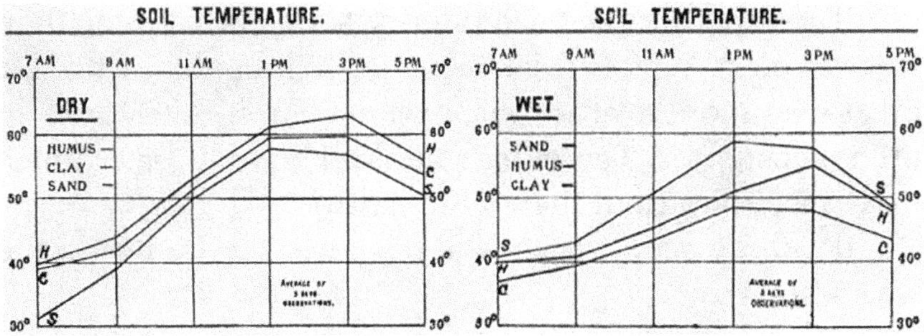

Fig. 32. Charts showing average temperature of a set of dry and wet soils during a period of five days. *H*, humus; *C*, clay; *S*, sand.

HOW SOILS LOSE HEAT

Wet one of your fingers and hold your hand up in the

air. The wet finger will feel colder than the others and will gradually become dry. This is because some of the heat of your finger is being used to dry up the water or change it into a vapor, or in other words to evaporate it.

In the same manner a wet soil loses heat by the evaporation of water from its surface.

Experiment – Heat an iron rod, take it from the fire and hold it near your face or hand. You will feel the heat without touching the rod. The heat is radiated from the rod through the air to your body and the rod gradually cools. In the same way the soil may lose its heat by radiating it into the air. A clay soil will lose more heat by radiation than a sandy soil because the clay is more compact.

CONDITIONS WHICH INFLUENCE SOIL TEMPERATURE

It will be noticed that the dry soils are warmer than the wet ones. Why is this? Scientists tell us that it takes a great deal more heat to warm water than it does to warm other substances. Therefore when soil is wet it takes much more heat to warm it than if it were dry.

It will be seen that of the dry soils the humus is the warmest. Why?

Experiment – Take two thermometers, wrap the bulb of one with a piece of black or dark colored cloth and the bulb of the other with a piece of white cloth, then place them where the sun will shine on the cloth covered bulbs. The mercury in both thermometers will be seen to rise, but in the thermometer with the dark cloth about the bulb it will rise faster and higher than in the other. This shows that the dark cloth absorbs heat faster than the white cloth. In the same manner a dark soil will absorb heat faster than a light colored soil; therefore it will be warmer if dry.

Why was the dry clay warmer than the dry sand?

Because its darker color helped it to absorb heat more rapidly than the sand, and, as the particles were smaller and more compact, heat was carried into it more rapidly by conduction.

Why were the wet humus and clay cooler than the wet sand?

As they were darker in color and the clay was more compact than the sand, they must have absorbed more heat, but they also held more water, and, therefore, lost more heat by evaporation.

1 2 3

Fig. 33. To show the value of organic matter. 1 contains clay subsoil; 2, clay subsoil and fertilizer; 3, clay subsoil and organic matter. All planted at the same time.

Of the dry soils, then, the humus averaged warmest, because, on account of its dark color, it absorbed heat more readily than the others. The dry clay was warmer than the sand on account of its color and compact texture. Of the wet soils the sand was the warmest, because, on account of its holding less moisture, less heat was required to raise its temperature and there was less cooling by evaporation, while the other soils, although they absorbed more heat than the sand, lost more on account of greater evaporation, due to their holding more moisture. Why are sandy soils called warm soils and clay soils said to be cold?

How may we check losses of heat from the soil?

If we make a mulch on the surface of the soil evaporation will be checked and therefore loss of heat by evaporation will be checked also. The mulch will also check the conduction of heat from the lower soil to the surface and therefore check loss of heat by radiation from the surface.

VALUE OF ORGANIC MATTER

Figure 33 illustrates a simple way to show the value of organic matter in the soil. The boxes are about twelve inches square and ten inches deep. They were filled with a clay subsoil taken from the second foot below the surface of the field. To the second box was added sufficient commercial fertilizer to supply the plants with all necessary plant food. To the third box was added some peat or decayed leaves, in amount about ten per cent of the clay subsoil. The corn was then planted and the boxes were all given the same care. The better growth of the corn in the third box was due to the fact that the organic matter not only furnished food for the corn but also during its decay prepared mineral plant food that was locked up in the clay, and also brought about better conditions of air and moisture by improving the texture of the soil. The plants in the second box had sufficient plant food, but did not make better growth because poor texture prevented proper conditions of air and moisture. "And that's another witness" for organic matter. Decaying organic matter or humus is really the life of the soil and it is greatly needed in most of the farm soils of the eastern part of the country. It closes the pores of sandy soils and opens the clay, thus helping the sand to soak up and hold more moisture and lessening excessive ventilation, and at the same time helping the roots to take a firmer hold. It helps the clay to absorb rain, helps it to pump water faster, helps it to hold water longer in dry weather, increases ventilation, favors root penetration and increases heat absorption. We can increase the amount of organic matter in the soil by plowing in stable manure, leaves and other organic refuse of the farm, or we can plow under crops of clover, grass, grain or other crops grown for that purpose.

CHAPTER VIII

Plant Food in the Soil

We learned in previous paragraphs that the roots of plants take food from the soil, and that a condition necessary for the root to do its work for the plant was the presence of available plant food in sufficient quantities.

What is plant food? For answer let us go to the plant and ask it what it is made of.

Experiment – Take some newly ripened cotton or cotton wadding, a tree branch, a cornstalk, and some straw or grass. Pull the cotton apart, then twist some of it and pull apart; in turn break the branch, the cornstalk and the straw. The cotton does not pull apart readily nor do the others break easily; this is because they all contain long, tough fibers. These fibers are called woody fiber or cellulose. The cotton fiber is nearly pure cellulose.

Experiment – Get together some slices of white potato, sweet potato, parsnip, broken kernels of corn, wheat and oats, a piece of laundry starch and some tincture of iodine diluted to about the color of weak tea. Rub a few drops of the iodine on the cut surfaces of the potatoes, parsnip, and the broken surfaces of the grains. Notice that it turns them purple. Now drop a drop of the iodine on the laundry starch. It turns that purple also. This experiment tells us that plants contain starch.

Experiment – Chew a piece of sorghum cane, sugar cane, cornstalk, beetroot, turnip root, apple or cabbage. They all taste sweet and must therefore contain sugar.

Examine a number of peach and cherry trees. You will

find on the trunk and branches more or less of a sticky substance called gum.

Experiment – Crush on paper seeds of cotton, castor-oil bean, peanuts, Brazil nuts, hickory nuts, butternuts, etc. They make grease spots; they contain fat and oil.

Experiment – Chew whole grains of wheat and find a gummy mucilaginous substance called wheat gum, or wet a pint of wheat flour to a stiff dough, let it stand about an hour, and then wash the starch out of it by kneading it under a stream of running water or in a pan of water, changing the water frequently. The result will be a tough, yellowish gray, elastic mass called gluten. This is the same as the wheat gum and is called an albuminoid because it contains nitrogen and is like albumen, a substance like the white of an egg.

If we crush or grate some potatoes or cabbage leaves to a pulp and separate the juice, then heat the clear juice, a substance will separate in a flaky form and settle to the bottom of the liquid. This is vegetable albumen.

Experiment – Crush the leaves or stems of several growing plants and notice that the crushed and exposed parts are moist. In a potato or an apple we find a great deal of moisture. Plants then are partly made of water. In fact growing plants are from 65 to 95 per cent water.

Experiment – Expose a plant or part of a plant to heat; the water is driven off and there remains a dry portion. Heat the dry part to a high degree and it burns; part passes into the air as smoke and part remains behind as ashes.

Fig. 34. Soy-bean roots. Showing nodules of tubercles, the homes of nitrogen-fixing bacteria.

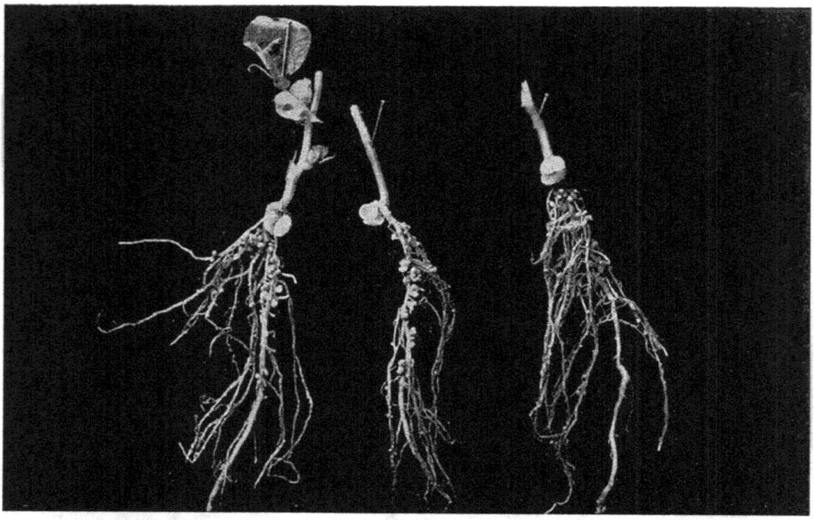

Fig. 35. Garden-pea roots, showing tubercles or nodules, the homes of nitrogen-fixing bacteria.

We have found then the following substances in plants: Woody fiber or cellulose, starch, sugar, gum, fats and oils, albuminoids, water, ashes. Aside from these are found certain coloring matters, certain acids and other matters which give taste, flavor, and poisonous qualities to fruits and vegetables. More or less of all these substances are found in all plants. Now these are all compound substances. That is, they can all be broken down into simpler substances, and with the exception of the water and the ashes, the plants do not take them directly from the soil.

The chemists tell us that these substances are composed of certain chemical elements, some of which the plant obtains from the air, some from the soil and some from water.

The following table gives the substances found in plants, the elements of which they are composed, and the sources from which the plants obtain them:

Substances found in plants	**Elements of which they are made**
Cellulose or woody fiber	
Starch	Carbon
Sugar	Oxygen
Gum	Hydrogen
Fat and Oil	
	Carbon
	Oxygen
Albuminoids	Hydrogen
	Nitrogen
	Sulfur
	Phosphorus
	Phosphorus
	Potassium
Ashes	*Calcium*
	Magnesium
	Iron
Water	Oxygen
	Hydrogen

Here is a brief description of these chemical elements.

- Oxygen, a colorless gas, forms one-fifth of the air.
- Hydrogen, a colorless gas, forms a part of water.
- Carbon, a dark solid, forms nearly one-half of all

organic matter; charcoal is one of its forms. The lead in your pencil is another example.

- Nitrogen, a colorless gas, forms four-fifths of the air. Found in all albuminoids.
- Sulfur, a yellow solid.
- Phosphorus, a yellowish white solid.
- Potassium, a silver white solid.
- Calcium, a yellowish solid. Found in limestone.
- Magnesium, a silver white solid.
- Iron, a silver gray solid.

Of these elements the nitrogen, sulfur, phosphorus, potassium, calcium, magnesium, and iron must not only exist in the soil but must also be there in such form that the plant can use them. The plant does not use them in their simple elementary form but in various compounds. These compounds must be soluble in water or in weak acids.

Of these seven elements of plant food the nitrogen, phosphorus, and potassium and calcium are of particular importance to the farmer, because they do not always exist in the soil in sufficient available quantities to produce profitable crops. Professor Roberts, of Cornell University, tells us that an average acre of soil eight inches deep contains three thousand pounds of nitrogen. The nitrogen exists largely in the humus of the soil and it is only as the humus decays that the nitrogen is made available. Here is another reason for keeping the soil well supplied with organic matter. The decay of this organic matter is hastened by working the soil; therefore good tillage helps to supply the plant with nitrogen.

If the nitrogen becomes available when there is no crop on the soil it will be washed out by rains and so lost. Therefore the soil, especially if it is sandy, should be covered with a crop the year through.

Many lands lose large amounts of plant food by being left bare through the fall and winter, especially in those parts of the country where the land does not freeze.

The phosphorus, potassium and calcium also exist in most soils in considerable quantities, but often are not available; thorough tillage and the addition of organic matter will help to make them available, and new supplies may be added in the form of fertilizers. Calcium is found in nearly all soils in sufficient quantities for most crops, but sometimes there is not enough of it for such crops as clover, cowpea, alfalfa, etc. It is also used to improve soil texture. The entire subject of commercial fertilizers is based almost entirely on the fact of the lack of these four elements in the soil in sufficient available quantities to grow profitable crops. The plant gets its phosphorus from phosphoric acid, its potassium from potash, and its calcium from lime.

There is a class of plants which have the power of taking free nitrogen from the air. These are the leguminous plants; such as clover, beans, cowpeas, alfalfa, soybean, etc. They do it through the acid of microscopic organisms called bacteria which live in nodules or tubercles on the roots of these plants (**Figs. 34-35**). Collect roots of these plants and find the nodules on them. The bacteria take nitrogen from the air that penetrates the soil and give it over to the plants. Here is another reason for good soil ventilation.

This last fact brings us to another very important property of soils. Soils have existing in them many very small plants called bacteria. They are so very small that it would take several hundred of them to reach across the edge of this sheet of paper. We cannot see them with the naked eye but only with the most powerful microscopes. Some of these minute plants are great friends to the farmer, for it is largely through their work that food is made available for the higher plants. Some of them break down the organic matter and help prepare the nitrogen for the larger plants. Others help the leguminous plants to feed on the nitrogen of the air. To do their work they need warmth, moisture, air, and some mineral food; these conditions we bring about by improving the texture of the soil by means of thorough tillage and the use of organic matter.

CHAPTER IX

Seeds

In the spring comes the great seed-planting time on the farm, in the home garden and in the school garden. Many times the questions will be asked: Why didn't those seeds come up? How shall I plant seeds so as to help them sprout easily and grow into strong plants? To answer these questions, perform a few experiments with seeds, and thus find out what conditions are necessary for seeds to sprout, or germinate. For these experiments you will need a few teacups, glass tumblers or tin cans, such as tomato cans or baking-powder cans; a few plates, either of tin or crockery; some wide-mouth bottles that will hold about half a pint, such as pickle, olive, or yeast bottles or druggists' wide-mouth prescription bottles; and a few pieces of cloth. Also seeds of corn, garden peas and beans.

Experiment – Put seeds of corn, garden peas, and beans (about a handful of each) to soak in bottles or tumblers of water. Next day, two hours earlier in the day, put a duplicate lot of seeds to soak. When this second lot of seeds has soaked two hours, you will have two lots of soaked seeds of each kind, one of which has soaked twenty-four hours and the other two hours. Now take these seeds from the water and dry the surplus water from them by gently patting or rubbing a few at a time in the folds of a piece of cloth, taking care not to break the skin or outer coating of the seed. Place them in dry bottles, putting in enough to cover the bottoms of the bottles about three seeds deep; cork the bottles. If you cannot find corks, tie paper over the mouths of the bottles. Label the bottles "Seeds soaked 24 hours," "Seeds soaked 2 hours," and let them stand in a warm place several days. If there is danger of freezing at night, the bottles of seeds may be kept in the kitchen or living room where it is warm, until they sprout.

Observe the seeds from day to day. The seeds that soaked twenty-four hours will sprout readily (**Fig. 36**), while most, if not all, of those that soaked only two hours will not sprout. Why is this? It is because the two-hour soaked seeds do not receive sufficient moisture to carry on the process of sprouting.

Our experiment teaches us that seeds will not sprout until they receive enough moisture to soak them through and through.

This also teaches that when we plant seeds we must so prepare the soil for them and so plant them that they will be able to get sufficient moisture to sprout.

Experiment – Soak some beans, peas or corn, twenty-four hours; carefully dry them with a cloth. In one half-pint bottle place enough of them to cover the bottom of the bottle two or three seeds deep; mark this bottle A. Fill another bottle two-thirds full of them and mark the bottle B (**Fig. 37**). Cork the bottles and let them stand for several days. Also let some seeds remain soaking in the water. The few seeds in bottle A will sprout, while, the larger number in bottle B will not sprout, or will produce only very short sprouts. Why do not the seeds sprout easily in the bottle that is more than half full?

To answer this question try the following experiment:

Experiment – Carefully loosen the cork in bottle B (the bottle containing poorly sprouted seeds), light a match, remove the cork from the bottle and introduce the lighted match. The match will stop burning as soon as it is held in the bottle, because there is no fresh air in the bottle to keep the match burning. Test bottle A in the same way. What has become of the fresh air that was in the bottles when the seeds were put in them? The seeds have taken something from it and have left bad air in its place; they need fresh air to help them sprout, but they have not sprouted so well in bottle B because there was not fresh air enough for so many seeds. The seeds in the water do not sprout because there is not enough air in the water. Now try another experiment.

A. *B.*

Fig. 36. To show that seeds need water for germination. The beans in bottle *A* were soaked 2 hours, those in bottle *B* were soaked 24 hours. They were then removed from the water and put into dry bottles.

A. B. C.

Fig. 37. Seeds need air for germination. The beans in both bottles were soaked 24 hours, and then were put into dry bottles Bottle *A* contained sufficient air to start the few seeds. Bottle *B* had not enough. The water in the tumbler *C* did not contain sufficient air for germination.

A. B.

Fig. 38. To show that seeds need air for germination. Corn planted in puddled clay in tumbler *A* could not get sufficient air for sprouting. The moist sand in tumbler *B* admitted sufficient air for germination.

Experiment – Fill some tumblers or teacups or tin cans with wet sand and others with clay that has been wet and then thoroughly stirred till it is about the consistency of cake batter or fresh mixed mortar. Take a tumbler of the wet sand and one of the wet clay and plant two or three kernels of corn in each, pressing the kernels down one-half or three-quarters of an inch below the surface; cover the seeds and carefully smooth the surface.

In other tumblers plant peas, beans, and other seeds. Cover the tumblers with saucers, or pieces of glass or board to keep the soil from drying. Watch them for several days. If the clay tends to dry and crack, moisten it, fill the cracks and smooth the surface.

The seeds in the sand will sprout but those in the clay will not (see **Fig. 38**). Why is this? Water fills the small spaces between the particles of clay and shuts out the fresh air that is necessary for the sprouting of the seeds.

This teaches us that when we plant seeds we must so prepare the soil, and so plant the seeds that they will get enough fresh air to enable them to sprout, or, in other words, the soil must be well ventilated.

Experiment – Plant seeds of corn and beans in each of two tumblers; set one out of doors in a cold place and keep the other in a warm place in the house. The seeds kept in the house will sprout quickly but those outside in the cold will not sprout at all. This shows us that seeds will not sprout without heat.

If the weather is warm place one of the tumblers in a refrigerator. Why don't we plant corn in December? Why not plant melons in January? Why not plant cotton in November?

The seeds of farm crops may be divided into two classes according to the temperatures at which they will germinate or sprout readily and can be safely planted.

Class A. Those seeds that will germinate or sprout at an average temperature of forty-five degrees in the shade, or at about the time the peach and plum trees blossom:

Barley	Beet
Oats	Carrot
Rye	Cabbage
Wheat	Cauliflower
Red Clover	Endive
Crimson Clover	Kale
Grasses	Lettuce

These can be planted with safety in the spring as soon as the ground can be prepared, and some of them, if planted in the fall, live through the winter.

Class B. Those seeds that will germinate or sprout at an average temperature of sixty degrees in the shade, or when the apple trees blossom:

Alfalfa	Soy Bean
Cow Pea	Pole Bean
Corn	String Bean
Cotton	Melon
Egg Plant	Okra

We are now ready to answer the question: What conditions are necessary for seeds to sprout or germinate? These conditions are:

- The presence of enough moisture to keep the seed thoroughly soaked.
- The presence of fresh air.
- The presence of more or less heat.

This teaches us that when we plant seeds in the window box or in the garden or on the farm we must so prepare the soil and so plant the seeds that they will be able to obtain sufficient moisture, heat, and air for sprouting. The moisture must be film water, for if it is free water or capillary water filling the soil pores, there can be no ventilation and, therefore, no sprouting.

SEED TESTING

In a previous experiment the seeds planted in the wet clay did not sprout (see **Fig. 38**). In answer to the question, "Why is this?" some will say the seeds were bad. It often happens on the farm that the seeds do not sprout well and the farmer accuses the seedsman of selling him poor seed, but does not think that he himself may be the cause of the failure by not putting the seeds under the proper conditions for sprouting. How can we tell whether or not our seeds will sprout if properly planted? We can test them by putting a number of seeds from each package under proper conditions of moisture, heat and air, as follows:

For large seeds take two plates (see **Fig. 39**) and a piece of cloth as wide as the bottom of the plate and twice as long. Count out fifty or one hundred seeds from a package, wet the cloth and wring it out. Place one end of the cloth on the plate, place the seeds on the cloth and fold the other end of the cloth over them. On a slip of paper mark the number of seeds and date, and place on the edge of the plate. Now cover the whole with another plate, or with a pane of glass to keep from drying. Set the plate of seeds in a warm room and examine occasionally for several days. If the cloth tends to dry, moisten it from time to time. As the seeds sprout take them out and keep a record of them. Or leave them in the plate and after four or five days count those that have sprouted. This will give the proportion of good seeds in the packages.

For small seeds fold the cloth first and place the seeds on top of it.

Another good tester for small seeds is made by running about an inch of freshly mixed plaster of Paris into a small dish or pan and moulding flat cavities in the surface by setting bottles into it.

The dish or pan and bottles should be slightly greased to prevent the plaster sticking to them. When the cast has hardened it should be turned out of the mold and set in a large dish or pan. One hundred small seeds are then counted out and put into one of the cavities, others are put into the other cavities. Water is then poured into the pan till it rises half way up the side of the plaster cast or porous saucer. The whole thing is then covered to keep in the moisture (**Fig. 40**).

Another method is to get boxes of finely pulverized sand or soil and carefully plant in it fifty or one hundred seeds of each kind to be tested. Then by counting those that come up, the proportion of good seeds can easily be found.

In every case the testers should be kept at a

temperature of about seventy degrees or about that of the living room.

HOW THE SEEDS COME UP

Plant a few seeds of corn, beans and garden peas in boxes or tumblers each day for several days in succession. Then put seeds of corn, beans and garden peas to soak. After these have soaked a few hours, examine them to find out how the seed is constructed. Note first the general shape of the seeds and the scar (**Fig. 41-4**) on one side as in the bean or pea and at one end or on one edge in the corn. This scar, also called hilum, is where the seed was attached to the seed vessel.

Cut into the bean and pea, they will be found to be protected by a tough skin or coat. Within this the contents of the seed are divided into two bodies of equal size lying close to each other and called seed leaves or cotyledons (**Fig. 41-5**). Between them near one end or one side will be found a pair of very small white leaves and a little round pointed projection. The part bearing the tiny leaves was formerly, and is sometimes now, called the *plumule*, but is generally called the epicotyl, because it grows above or upon the cotyledons. The round pointed projection was formerly called the radicle, but is now spoken of as the hypocotyl, because it grows below or under the cotyledons.

Examine a dry kernel of corn and notice that on one side there is a slight oval-shaped depression (**Fig. 41-1**). Now take a soaked kernel and cut it in two pieces making the cut lengthwise from the top of the kernel through the center of the oval depression and examine the cut surface. A more or less triangular-shaped body will be found on the concave side of the kernel (see **Figs. 41-2 and 41-3**). This is the one cotyledon of the corn. Besides this will be found quite a mass of starchy material packed in the coverings of the kernel and in close contact with one side of the cotyledon. This is sometimes called the endosperm.

Within the cotyledon will be found a little growing shoot pointed toward the top of the kernel. This is the epicotyl, and another growing tip pointed toward the lower end of the kernel; this is the hypocotyl or the part that penetrates the soil and forms roots.

Now examine the seeds that were planted in succession. Some will be just starting a growing point down into the soil. Some of them have probably come up and others are at intermediate stages.

How did the bean get up?

After sending down a root the hypocotyl began to develop into a strong stem which crooked itself until it reached the surface of the soil and then pulled the cotyledons or seed-leaves after it (**Fig. 42**). These turn green and after a time shrink and fall off.

The pea cotyledons were left down in the soil, the epicotyl alone pushing up to the surface. The corn pushed a slender growing point to the surface leaving the cotyledon and endosperm behind in the soil but still attached to the little plant (**Fig. 43**).

USE OF COTYLEDONS AND ENDOSPERM

Experiment – Plant some beans in a pot or box of soil and as soon as they come up cut the seed-leaves from some of them and watch their growth for several days. It will soon be seen that the plants on which the seed leaves were left increase in size much more rapidly than those from which the seed leaves were removed (see **Figs. 43 and 44**). Sprout some corn in the seed tester. When the seedlings are two or three inches long, get a wide-mouthed bottle or a tumbler of water and a piece of pasteboard large enough to cover the top. Cut a slit about an eighth of an inch wide from the margin to the center of the pasteboard disk. Take one of the seedlings, insert it in the slit, with the kernel under the pasteboard so that it just touches the water. Take another seedling of the same size, carefully remove the kernel from it without injuring the root, and place this seedling in the slit beside the first one (**Fig. 45**). Watch the growth of these two seedlings for a few days. Repeat this with sprouted peas. In each case it will be found that the removal of the seed leaves or the kernel checks the growth of the seedling. Therefore, it must be that the seed leaves that appear above ground, as in the case of the bean, or the kernel of the corn that remains below the surface of the soil, furnish the little plant with food until its roots have grown strong enough to take sufficient food from the soil.

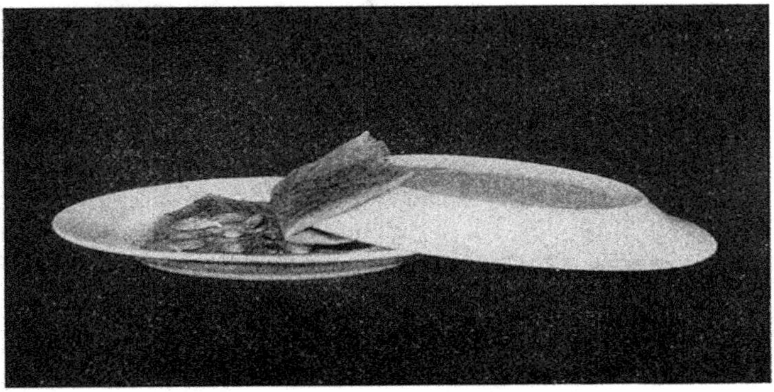

Fig. 39. Seed-tester, consisting of two plates & moist cloth.

Fig. 40. – Seed-Tester. A plaster cast with cavities in the surface for small seeds.

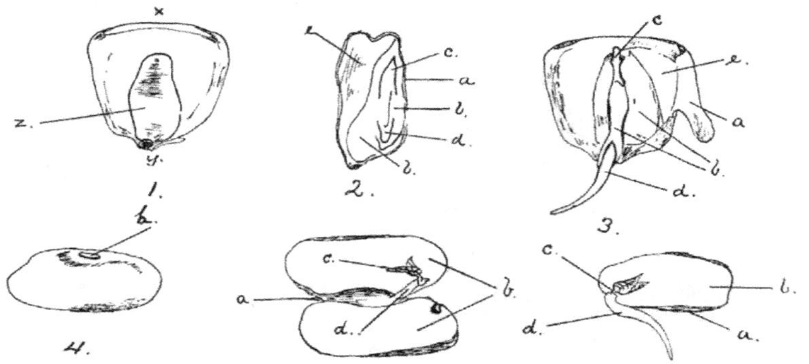

Fig. 41.□1. Corn-kernel showing depression at *z*. 2. Section of same after soaking. 3. Corn-kernel after germination has begun. The seed-coat *a* has been partly removed. 4. Bean showing scar or hilum at *h*.

5. The same, split open. 6. Bean with one cotyledon removed, after sprouting had begun. *a*, Seed-coat; *b*, cotyledon; *c*, epicotyl; *d*, hypocotyl; *e*, endosperm. □(Drawings by M.E. Feltham.)

CHAPTER X

Seed Planting

How deep should seeds be planted?

Experiment – Plant several kernels of corn in moist soil in a glass tumbler or jar. Put one kernel at the bottom and against the side of the glass, place the next one a half-inch or an inch higher and an inch and a half to one side of the first seed and against the glass. Continue this till the top of the glass is reached (**Fig. 2**). Leave the last seed not more than one-fourth inch below the top of the soil. The soil should be moist at the start and the seeds should all be against the glass so they can be seen. This can best be done by planting as you fill the glass with soil. Plant peas and beans in the same way. Do not water the soil after planting. Set aside in a warm place and wait for the seeds to come up.

Another method of performing this experiment is to make a box having one side glass (**Fig. 46**). The length and the depth of the box will depend upon the size of the glass you use. Fill the box nearly full of moist soil and plant seeds of corn and beans and peas at depths of one-quarter inch, one inch, two inches, three inches, and four inches. These seeds can best be put in as the box is being filled. Hold each individual seed against the glass with a stick so that when planted they may be seen through the glass. Protect the seeds and roots from light by using a sheet of cardboard, tin or wrapping paper or a piece of board, and set in a warm place.

Many of the seeds planted only one-quarter inch deep

will not sprout because the soil about them will probably dry out before they take from it enough moisture to sprout. The one and two-inch deep seeds will probably come up all right. Of the three and four-inch deep seeds, the corn and peas will probably make their way to the surface because they send up only a slender shoot, which can easily force its way through the soil. The deep-planted beans will make a strong effort but will not succeed in forcing their way to the surface because they are not able to lift the large seed-leaves through so much soil, and will finally give up the struggle. If any of the deeper beans do get up, the seed-leaves will probably be broken off and the little plant will starve and be dwarfed. This experiment teaches us that we should plant seeds deep enough to get sufficient moisture for sprouting and yet not so deep that the young seedlings will not be able to force their way to the surface.

Seeds which raise their cotyledons above the soil should not be planted as deep as those which do not. Large, strong seeds like corn, peas, etc., which do not lift their cotyledons above the surface, can be planted with safety at a depth of from one to four or five inches.

Seeds of carrot, celery, parsley, parsnip and eggplant are weak and rather slow in germinating. It is customary to plant them rather thickly in order that by the united strength of many seeds they may more readily come to the surface. This point should be observed also in planting seeds in heavy ground that is liable to pack and crust over before the seeds germinate. Seed should always be sown in freshly stirred soil and may be planted by hand or with a machine.

Fig. 42 To show how the bean plant gets up. Notice the curved hypocotyls pulling the seed-leaves or cotyledon out of the soil.

Fig. 43 To show how the corn-plant gets out of the soil. A slender growing point pushes straight up through the soil, leaving the kernel behind.

Fig. 44. To show the use of the cotyledons. These are the plants shown in tumbler 2, Fig 42, forty-eight hours after removing the cotyledons from plant *B*. Plant *B*, although first up, has been handicapped by the loss of its cotyledons.

For the home garden and the school garden, and when only small quantities of any one variety are planted, a machine is hardly desirable and hand planting is preferable.

The rows are marked out with the garden marker, or the end of a hoe or rake handle (**Fig. 47**), using a line or the edge of a board as a guide. The seeds are then carefully and evenly dropped in the mark or furrow.

The covering is done with the hand or a rake or hoe, and the soil is pressed over the seeds by patting it with the covering tool or walking on the row and pressing it with the feet. This pressing of the soil over the seeds is to bring the particles of soil close to each other and to the seed so that film water can climb upon them and moisten the seed sufficiently for sprouting.

A convenient way of distributing small seeds like those of turnip and cabbage, is to take a small pasteboard box or tin spice or baking-powder box, and punch a small hole in the bottom near one end or side. Through this the seeds can be sifted quite evenly.

For the larger operations of the farm and market garden, hand and horse-power drills and broadcasters are generally used, though some farmers still plant large fields by hand.

The grasses and clovers are generally broadcasted by hand or machine, and are then lightly harrowed and are generally rolled.

The small grains (wheat, oats, etc.) are broadcasted by many farmers, but drilling is considered better. With the grain drill the seed is deposited at a uniform depth and at regular intervals. In broadcasting, some of the seeds are planted too deep, and some too shallow, and others are left on the surface of the soil.

From experiment it has been found that there is a loss of about one-fifth of the seed when broadcasted as compared with drilling.

As in the case of grass seed, the grains are generally rolled after sowing.

Corn is planted by hand, or by hand- and horse-corn-planters, which drop a certain number of seeds at any required distance in the row.

There are a number of seed drills made for planting vegetable seeds which are good machines.

The main points to be considered in seed drills or seed planting machines are:

Simplicity and durability of structure.

Ease of draft.

Uniformity in quantity of seed planted, and in the distances apart and depth to which they are planted.

The distances apart at which seeds are planted vary according to the character of the plant. Bushy, spreading plants and tall plants require more room than low and slender-growing plants.

Visit the neighboring hardware stores and farms and examine as many seed-growing tools as possible to see how they are constructed and how properly used. Practice planting with these tools, if possible.

Illustrations of grain drills and other seed-planting machines will be found in seed catalogues, hardware catalogues, and in the advertising columns of agricultural papers.

SEED CLASSIFICATION

In order to become familiar with the farm and garden seeds, obtain samples of as many of them as possible. Put them in small bottles – homeopathic vials for instance – or stick a few of each kind on squares of cardboard. Arrange them in groups according to resemblances or relationships, comparing not only the seeds but also the plants on which they grew. If you cannot recall the plants, and there is no collection available, study the illustrations in seed catalogs that can be obtained from seedsmen. The following groups contain most of the farm and garden seeds, excepting flower seeds:

Grass Family:
Corn,
Wheat,
Oats,
Rye,
Barley,
Sorghum,
Orchard Grass,
Red Top Grass,
Timothy,
Kentucky Blue Grass.

Gourd Family:
Cantaloupe,
Citron,
Cucumber,
Gourd,
Muskmelon,
Pumpkin,
Squash,
Watermelon,
Cymling.

Parsley Family:

Mustard Family:
Mustard,
Cabbage,
Cauliflower,
Collards,
Brussels Sprouts,
Kale,
Kohl Rabi,
Radish,
Rutabaga,
Turnips,
Watercress.

Thistle Family:
Artichoke,
Cardoon,
Chicory,
Dandelion,
Endive,
Lettuce,
Salsify,
Sunflower,
Tansy.

Caraway,
Carrot,
Celery,
Coriander,
Cumin,
Fennel,
Parsley,
Parsnip.

Lily Family:
Asparagus,
Garlic,
Leek,
Onion.

Fig. 45 To show the use of the kernel to the young corn-plant. The kernel was carefully removed from the plant on the right when both plants were of the same size. The result is a dwarfing of the plant.

Fig. 46 To show how deeply seeds should be planted. Seeds 1 and 5 did not sprout because they were not deep enough to get sufficient moisture. The corn-plants from sprouting seeds 2, 3 and 4 all pushed their slender growing points to the surface. Of the beans, No. 6 succeeded in pulling the cotyledons to the surface, and has made a good plant. Nos. 7 and 8, although they made a hard struggle, were not able to raise the cotyledons through so great a depth of soil, and finally gave up the struggle.

TRANSPLANTING

The seeds of some crops – cabbage, tomato, lettuce, for example – are planted in window boxes, hot-beds, cold frames or a corner of the field or garden. When the seedlings have developed three or four leaves or have become large enough to crowd one another, they are thinned out or are transplanted into other boxes, frames or plots of ground, or are transplanted into the field or garden.

The time and method of transplanting depend largely on:

- The condition of the plant.
- The condition of the soil.
- The condition of the atmosphere.

For best results in field planting the plant should be well grown, strong and stocky, with well-developed roots and three or four strong leaves.

The soil should be thoroughly prepared, moist and freshly stirred. A moist day just before a light shower is the best time. These conditions being present, the plants are carefully lifted from the seed bed with as little disturbance of the roots as possible and carried to the field or garden. Some plants, like cabbage, will stand considerable rough treatment, while others, like the eggplant, require greater care.

In the field or garden a hole is made for each plant with the hand, a stick or dibber or any convenient tool, the roots of the plant are carefully placed in it and the soil is pressed about them. If the soil is moist and freshly stirred, new roots will generally start in a very short time.

Plants that have been grown in pots, small boxes or tin cans, as tomatoes and eggplants are sometimes grown, may be quickly transplanted in the field in the following manner: Open the furrow with a small plow, knock the plants out of the pots or cans and place them along the land side of the furrow at the proper distances, then turn the soil back against them with the plow.

When there is a large number of plants to be set, as in planting cabbage, sweet potatoes, etc., by the acre, it is not always convenient to wait for a cloudy day or to defer operations till the sun is low in the afternoon. In such cases the roots of the plants should be dipped in water or in thin mud just before setting them, or a little water may be poured into each hole as the plant is put in. The soil should always be well firmed about the roots. The firming of the soil about the roots of a newly set plant is as important as firming it over planted seeds. The soil should be packed so tightly that the individual leaves will be torn off when an attempt is made to pull the plant up by them.

In dry or warm weather it is a good plan to trim the tops of plants when setting them. This can be done readily with some plants, such as cabbage and lettuce, by taking a bundle of them in one hand and with the other twisting off about half of their tops.

Fig. 47. Seed planting: 1, making the drill; 2, dropping the seeds; 3, covering the seeds; 4, packing soil over the seeds.

Fig. 48. A collection of planting machines. The large central machine is a grass and grain planter. The one on the left, a potato planter. The one on the right, a corn, bean, and pea planter. The three smaller machines in front are hand seed planters.

The proper time to transplant fruit and ornamental trees and shrubs is during the fall, winter and early spring, which is their dormant or resting season, as this gives the injured roots a chance to recover and start new rootlets before the foliage of the plant makes demands on them for food and moisture.

In taking up large plants many roots are broken or crushed. These broken and injured roots should be trimmed off with a smooth cut. The tree or shrub is then placed in the hole prepared for it and the soil carefully filled in and packed about the roots. After the plant is set, the top should be trimmed back to correspond with the loss of root. If the plant is not trimmed, more shoots and leaves will start into growth than the damaged roots can properly furnish with food and water, and the plant will make a weak growth or die.

There are on the market a number of hand transplanting machines that, from their lack of perfection, have not come into general use. Many of them require more time to operate than is consumed in hand planting. A number of large machines for transplanting are in successful and satisfactory use on large truck and tobacco farms. These machines are drawn by horses and carry water for watering each plant as it is set.

Practice transplanting in window boxes or in the open soil and see how many of your plants will survive the operation.

CHAPTER XI

Spading and Plowing

We have learned the important conditions necessary for the sprouting of seeds and for the growth and development of roots. We have also learned something about the soil, its properties, and its relation to, or its behavior toward these important conditions. We are therefore prepared to discuss intelligently methods of treating the soil to bring about, or maintain, these conditions.

SPADING THE SOIL

The typical tool for preparing the soil for root growth is a spade or spading fork (**Fig. 49**). With this tool properly used we can prepare the soil for a crop better than with any other.

In spading, the spade or fork should be pushed into the soil with the foot the full length of the blade and nearly straight down. The handle is then pulled back and the spadeful of earth is pried loose, lifted slightly, thrown a little forward, and at the same time turned. The lumps are then broken by striking them with the blade or teeth of the tool. All weeds and trash should be covered during the operation. A common fault of beginners is to put the spade in the soil on a slant and only about half the length of the blade, and then flop the soil over in the hole from which it came, often covering the edge of the unspaded soil. The good spader works from side to side across his piece of ground, keeping a narrow trench or furrow between the spaded and unspaded soil, into which weeds and trash and manure may be drawn and thoroughly covered, and also to prevent covering the unspaded soil. If this work has been well done with the ordinary spade or fork and finished with a rake, the result will be a bed of soil twelve to fifteen inches deep, fine and mellow and well prepared for root penetration, for good ventilation, for the absorbing and holding of moisture and warmth.

This method should always be employed for small gardens and flower beds.

PLOWING

For preparing large areas of soil the plow is the tool most generally used.

WHY DO WE SPADE AND PLOW?

To break and pulverize the soil and make it soft and mellow, so the roots of plants may enter it in search of food, and get a firm hold for the support of the plant that is above ground.

To make the soil open and porous, so that it can more readily absorb rain as it falls on the surface.

To check loss of water by evaporation.

To admit air to the roots of plants. Also to allow air to act chemically on the mineral and organic matter of the soil and make them available to the crop.

To raise the temperature of soils in the spring, or of damp soils at any time.

To mix manures and organic matter with the soil.

Fig. 49. – SPADING-FORK AND SPADE

The more thoroughly manure is distributed through

the soil the more easily plants will get it and the greater will be its effect on the soil.

To destroy the insect enemies of the plant by turning them up to the frost and the birds.

To kill weeds. Weeds injure crops:

They waste valuable moisture by pumping it up from the soil and sending it out into the air through their leaves. In this way they do their greatest injury to crops.

They crowd and shade the crop.

They take plant food that the plant should have.

Spading and plowing bring about conditions necessary for the sprouting or germination of seeds.

Spading and plowing also tend to bring about conditions necessary for the very important work of certain of the soil bacteria.

PARTS OF A PLOW

It will be found that a good farm plow has the following parts (**Fig. 50**):

A standard or stock, the central part of the plow to which many of the other parts are attached.

A beam, to which the power is attached by which the plow is drawn.

Some plows have wooden beams and others have iron beams.

Handles by which the plowman guides and steadies the plow and also turns it at the corners of the plowed ground in going about the field.

A clevis, which is attached to the end of the beam and is used to regulate the depth of plowing.

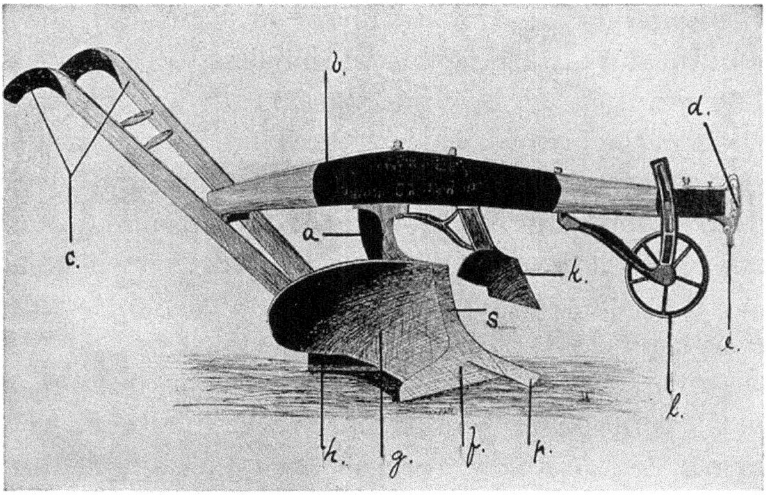

Fig. 50. – A WOOD BEAM-PLOW *a*, stock; *b*, beam; *c*, handles; *d*, clevis, *e*, shackle, *f*, share; *g*, moldboard; *h*, landside; *k*, jointer or skimmer, *l*, truck or wheel, *p*, point or nose, *s*, shin.

To the clevis is attached a *draft ring* or *shackle*, to which the horse or team is fastened. To make the plow run deep the draft ring or shackle is placed in the upper holes or notches of the clevis; to make it run shallow the ring is placed in the lower holes. On some plows there are only notches in the clevis for holding the ring, they answer the same purpose as holes. The clevis is also used on some plows to regulate the width of the furrow. By moving the draft ring or shackle towards the plowed land the plow is made to cut a wider furrow, moving it away from the plowed land causes the plow to cut narrower.

Some plows have a double clevis so that the draft ring may be raised or lowered, or moved to right or left. With some plows the width of the furrow is adjusted by moving the beam at its attachment to the handles.

A share, called by some the point, which shears the bottom of the furrow slice from the land. The share should be sharp, especially for plowing in grass land and land full of tough roots. If the share, particularly the point, becomes worn so that it bevels from beneath upwards it will be hard to keep the plow in the soil, for it will tend to slide up to the surface. If this happens the share must be renewed or sharpened. Plows are being made now with share and point separate, and both of these reversible (**Fig. 51**), so that if either becomes worn on the under side it can be taken out and turned over and put back and it is all right, they thus become self-sharpening.

A moldboard. This turns and breaks the furrow slice. The degree to which the moldboard pulverizes depends on the steepness of its slant upward and the abruptness of its curve sidewise.

The steeper it is and the more abrupt the curve, the greater is its pulverizing power. A steep, abrupt moldboard is adapted to light soils and to the heavier soils when they are comparatively dry. This kind of a plow is apt to puddle a clay soil if it is quite moist. For breaking new land a plow with a long, gradually sloping share and moldboard is used.

A landslide, which keeps the plow in place.

A coulter. Some plows have a straight knife-like coulter (**Fig. 52**) that is fastened to the beam just in front of the moldboard and serves to cut the furrow slice from the land. In some plows this is replaced by an upward projection of the share; this is wide at the back and sharp in front and is called the shin of the plow from its resemblance to the shin bone. The coulter is sometimes made in the form of a sharp, revolving disk (**Fig. 53**), called a rolling coulter. This form is very useful in sod ground and in turning under vines and tall weeds. It also lessens the draft of the plow.

A jointer or skimmer that skims stubble and grass from the surface of the soil and throws them into the bottom of the furrow where they are completely covered. The jointer helps also to pulverize the soil.

A truck or wheel, attached under the end of the beam. This truck makes the plow run steadier. This is sometimes used to make the plow run shallower by setting it low down. This is not right, for it then acts as a brake and makes the plow draw harder. The depth of the furrow should be adjusted at the clevis.

A plow not only has parts but it has character also.

CHARACTERISTICS OF A GOOD PLOW

- A good plow should be strong in build and light in weight.
- The draft should be as light as possible.
- The plow should run steadily.
- A good plow should not only turn the soil but should pulverize it as well.

When plowing, the team should be hitched to the plow with as short traces as possible, and the plow should be so adjusted that it will cut furrows of the required width and thickness with the least possible draft on the team and the least exertion on the part of the plowman.

THE FURROW SLICE

In plowing, the furrow slice may be cut thin and wide and be turned over flat. This method is adapted to breaking new land and heavy sod land.

It may be cut thick and narrow and be turned up on edge.

Or it may be cut of such a width and depth that the plow will turn it at an angle of about forty-five degrees. By this last method the greatest amount of soil can be turned at least expense of labor; the furrow slice can be more thoroughly broken; the greatest surface is exposed to the action of the air, and plant food is more evenly distributed through the soil.

HOW DEEP SHALL WE PLOW?

We learned in a previous chapter that the roots of farm plants develop largely in that part of the soil which is worked by the plow; therefore, to have as much tilled soil as possible for root growth, we should generally plow as deep as possible without turning too much of the subsoil to the surface. Lands that have been plowed deep should be deepened gradually by plowing up a half-inch to an inch of subsoil each year until the plow reaches a depth of at least nine or ten inches.

There is an opinion among many farmers that sandy soils should not be plowed deep. But as these soils are apt to be leachy it seems best to fill them with organic matter to as great a depth as possible to increase their water-holding power, and plowing farm manures in deep can best do this.

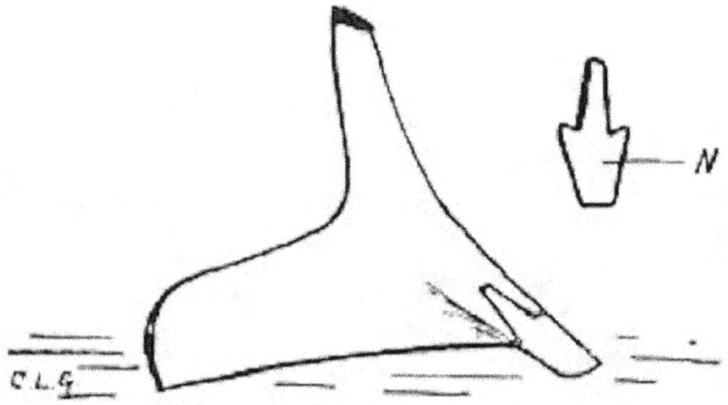

Fig. 51. – A SLIP-NOSE SHARE. *N*, A SLIP-NOSE.

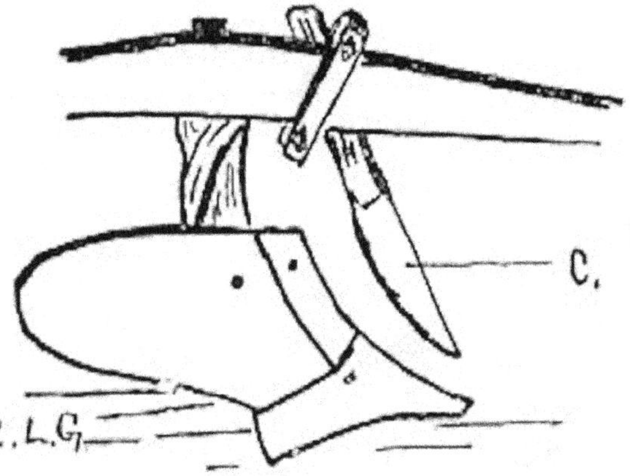

Fig. 52. – *C*, STRAIGHT KNIFE COULTER.

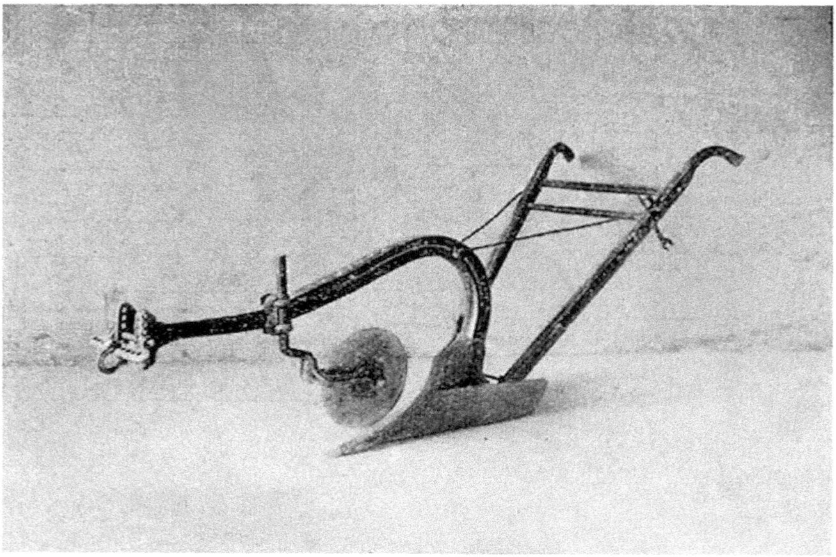

Fig. 53. An iron beam-plow, with rolling coulter and double clevis.

Fig. 54. – A ROLLING COULTER HARROW.

Fig. 55. – SPRING-TOOTHED HARROWS.

In many parts of the South the farmers use very small plows and small animals to draw them. The result is that the soil is not prepared to a sufficient depth to allow of the large root development necessary for large crops. These farmers need larger tools and heavier animals if they expect to make much improvement in the yield of their crops. These small plows and this shallow plowing have done much to aid the washing and gullying of the hill farms by rain. The shallow layer of loose soil takes in the rain readily, but as the harder soil beneath does not take the water as readily, the shallow plowed soil soon fills, then becomes mud, and the whole mass goes down the slope. The land would wash less if it had not been plowed at all, and least of all if it were plowed deep, for then there would be a deep reservoir of loose soil which would be able to hold a large amount of water until the harder lower soil could take care of it.

BREAKING OUT THE MIDDLES

Some farmers have a way when getting the land ready for a crop, of plowing the rows first and then "breaking out the middles" or spaces between after the crop is planted. This is a poor practice, as it interferes with thorough preparation of the soil. The ground can be more thoroughly plowed and broken up before the crop is planted than afterwards. This practice of leaving the middles interferes with proper harrowing and after-cultivation.

THROWING THE LAND UP IN RIDGES

Many farmers throw the land up into ridges with the plow and then plant on the ridge. When land is thrown into ridges a greater amount of surface is exposed to the air and a greater loss of moisture by evaporation takes place, therefore ridge culture is more wasteful of soil water than level culture. For this reason dry soils everywhere and most soils in dry climates should, wherever practicable, be left flat. On stiff, heavy soils that are slow to dry out, and on low bottom lands it may be desirable to ridge the land to get the soil dried out and warmed quicker in the spring. Late fall and early planter truck crops are often planted on the southern slopes of low ridges thrown up with the plow for warmth and protection from cold winds.

TIME TO PLOW

The time of plowing will depend somewhat on the nature of the soil, climate and the crop.

More plowing is done in the spring just before planting spring and summer crops than at any other time, excepting in localities that plant large areas of winter grain and truck. This spring plowing should be done early, for the spring plowing tends to dry the loosened soil somewhat and allows it to become warm at an earlier date, and at the same time the loosened soil tends to hold water in the lower soil for future use by the crop and allows the soil to take in spring rains more readily. If a cover crop or green manure crop is to be turned under in the spring it should be done early so as to prevent the crop to be turned under from pumping too much water out of the soil and thus interfering with the growth of the crop for which the land is being prepared.

There are some particular advantages to be gained by fall plowing in heavy soils:

Immediately after harvest the land is usually dry and easy to work.

The soil plowed at this time and left rough is acted upon physically by frost, which pulverizes it, and chemically by rain and air, which renders plant food available.

Insects are turned up and exposed to frost and birds.

A great number of weeds are destroyed and the land is more easily fitted for crops in the spring. Fall plowing should be done as early as possible, especially in the dryer regions, to catch all water possible. It is not advisable to plow sandy soils in the fall lest plant food be washed out of them.

When possible a cover crop should be put on fall plowed land where there is likely to be loss of plant food by leaching.

BARE FALLOW

The term "fallowing" is sometimes applied to the operation of plowing, and sometimes the land is left bare without a crop sometime after plowing; this is called "bare fallowing" the land.

Bare fallowing should not be practiced on all soils. It is adapted:

To dry climates and dry seasons where it is desirable to catch and save every possible drop of rainfall, and where plant food will not be washed out of the exposed soils by rains.

To heavy clay lands.

To lands that are foul with weeds and insects.

To sour soils which are sweetened by exposure to air and rain.

Light sandy soils should not be subjected to bare fallow unless they are very foul with weeds. They should always be covered with a crop to prevent loss of plant food by leaching.

CHAPTER XII

Harrowing and Rolling

After spading or plowing the next operation in the preparation of the soil is generally raking, harrowing or dragging. The objects of these operations are:

To break lumps and clods left by the plow and spade and to further pulverize the soil.

Harrowing and raking aid in controlling soil ventilation, and put the soil in better condition to absorb moisture.

They check the loss of moisture by making a mulch of fine loose earth on the surface.

The harrow and rake destroy the weeds.

The harrow brings about conditions favorable to the even distribution of seeds.

It is also the tool generally used to cover seeds sown broadcast.

Harrowing is generally done just before planting, and with some crops just after, to cover seeds or to smooth the ground. Harrowing is also done in the first stages of growth of some crops to kill weeds and make a soil mulch.

The harrow should always follow the plow within a few hours unless it is desired to leave the land in a bare fall or winter fallow.

At other times of the year the lumps of earth are apt to dry out and become hard and difficult to break. If there is but one work team on the farm it is a good plan during the plowing season to stop the plow in time to harrow the day's plowing before the day's work ends.

HARROWS

There are several types of harrows in use. They may be classified according to the style of their teeth or cutting parts; they are as follows:

Rolling cutter harrows. Spring-toothed harrows. Spike-toothed harrows. Coulter-toothed harrows. Chain harrows. Brush harrows. Plank or drag harrows.

These types vary in the depth to which they cut, and the degree to which they pulverize the soil.

Rolling cutter harrows. Harrows of this type (see **Fig. 54**) consist of one or more revolving shafts on which are arranged a number of concave disks. These disks are either entire, notched, or made of several pieces fastened together. Examples of these are the disk, cutaway and spading harrows. These harrows cut and move the soil deeper than the other types. They are especially adapted to work on heavy clay soils.

The value of this type of harrow as moisture preservers depends on the manner in which they are used. If the disks are so set that they cover but a portion of the surface with a mulch of fine earth they leave a ridge exposed to the action of the wind and sun and the rate of evaporation is greatly increased. The disks should be set at such an angle that the whole surface shall be stirred or covered. Soils that need the disk harrow should generally be gone over again with some shallower working tool to smooth the surface. An objection to the rolling cutters is that unless great care is taken they will leave the land in ridges and valleys.

The two gangs of disks throw the earth in opposite directions. They are generally set to throw it from the center and the result is a shallow double furrow the width of the machine.

By lapping each time the furrow is partially filled, but to get the land smooth a smoothing harrow should be used after the rolling cutter.

Spring-toothed harrows (**Fig. 55**). Spring-toothed harrows with their curved spring teeth enter the soil readily, draw moderately easy and pass over obstructions without much difficulty.

They are very useful in new land that is full of roots and stumps and also stony land. They pulverize the soil to an average depth. They leave the soil in ridges. The ridges can be leveled by a smoother in the shape of a piece of plank attached to the rear of the harrow. On newly plowed grass land they tend to tear up the sod and leave it on the surface. They also tend to drag out coarse manures when plowed in.

The original and more common form of the spring-toothed harrow is a floating harrow when at work. That is, it rests on the points of the teeth and is dragged or floated over the ground.

A newer form of spring-toothed harrow, sometimes called the fallow cultivator, is mounted on high wheels and they largely control its action. This form of harrow is claimed to do much better work than the floating harrow and may in a large measure displace the rolling cutter. The weight of this harrow is entirely taken from the soil except in the wheel tracks, and the entire action is that of pulverizing and lightening the soil.

Spike-toothed harrows (**Fig. 56**). The teeth of these harrows are round, square or diamond-shaped spikes fastened into a wood or iron frame. The teeth are set in a vertical position or are inclined to the rear.

These harrows are shallow in their action; they run easily but tend to compact the soil more than the other types and are therefore better adapted to loose soils and to finishing off after the work of the deep cutting harrows. They are also used for covering seeds.

Coulter-toothed harrows. The coulter-toothed harrows (**Fig. 57**) have teeth resembling the coulter of a plow twisted or bent into various shapes. The Acme is a good example of this class of harrow. It cuts, turns and pulverizes the surface soil somewhat after the manner of the plow. It prepares a fine mulch and leaves an excellent seed bed.

Fig. 56. – SPIKE-TOOTHED HARROWS.

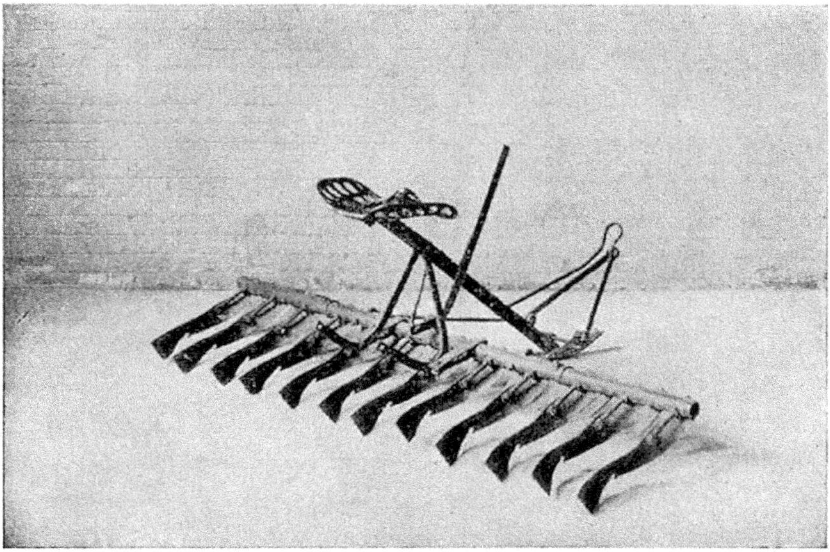

Fig. 57. – A COULTER-TOOTHED HARROW.

Fig. 58. – A PLANK HARROW.

It is an excellent harrow to finish off with after using a

rolling cutter.

Chain harrows. The chain harrow consists of a web of chains linked together. They have a wonderful power for breaking clods and are useful for collecting weeds. They shake the dirt from the weeds and roll them into heaps. Chain harrows tend to compact the soil.

Brush harrows. The brush harrow is a primitive form made by fastening brush to a long pole. Brush harrows are quite useful for brushing in seed and for pulverizing manure broadcasted on grass lands.

Plank harrows. The plank harrow (see **Fig. 58**) is made of several planks fastened together so that each plank overlaps the next one to it, like the clapboards of a house. This harrow is as good as a roller in fining and smoothing the surface soil. It is an excellent tool to use alternately with a spike or coulter-toothed harrow on lumpy soil.

This tool rasps or grinds many of the lumps or clods which slip by the harrow teeth and presses others into the ground so that the harrow following can get a grip on them. It is a harrow that can be made on any farm. This planker is an excellent tool to smooth the surface, for broadcasting small seeds and for planting truck crops.

ROLLING

The objects of rolling are:

To compress the surface soil so that the harrow will do its work more efficiently, also to break clods or lumps that may have resisted the action of the harrow.

To smooth the surface of the soil for an even distribution of small seeds, and to firm the soil around such seeds after they are planted so that they will keep moist and sprout readily.

To give compactness to soils that are light and loose and thus enable them to hold moisture and plant food better.

To press into the ground the roots of plants partly dislodged by the frost.

To remove the conditions favorable to the development of many kinds of insects.

To sink surface stones so that they will not interfere with harvesting the crop.

Light porous soils may be rolled at any time, but clay soils can be rolled to advantage only when they are stiff and cloddy.

Spring-sown grain is often rolled as soon as sown. This is all right in ordinary spring weather, but if showers are frequent and the soil is quite moist the rolling should be omitted till after the grain is up.

The same practice will apply to autumn-sown grain also. If the soil is dry the rolling helps it to pump water up to the seeds. But if it is moist and showers are frequent the combined action of the roller and the rain is to make so thick a crust that many of the seeds will not be able to force their way through it or will be smothered by poor ventilation.

After the grain is up the rolling may be done to advantage, as it then makes a firm soil about the roots of the plants, a condition of benefit to grain crops.

The simplest form of roller is a solid or hollow cylinder of wood fastened into a frame by which it is drawn. Some rollers have spikes or blunt attachments fastened to their surfaces for breaking clods. A roller that is quite popular consists of a cylinder of pressed steel.

CHAPTER XIII

Leaves

We found in an earlier lesson that all of our farm plants have roots, stems, leaves, flowers, fruit and seeds. We studied the root first as being the most important part of the plant to the farmer. The seed was the next part studied, for that was considered the next most important, because the seed is the main reliance for new plants. The part next in importance is the leaf and that we will now study.

If you will go into the field and observe the leaves on a number of plants, you will find that the following facts are true:

They are all green.

They are flat and thin.

Many of them are very broad.

Some of the leaves on a single branch are larger than others on the same branch, and some have longer stems than others.

Most of them have a rather dark glossy upper surface and a lighter rougher under surface.

The leaves on the lower branches of the trees are spread out in a more or less flat layer and have their glossy surfaces all turned up, while those on branches in the tops of trees or shrubs are arranged all around the branch, the glossy surface being turned up.

What are the reasons for these facts? A study of the work of the leaves and the conditions necessary for them to perform their work will help us to answer this question.

Fig. 59. To show transpiration. Plant *A* was set in the sunlight, plant *B* was left in the darker part of the room. *A* has transpired much more than *B*, showing that sunlight is necessary for this work.

THE USES OF LEAVES TO PLANTS

Experiment – (See **Fig. 59**). Take a pot or tumbler in which a young plant is growing, also a piece of pasteboard large enough to cover the top of the pot; cut a slit from the edge to the center of the pasteboard, then place it on the top of the pot, letting the plant enter the slit. Now close the slit with wax or tallow, making it perfectly tight about the stem. If the plant is not too large, invert a tumbler over it, letting the edge of the tumbler rest on the pasteboard; if a tumbler is not large enough use a glass jar. If a potted plant is not convenient a slip or a seedling bean or pea placed in a tumbler of water will serve the purpose.

Fig. 60. – AMOUNT OF TRANSPIRATION This plant transpired within 48 hours an amount of water equal to the colored liquid in the bottle standing on the jar, more than 6 ounces.

Prepare several and place some in a sunny window and leave others in the room where it is darker, and observe them from time to time. In the case of those plants that were set in the sunny window moisture will be seen collecting on the inner surface of the tumbler. Where does this come from? It is absorbed from the soil by the roots and is sent with its load of dissolved plant food up through the stems to the leaves. There most of the water is passed from the leaves to the air and is condensed on the sides of the glass. A work of leaves then is to throw off or to transpire moisture and thus make room for a new supply of food-laden moisture. This water is thrown off through little pores or mouths or stomata which are very small and very numerous on the under side of the leaf. It will be noticed that the plant not placed in the sunlight transpires very little moisture, showing that sunlight helps the leaves in this work of transpiration.

How much water does a plant transpire or throw off from its leaves?

Experiment – (See **Fig. 60**). Fill a common quart fruit jar or can with soil and plant in it a kernel of corn, a bean, a cotton seed or seed of some other plant. After the plant has grown to be twelve or fifteen inches high, cut a piece of pasteboard a little larger than the top of the jar, cut a hole in the center as large as the stem of the plant and make a slit from edge to center. Soak the pasteboard in melted wax or paraffin candle. Cool it and then place it over the jar, slipping it around the plant stem. Now solder the pasteboard to the jar with melted candle making the joints tight all the way around. Then close up the slit and the hole about the stem. The jar is now completely sealed and there is no way for water to escape except through the plant. The plant should be well watered before the jar is closed. Now weigh the jar and set in the sunlight. Weigh again the next day. The difference in the two weights will represent the amount of water transpired by the plant. The weighings may be repeated until moisture gives out. If it is desired to continue this experiment some time, a small hole should be cut in the pasteboard before it is fastened to the jar. This hole is for adding water to the jar from time to time. The hole should be kept closed with a cork. The amount of water added should always be weighed and account taken of it in the following weighings. While this plant is growing it will be well to wrap the jar with paper to protect the roots from the light.

It has been found that the amount of water necessary to grow a plant to maturity is equal to from 300 to 500 times the weight of the plant when dry.

This gives us an idea of the very great importance of water to plants.

Experiment – Take a few leaves from a plant of cotton, bean, clover or other plant that has been growing in the sunlight; boil them for a few minutes to soften the tissues, then place them in alcohol for a day or until the green coloring matter is extracted by the alcohol. Wash the leaves by taking them from the alcohol and putting them in a tumbler of water. Then put them in saucers in a weak solution of iodine. The leaf will be seen to gradually darken; this will continue until it becomes dark purple or almost black (**Fig. 61**). We have already learned that iodine turns starch this color, so we conclude that leaves must contain starch. (Five or ten cents worth of tincture of iodine from a drug store diluted to about the color of weak tea will be sufficient for these leaf experiments.)

Experiment – If a potted plant was used for the last experiment, set it away in a dark closet after taking the leaves for the experiment. A day or two after, take leaves from it before removing it from the closet. Boil these leaves and treat them with alcohol as in the previous experiment. Then wash them and test them with iodine as before. No starch will be found in the leaves (**Fig. 62**). The starch that was in them when placed in the closet has disappeared. Now paste some thick paper labels on some of the leaves of a plant exposed to the sunlight. After a few hours remove the leaves that have the labels on them, boil, treat with alcohol and test with the iodine. In this case starch will be found in all parts of the leaf except the part over which the label was pasted (**Fig. 63**). If the sunlight is intense and the label thin, some starch will appear under it.

According to these last experiments, leaves contain starch at certain times, and this starch seems to appear when the leaf is in the sunlight and to disappear when the light is cut off. The fact is that the leaves manufacture starch for the plant and sunlight is necessary for this work. The starch is then changed to sugar, which is carried by the sap to other parts of the plant where it is again changed to starch to be built into the plant structure, or stored for future use.

Experiment – Take leaves from a plant of silver-leaf geranium growing in the sunlight. If this plant cannot be had, the leaves from some other variegated white and green leaved plant will do. Boil these leaves, treat with alcohol, wash and test with iodine (**Fig. 64**). Starch will be found in the leaf wherever there was green coloring matter in it, while the parts that were white will show no starch. The green coloring matter seems to have something to do with the starch making, in fact starch is manufactured only where it is present. This coloring matter is called chlorophyll or leaf green.

The chemists tell us that this starch is made from carbon and water. There exists in the air a gas called carbonic acid gas; this gas is composed of carbon and oxygen. It is breathed out of the lungs of animals and is produced by the burning and decay of organic matter. The under side of the leaf contains hundreds of little pores or mouths called stomata. This gas mixed with air enters these mouths. The green part of the leaf aided by the sun takes hold of the gas and separates the carbon from the oxygen. The oxygen is allowed to go free, but the carbon is made to unite with water and form starch.

Experiment – The escape of this oxygen gas may be seen by taking some water weed from either fresh or salt water and placing it in a glass jar of the kind of water from which it came, then set the jar in the sunlight. After a time bubbles of gas will be seen collecting and rising to the surface. If a mass of weed like the green scum of fresh water ponds or green sea lettuce be used, the bubbles of gas will become entangled in the mass and will cause it to rise to the surface of the water. At the same time prepare another jar of the weed and place it somewhere out of the sun; very few bubbles will be seen to rise and the weed will settle to the bottom of the jar (**Fig. 65**).

All of the food of the plant, whether taken from the air

or from the soil is digested in the leaves, and sunlight and air are necessary for this work.

Another function of leaves then is to digest food for the plant.

Important functions of leaves then are:

To transpire moisture sent up by the roots.

To manufacture starch by combining some of the water sent up by the roots with carbon taken from the air.

To digest the starch and food sent up by the roots.

To do these things well leaves must be connected with a strong, healthy root system and must have plenty of light and air.

We are now ready to give reasons for the facts about leaves mentioned in the first part of the chapter.

Leaves are green because the green coloring matter is necessary for the leaf to do its work.

Leaves are flat and thin and broad in order that they may present a large surface to the air and sunlight.

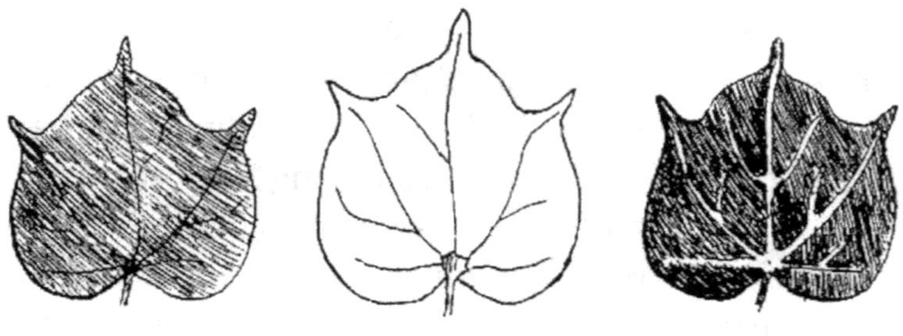

1 2 3

Fig. 61. To show that growing leaves contain starch. 1. Represents a green cotton leaf as picked from the plant. 2. Is the same leaf after taking out the green coloring matter; the leaf is white. 3. The same leaf after treatment with weak iodine turned to a dark purple, showing the presence of starch. (Drawings by M.E. Feltham.)

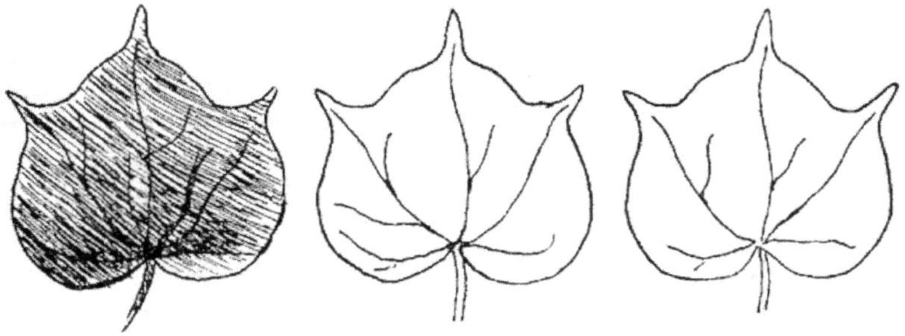

4 5 6

Fig. 62. To show that starch disappears from the leaf when the plant is placed in the dark. The plant from which was taken the leaf represented in Fig 61, was immediately placed in a dark closet for 24 hours. Then leaf 4 was taken from it; 5 represents this leaf after the chlorophyll was taken from it: it is white; 6 is the same after treatment with iodine. The leaf remains white, showing no starch. (Drawings by M.E. Feltham.)

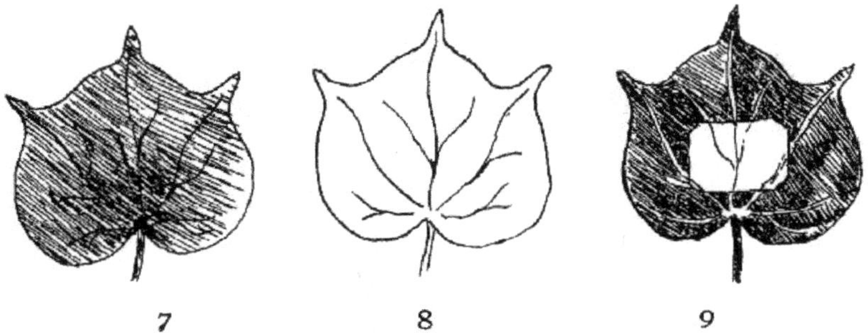

7 8 9

Fig. 63. To show that sunlight is necessary for starch-making by leaves. Leaf 7 had a paper label stuck to its upper surface a couple of hours while the plant was exposed to sunlight; 8 is the same leaf after the chlorophyll was taken out, and 9 represents it after treatment with iodine. The leaf turned purple in all parts except the part that was shaded by the label. Starch was removed from the portion under the label, but was not renewed because the label kept out the necessary sunlight. (Drawings by M.E. Feltham.)

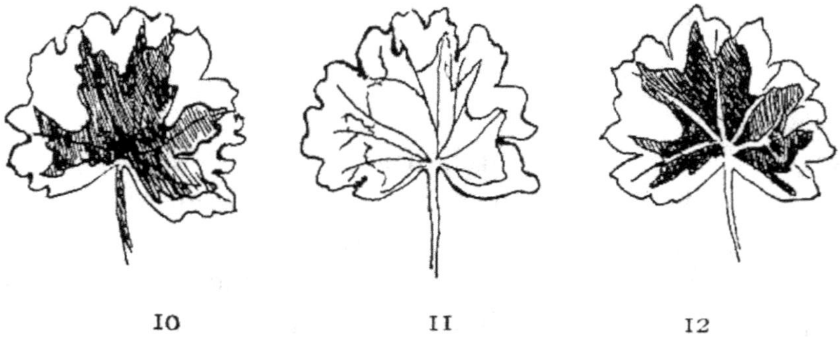

Fig. 64. To show that chlorophyll is necessary for starch formation in the leaf. 10 is a variegated leaf from a silver-leaved geranium; the center is an irregular patch of green, with an irregular border of white. 11, after taking out the green. 12, after iodine treatment, the leaf turns purple only where it was originally green, showing that no starch forms in the white border. (Drawings by M.E. Feltham.)

Some leaves on the branch are larger than others because in the struggle for light and air they have had a better chance than the others or they have had more of the food that has come up from the root.

Some of the leaves have developed longer stems than others in their effort to reach out after light and air.

Most leaves have the little mouths through which air is taken in and water and oxygen given out on the rough side, and that side is turned down toward the earth probably so that rain and dust will not choke the little pores.

The leaves of the lower branches tend to spread out in a broad, flat plane because in the effort to get light no leaf will grow directly under and in the shadow of another, while on those branches which grow straight up from the top of the tree the leaves can get light from all sides and so arrange themselves around the stem.

Is it of any value to the plant grower to know these facts about leaves? It is, for knowing these things he can better understand the necessity of caring for the leaves of his growing plants to see that their work is not interfered with.

HOW THE WORK OF SOME LEAVES IS INTERFERED WITH

Many people who grow house plants have trouble in keeping them well clothed with leaves, for instance, the geranium and the rubber plant. The leaves are constantly turning yellow and dropping off or drying up. This sometimes occurs from over-watering or not sufficiently watering the soil in the pot or box. If the watering is all right the trouble may occur in this way:

The air of the house is quite dry, especially in winter. As a result transpiration from the leaf may be excessive.

More water is transpired than is necessary, consequently the roots pump more and with it more food is sent to the leaf than it can take care of. As the excess of water is transpired the excess of food is left in the leaf. The tendency is to clog its pores and therefore interfere with its work, and gradually weaken and finally kill it.

The remedy for this is to spray the leaves frequently so as to keep the air about them moist and so check transpiration. Keeping a vessel of water near them helps also as this tends to keep the air moist. Dust sometimes chokes the leaves. Washing or spraying remedies this.

Sometimes house plants, and out-door plants as well, become covered with a small, green insect called the plant louse or aphis. This insect has a sharp beak like a mosquito and it sucks the juices from the leaf and causes it to curl up, interfering with its work and finally killing it. Frequent spraying with water will tend to keep these away.

A surer remedy against them is to spray the plants with weak tobacco water made by soaking tobacco or snuff in water, or to fumigate them with tobacco smoke. Sometimes the under side of the leaf becomes infested with a very small mite called red spider because it spins a web. These mites injure the leaf by sucking sap from it.

They can be kept in check by frequent spraying for they do not like water. If, then, we are careful to frequently spray the leaves of our house plants we will have very little trouble from aphis, red spider or over transpiration. The aphis, or plant louse, is often very numerous on out-door plants, for instance, the rose, chrysanthemum, cabbage, and fruit trees. They vary in color from green to dark brown or black. They are treated in the same way as those on the house plants. Some familiar out-door insects which interfere with leaf work are the common potato bug, the green cabbage worm, the rose slug, the elm tree leaf beetle, the canker worm, the tomato worm. These insects and many others eat the leaves (**Fig. 67**). They chew and swallow their food and are called chewing insects. All insects which chew the leaves of plants can be destroyed by putting poison on their food. The common poisons used for this purpose are Paris green and London purple, which contain arsenic, and are used at the rate of one teaspoonful to a pail of water or one-fourth pound to a barrel of water. This is sprinkled or sprayed on the leaves of the plants. Another poison used is white hellebore. This loses its poisoning qualities when exposed to the air for a time. Therefore it is safer to use about the flower garden and on plants which are soon to be used as food or whose fruit is to be used soon, like cabbages and current bushes. This hellebore is sifted on the plant full strength, or it may be diluted by mixing one part of hellebore with one or two parts of flour, plaster, or lime. It is also used in water, putting one ounce of hellebore in three gallons of water and then spraying it on the plants. Plants may be sprayed by using a watering pot with a fine rose or sprinkler, or an old hair-brush or clothes-brush.

For large plants or large numbers of smaller plants spray pumps of various sizes are used. Sometimes chewing insects on food plants and sucking insects on all plants are treated by spraying them with soapy solutions or oily solutions that injure their bodies.

The work of the leaf is also interfered with by diseases that attack the leaves and cause parts or the whole leaf to turn yellow or brown or become blistered or filled with holes.

The common remedy for most of these diseases is called the "Bordeaux Mixture." It is prepared as follows:

Dissolve four pounds of blue vitriol (blue stone, or copper sulfate) in several gallons of water. Then slake four pounds of lime. Mix the two and add enough water to make a barrelful. The mixture is then sprayed on the plants.

For more detailed directions for spraying plants and combating insects and diseases write to your State Experiment Station and to the United States Department of Agriculture at Washington, D.C.

Fig. 65. To show the giving off of gas by leaves, and that sunlight is necessary for it. The jars contain seaweed. *A* was set in the sun and developed enough gas to float part of the plant. *B* was left in the darker part of the room and developed very little gas.

The work of the leaves of houseplants is often interfered with by not giving them sufficient sunlight. Garden and field plants are sometimes planted so thick that they crowd each other and shut the light and air from each other, or weeds are allowed to grow and do the same thing, the result being that the leaves cannot do good work and the plant becomes weak and sickly. Pulling them up and exposing their roots to the sun destroy weeds. This should be done before the weeds blossom, to prevent them from producing fresh seeds for a new crop of weeds.

Some weeds have fleshy roots – for example, dock, thistle – in which food is stored; these roots go deep in the ground, and when the upper part of the plant is cut or broken off the root sends up new shoots to take the place of the old. Some have underground stems in which food is stored for the same purpose. The surest way to get rid of such weeds, in fact, of all weeds, is to prevent their leaves from growing and making starch and digesting food for them. This is accomplished by constantly cutting off the young shoots as soon as they appear above the soil, or by growing some crop that will smother them. The constant effort to make new growth will soon exhaust the supply of stored food and the weed will die.

Fig. 66. Seedling radishes reaching for light.

Fig. 67. Elm leaves injured by the "imported elm-tree leaf beetle," a chewing insect.

CHAPTER XIV

Stems

What are stems for? Visit the farm or garden and the fields to examine stems and study their general appearances and habits of growth. Notice that many plants, like the trees, bushes and many vegetable and flowering plants, have stems which are very much branched, while others have apparently single stems with but few or no branches. Examine these stems carefully and note that there are leaves on some part of all of them and that just above the point where each leaf is fastened to the stem there is a bud which may sometime produce a new branch (**Fig. 68**). If the stems of trees and other woody plants be examined in the winter after the leaves have fallen, it will be seen that the buds are still there, and that just below each bud is a mark or leaf scar left by the fallen leaf. These buds are the beginnings of new branches for another year's growth. On some branches will be found also flowers and fruit or seed vessels.

Buds and leaves or buds and leaf scars distinguish stems from roots. Some plants have stems under the soil as well as above it. These underground stems resemble roots but can be distinguished from them by the rings or joints where will be found buds and small scale-like leaves (**Fig. 69**). Quitch-grass or wiregrass, Bermuda grass, white potato and artichoke are examples of underground stems.

Now study the habit of growth of these stems. Notice that:

Some plants grow erect with strong, stiff stems, for example, corn, sunflower, maple, pine, elm and other trees. Many of these erect stems have branches reaching out into the air in all directions. Stand under a tree close to the stem or trunk and look up into the tree and notice that the leaves are near the outer ends of the branches while in the center of the tree the branches are nearly bare. Why is this? If you remember the work of leaves and the conditions necessary for their work you will be able to answer this question. Leaves need light and air for their work, and these erect, branching stems hold the leaves up and spread them out in the light and air.

Notice that where several trees grow close together, they are one-sided, and that the longest and largest branches are on the outside of the group and that they have more leaves than the inner branches. Why? Why do the trees in thick woods have most of the living branches and bear most of their leaves away up in the top of the tree?

Some stems instead of standing up erect climb up on other plants or objects by means of springlike tendrils that twist about the object and so hold up the slender stem. On the grape vine these tendrils are slender branches. On the sweet pea and garden pea they are parts of the leaves. The trumpet creeper and English ivy climb by means of air roots. The nasturtium climbs by means of its leaf stems.

Other stems get up into the light and air with their leaves by twining about upright objects. For example, the morning glory and pole bean.

Some stems will be found that spread their leaves out to the sun by creeping over the ground. Sweet potato, melon, squash, and cucumber vines are examples of such plants.

One use of the stems of plants then is to support the leaves, flowers and fruit, and expose them to the much needed light and air.

Experiment – Get a piece of grape vine and cut it into pieces four or five inches long; notice that the cut surface appears to be full of little holes. Cut a piece from between joints, place one end in your mouth and blow hard. It will be found that air can be blown through the piece of vine. Now pour about an inch of water in a tumbler or cup and color it with a few drops of red ink. Then stand some of the pieces of grape vine in the colored water. In a few hours the colored water will appear at the upper ends of the sticks. Capillary force has caused the colored water to rise through the small tubes in the vine. Repeat this experiment with twigs of several kinds of trees and soft green plants, as elm, maple, sunflower, corn, etc. It will not be possible to blow through these twigs, but the red water will rise through them by osmosis, and in a few hours will appear at the upper ends. If some leaves are left on the stems the colored water will appear in them. Some white flowers can be colored in this way.

In this manner the stem carries plant food dissolved in water from the roots to the leaves, and after the leaves have digested it carries it back to various parts of the plant.

The stem then serves as a conductor or a passage for food and moisture between roots and leaves.

Visit a strawberry bed or search for wild strawberry plants. Notice that from the older and larger plants are sent out long, slender, leafless stems with a bud at the tip.

These stems are called runners. Find some runners that have formed roots at the tip and have developed a tuft of leaves there, forming new plants. Find some black raspberry plants and notice that some of the canes have bent over and taken root at the tips sending up a new shoot and thus forming a new plant. You know how rapidly wire grass and Bermuda grass will overrun the garden or farm. One way in which they do this is by sending out underground stems that take root at the joints and so form new plants.

Another use of the stem then is to produce new plants.

On the farm we make use of this habit of stems when we wish to produce new white potato plants. We cut an old potato in pieces and plant them. The buds in the eyes grow and form new plants. One way of getting new grape plants is to take a ripened vine in the fall and cut it in pieces with two or three buds and plant them so that one or both of the buds are covered with soil. The pieces will take root and in the spring will send up new shoots and thus form new plants.

You can obtain new plants from geranium, verbena, nasturtium and many other flowering plants, by cutting and planting slips or parts of the stems from them.

In parts of the South new sweet potato plants are obtained by cutting parts of the stems from growing plants and planting them.

Florists produce large numbers of new plants by taking advantage of this function of stems.

Experiment – Take a white potato which is a thickened stem and place it in a warm, dark place. It will soon begin to sprout or send out new stems, and as these new stems grow the potato shrinks and shrivels up. Why is this? It is because the starch and other material stored in the potato are being used to feed the new branches. When we plant potatoes in the garden and field the new plants produced from the eyes of the potato are fed by the stored material until they strike root and are able to take care of themselves.

All stems store food for the future use of the plant.

Annual plants, or those which live but one year, store food in their stems and leaves during the early part of their growth. During the fruiting or seed forming season this food material is transferred to the seeds and there stored, and the stems become woody. This is a fact to bear in mind in connection with the harvesting of hay or other fodder crops. If we let the grass stand until the seeds form in the head, the stem and leaves send their nourishment to the seeds and become woody and of less value than if cut before the seeds are fully formed.

In plants of more than one year's growth the stored food is used to give the plant a start the following season, or for seed production.

The rapid growth of leaf and twig on trees and shrubs in spring is made from the food stored in the stem the season before.

Sago is a form of starch stored in the stem of the sago palm for the future use of the plant.

Maple sugar is made from the food material stored in the trunk of the maple tree for the rapid growth of twig and leaf in the spring.

Cane sugar is the food stored in the sugar cane to produce new plants the next season.

If we examine the stem of a tree that has been cut down we find that it is woody, that the wood is arranged in rings or layers and that the outer part of the stem is covered with bark. We will notice also that the wood near the center of the tree is darker than the outer part. This inner part is called the heart wood of the tree. The lighter wood is called the sap wood. It is through the outer or sap wood that the water taken in by the root is passed up to the leaves where the food that it carries is digested and then sent back to the plant. The returning digested food is sent back largely through the bark. Between the bark and the wood is a very thin layer that is called cambium. This is the active growing tissue of the stem. In the spring it is very soft and slippery and causes the bark to peel off easily. This cambium builds a new ring of wood outside of the old wood and a new ring of bark on the inside of the bark. In this way the tree grows in diameter.

Now if the bark is injured, or any part of the stem, all parts below the wound are cut off from the return supply of digested food and their growth is checked. When such a wound does occur, or if cutting off a branch makes a wound, the cambium sets to work to repair the damage by pushing out a new growth that tends to cover the wound. We can help this by covering the wound and keeping the air from it to prevent its drying and to keep disease from attacking it before it is healed.

HOW THE WORK OF THE STEM MAY BE INTERFERED WITH

If there are any peach trees near by, examine the trunks close to the ground, even pulling away the soil for a few inches. You will very likely find a mass of gummy substance oozing from the tree. Pull this away and in it and in the wood under it will be found one or more yellowish white worms. These are tree borers. They will be found in almost all peach trees. They interfere with the work of the stem and in many cases kill the trees. These worms may be kept somewhat in check by keeping papers wrapped about the lower part of the tree. But the surest way to keep them in check is to dig them out, spring and fall, with a knife and wire.

Borers attack the other fruit trees and also ornamental trees and shrubs.

Rabbits sometimes gnaw the bark from trees during severe winters.

Careless workmen sometimes injure the bark of trees by allowing plows and mowing machines or other tools which they are using among them to come in contact with the trees and injure the bark.

Young trees purchased from the nursery generally have a label fastened to them with a piece of wire. Unless this wire is removed or is carefully watched and enlarged from time to time it will cut into the bark as the stem grows and interfere with its work and often kill the top of the tree or injure a main branch.

These are a few ways in which the work of the stem is sometimes checked and the plant injured thereby.

CHAPTER XV

Flowers

In our study of the parts of plants the flower and fruit have been given the last place because in the growing of most farm plants a knowledge of the functions of the flower is of less importance than that of the roots, leaves and stems. However, a knowledge of these parts is necessary for successful fruit culture and some other horticultural industries.

As with the other parts of the plant our study will not be exhaustive but will be simply an attempt to bring out one or two important truths of value to most farmers.

In the study of flowers the specimens used for study will depend upon the time of the year in which the studies are made and need not necessarily be the ones used here for illustration.

FUNCTION OR USE OF FLOWERS TO PLANTS

Of what use is the flower to the plant?

You have doubtless noticed that most flowers are followed by fruit or seed vessels. In fact, the fruit and seeds are really produced from the flower, and the work of most flowers is to produce seeds in order to provide for new plants.

To understand how this comes about it will be necessary to study the parts of the flower and find out their individual uses or functions.

Fig. 68. A horse-chestnut stem showing leaves, buds, and scars where last year's leaves dropped off.

Fig. 69. – AN UNDERGROUND STEM Buds show distinctly at points indicated by *b*.

PARTS OF A FLOWER

If we take for our study any of the following flowers: cherry, apple, buttercup, wild mustard, and start from the outside, we will find an outer and under part which in most flowers is green. This is called the calyx (**Figs. 70-73** and **74**). In the buttercup and mustard the calyx is divided into separate parts called sepals. In the cherry, peach and apple, the calyx is a cup or tube with the upper edge divided into lobes.

Above the calyx is a broad spreading corolla, which is white or brightly colored and is divided into several distinct parts called petals. The petals of one kind of flower are generally different in shape, size and color from those of other flowers. In some flowers the petals are united into a corolla of one piece which may be funnel-shaped, as in the morning glory or petunia of the garden, or tubular as in the honeysuckle, wheel-shaped as in the tomato and potato, or of various other forms.

Within the corolla are found several bodies having long, slender stems with yellow knobs on their tips. These are called stamens. The slender stems are called stalks or filaments and the knobs anthers. The anthers of some of the stamens will very likely be found covered with a fine, yellow powder called pollen. This pollen is produced within the anther which, when ripe, bursts and discharges the pollen.

The stamens vary greatly in number in different kinds of flowers. In the center of the cherry, peach, or mustard flower will be found an upright slender body called the pistil. In the peach and cherry the pistil has three parts, a lower rounded, somewhat swollen part called the ovary, a slender stem arising from it called the style, and a slight enlargement at the top of the style called the stigma. The stigma is generally roughened or sticky. If the ovary is split open, within it will be found a little body called an ovule, which is to develop into a seed.

In the apple flower the pistils will be found to have one ovary with five styles and stigmas and in the ovary will be several ovules.

In the buttercup will be found a large number of small pistils, each consisting of an ovary and stigma.

The parts of different flowers will be found to vary in color, in shape, in relative size and in number. In some flowers one or more of the parts will be found wanting.

Examine a number of flowers and find the parts.

FUNCTIONS OF THE PARTS OF THE FLOWERS

Now what are the uses of these parts of the flower?

If we watch a flower of the peach or cherry from week to week, we will see that the pistil develops into a peach or cherry, which bears within a seed from which a new plant will be produced if the seed is placed under conditions necessary for germination or sprouting.

The pistils of the flowers of other plants will be found to develop into fleshy fruits, hard nuts, dry pods or husks containing one or more seeds.

The work of the pistil or pistils of flowers then is to furnish seeds for the production of new plants.

The botanists tell us that a pistil will not produce seeds unless it is fertilized by pollen from the same kind of flower falling on its stigma.

Fig. 70. – FLOWER OF CHERRY. *a*, pistil; *b*, stamen; *c*, corolla; *d*, calyx; *e*, section of flower showing ovary with ovule. (Drawing by M.E. Feltham.)

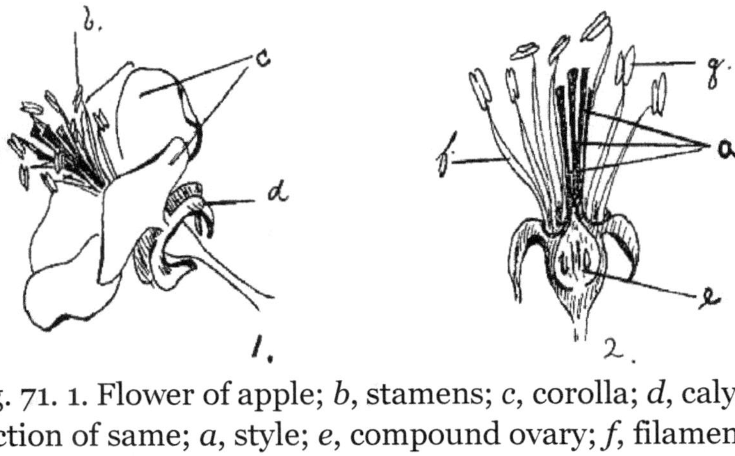

Fig. 71. 1. Flower of apple; *b*, stamens; *c*, corolla; *d*, calyx. 2. Section of same; *a*, style; *e*, compound ovary; *f*, filament; *g*, anther. (Drawing by M.E. Feltham.)

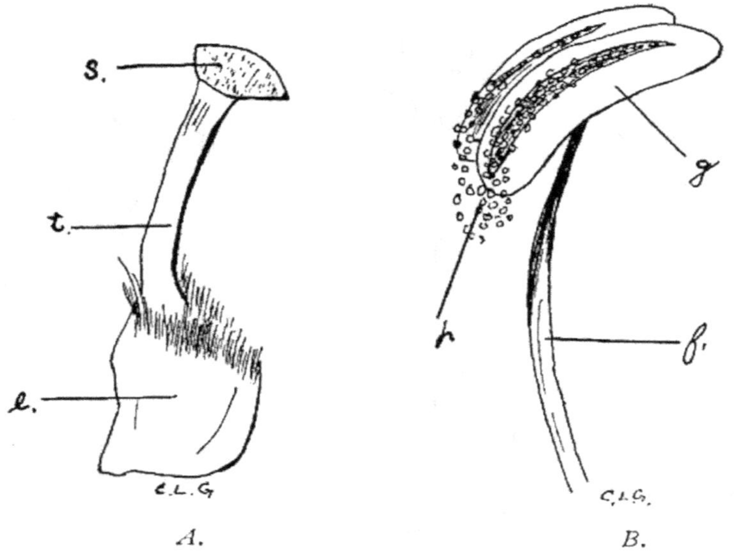

Fig. 72. *A*. Pistil of flowering raspberry; *e*, ovary; *t*, style; *s*, stigma. *B*. Stamen of flowering raspberry; *f*, filament; *g*, anther; *p*, pollen.

The work of the stamen then is to produce pollen to fertilize the pistils. Pistils and stamens are both necessary for the production of fruit and seed. They are therefore called the essential or necessary parts of the flower.

The botanists also tell us that nature has provided that in most cases the pistils shall be fertilized by the pollen of some other flower than their own, as this produces stronger seeds.

How is the pollen carried from flower to flower?
Go into the garden or field and watch the bees and butterflies flying about the flowers, resting on them and crawling into them.

They are seeking for nectar which the flower secretes. As they visit plant after plant, feeding from many flowers, their bodies become more or less covered with pollen as they brush over the stamens. Some of this pollen in turn gets rubbed off on the stigmas of the pistils and they become fertilized. Thus the bees and some other insects have become necessary as pollen carriers for some of the flowers and the flowers in turn feed them with sweet nectar.

This gives us a hint as to one use of the corollas, which spreads out such broad, brightly colored, conspicuous petals. It must be that they are advertisements or sign boards to attract the bees and to tell them where they can find nectar and so lead them unconsciously to carry pollen from flower to flower to fertilize the pistils. The act of carrying pollen to the pistil is called pollination, and carrying pollen from the stamens of one flower to the pistil of another flower is called cross-pollination.

If we examine a blossom bud just before it opens we will see only the calyx. Everything else will be wrapped up inside of it. Evidently, then, the calyx is a protecting covering for the other parts of the flower until blossoming time.

The corolla will be found carefully folded within the calyx and also helps protect the stamens and pistil.

Some flowers do not produce bright-colored corollas to attract the bees, for examples, the flowers of the grasses, wheat, corn, and other grains, the willows, butternuts, elms, pines and others. But they produce large amounts of pollen that is carried by the wind to the pistils.

Fig. 73. – FLOWER OF BUTTERCUP. *c*, petals; *d*, sepals; *h*, ripened pistils, or fruit. (Drawing by M.E. Feltham.)

You have sometimes noticed in the spring that after a rain the pools of water are surrounded by a ring of yellow powder and you have perhaps thought it was sulfur. It was not sulfur but was composed of millions of pollen grains from flowers. One spring Sunday I laid my hat on the seat in church. When I picked it up at the end of the service I found considerable dust on it. I brushed the dust off, but on reaching home I found some remaining and noticed that is was yellow, so I examined it with a magnifying glass and found that it was nearly all pollen grains. Then I rubbed my finger across a shelf in my room and found it slightly dusty; the magnifying glass showed me that this dust was half pollen. This shows what a great amount of pollen is produced and discharged into the air, and it shows that very few pistils could escape even if they were under cover of a building.

To make sure of cross pollination nature has in some cases placed the stamens and pistils in different flowers on the same plant. This will be found true of the flowers of the squashes, melons and cucumber. Below some of the flower buds will be seen a little squash, melon or cucumber (**Fig. 75**). These are the ovaries of pistils and the stigmas will be found within the bud or will be seen when the bud opens. But no stamen will be found here.

Other flowers on these plants will be found to possess only stamens. These staminate flowers produce pollen and then die. They do not produce any fruit, but their pollen is necessary for the little cucumbers, squashes and melons to develop.

Another example is the corn plant. Here the pistils are on the ear, the corn silk being the styles and stigmas, while the pollen is produced in the tassel at the top of the plant.

With some plants we find that not only are the pistils and stamens in separate flowers but also the staminate and pistillate flowers are placed on different plants. This will be found true of the osage orange and the willow.

In many flowers that have both stamens and pistils or

are perfect flowers the stigmas and pollen ripen at different times. With some varieties of fruit it is found that the pistils cannot be fertilized by pollen of the same variety. This is true of most of our native plums. For example, the pistils of the wild goose plum cannot be fertilized by pollen of wild goose plums even if it comes from other trees than the one bearing the pistils. They must have pollen from another variety of plum.

VALUE OF A KNOWLEDGE OF THE FLOWER

Many times it happens that a farmer or a gardener wants to start a strawberry bed and buys plants of a variety of berries that have the reputation of being very productive. He plants them and cultivates them carefully, and at the proper time they blossom very freely, and there is promise of a large crop, yet very few berries appear and this continues to be the case. Not satisfied with them he buys another variety and plants near them, and after that the old bed becomes very productive. Now why is this?

It happens that the flowers of some varieties of strawberries have a great many pistils but no stamens, or very few stamens, and there is not pollen enough to fertilize all of the blossoms, and when such a variety is planted it is necessary to plant near it some variety that produces many stamens and therefore pollen enough to fertilize both varieties in order to be sure of a crop. Those strawberries which produce flowers with only pistils are called pistillate varieties, while those with both stamens and pistils are called perfect varieties (**Fig. 78**). In planting them there should be at least one row of a perfect variety to every four or five pistillate rows.

Fig. 74. A magnolia flower showing central column of pistils and stamens, the pistils being above and the stamens below them.

A. B.

Fig. 75. – FLOWERS OF SQUASH. *A*, pistillate flower; *B*, staminate flower. A means of insuring cross-pollination.

We have learned that certain varieties of plums cannot be fertilized by pollen from the same variety, and to make them fruitful some other variety must be planted among them to produce pollen that will make them fruitful. This is more or less true of all our fruits. Therefore it is not best generally to plant one variety of fruit by itself. Not knowing this some orchardists have planted large blocks of a single variety of fruit which has been unfruitful till some other varieties have been planted near them or among them.

A knowledge of the necessity of pollination is very important to those gardeners who grow cucumbers, tomatoes, melons and other fruiting plants in greenhouses. Here in most cases the pollination is done by hand.

We noticed that nature provides that most of the flowers shall be cross pollinated. This is particularly true of the flowers of the fruit trees, and for this reason it is impossible to get true varieties of fruit from seed. For example, if we plant seeds of the wine sap apple, the new trees produced from them will not produce the same kind of apple but each tree will produce something different and they will very likely all be poorer than the parent fruit. This is because of the mixture of pollens that fertilize the pistils. Knowing this fact the nurseryman plants apple seeds and grows apple seedlings. When these get to be the size of a lead pencil he grafts them, that is, he digs them up, cuts off the tops away down to the root and then takes twigs from the variety he wishes to grow and sets or splices these twigs in the roots of the seedlings and then plants them. The root and the new top unite and produce a tree that bears the same kind of fruit as that produced by the tree from which the twig was taken.

These are a few of the reasons why it is well to know something about flowers and their work.

Fig. 76. – FLOWER OF A LILY. Notice how the stigma and the anthers are kept as far as possible from each other to guard against self-pollination and to insure cross-pollination.

FRUIT

The pistil develops and forms the fruit of the plant. This fruit bears seed for the production of new plants. This fruit may be a dry pod like the bean or pea, or it may be a fleshy fruit like the apple or plum. Now the developing pistil or fruit may be checked in its work of seed production by insects and diseases, and to secure good fruit it is in many cases necessary to spray the fruits just as the leaves are sprayed, to keep these insects and diseases in check.

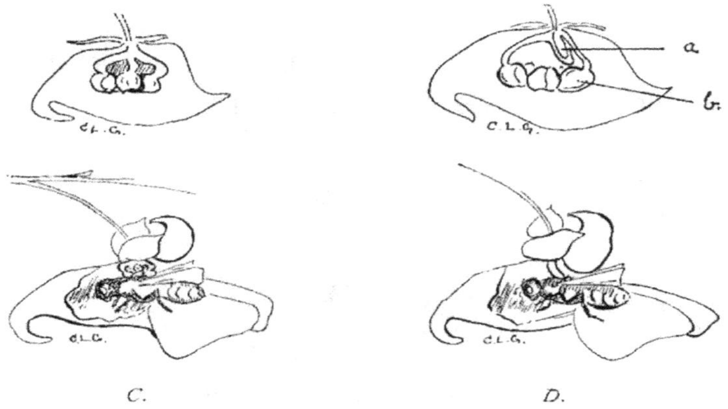

Fig. 77. Bud and flower of jewelweed, or “touch-me-not.” *A*. Interior of bud. Stamens are seen, but there appears to be no pistil. *B*. Section of bud showing the pistil concealed behind the stamens. *C*. Bee entering flower comes in contact with stamens and is loaded with pollen. *D*. Same bee entering older flower. The stamens have ripened and been pushed off by the lengthened pistil, which is brushed by the back of the bee, and thus is pollinated. This is a contrivance to insure cross-pollination.

The fruits of most plants, like the leaves, need light and air for their best development, and it sometimes happens that the branches of the fruit trees grow so thick that the fruits do not get sufficient light and air. This makes it necessary to thin the branches or in other words to prune the tree. Some trees also start more fruit than they can properly feed and as a result the ripened fruits are small and the tree is weakened. This makes it necessary to thin the fruits while they are young and undeveloped.

Fig. 78. *A*. Pistillate flower of strawberry. *B*. Perfect flower of strawberry. (Drawing by M.E. Feltham.)

Part II

Soil Fertility as Affected by Farm Operations and Farm Practices

CHAPTER XVI

A Fertile Soil

What is a fertile soil? The expression "a fertile soil" is often used as meaning a soil that is rich in plant food. In its broader and truer meaning a fertile soil is one in which are found all the conditions necessary to the growth and development of plant roots.

These conditions, as learned in Chapter II, are as follows:

The root must have a firm yet mellow soil. It must be well supplied with moisture. It must be well supplied with air. It must have a certain amount of heat. It must be supplied with available plant food.

In order to furnish these needs or conditions the soil must possess certain characteristics or properties.

These properties may be grouped under three heads:

Physical properties; the moisture, heat and air conditions needed by the roots.

Biological properties; the work of very minute living organisms in the soil.

Chemical properties; plant food in the soil.

PHYSICAL PROPERTIES OF A FERTILE SOIL

Three very important physical properties of a fertile soil are its

Power to take water falling on the surface. Power to absorb water from below. Power to hold water.

The fertile soil must possess all three of these powers. The relative degrees to which these three powers or properties are possessed determine more than anything else the kind of crops or the class of crops that will grow best on a given soil.

These powers depend, as we learned in Chapter IV, on the texture of the soil or the relative amounts of sand, silt, clay and humus contained in the soil.

The power of admitting a free circulation of air through its pores is also an important property of a fertile soil, for air is necessary to the life and growth of the roots. This property is dependent also on texture.

Two other important properties of a fertile soil are power to absorb and power to hold heat. These depend upon the power of the soil to take in warm rain and warm air, and also upon density and color. The denser or more compact soil and the darker soil having greater power to absorb heat.

The compactness of the soil which gives it greater powers to absorb heat weakens its powers to hold it, because the compactness allows more rapid conduction of heat to the surface, where it is lost by radiation.

The more moisture a soil holds, the weaker is its heat-holding power, because the heat is used in warming and evaporating water from the surface of the soil.

These important properties or conditions of moisture, heat and air, are, as we have seen, dependent on soil texture and color, which in turn are dependent upon the relative amounts of sand, clay and humus in the soil. We are able to control soil texture and therefore these physical properties to a certain degree by means of tillage and the addition of organic matter or humus (see Chapter IV).

BIOLOGICAL PROPERTIES OF A FERTILE SOIL

Biology is the story or science of life; and the biological properties of the soil have to do with living organisms in the soil.

The soil of every fertile field is full of very small or microscopic plants called bacteria or germs. They are said to be microscopic because they are so small that they cannot be seen without the aid of a powerful magnifying glass or microscope. They are so small that it would take about 10,000 average-sized soil bacteria or soil germs placed side by side to measure one inch.

A knowledge of three classes of these soil germs is of great importance to the farmer. These three classes of germs are:

Nitrogen-fixing germs. Nitrifying germs. Denitrifying germs.

NITROGEN-FIXING GERMS

We learned in Chapter VIII that nitrogen is one of the necessary elements of plant food, and that although the air is four-fifths nitrogen, most plants must take their nitrogen from the soil. There is, however, a class of plants called legumes which can use the nitrogen of the air. Clover, alfalfa, lucerne, cowpea, soy bean, snap bean, vetch and similar plants are legumes. These legumes get the nitrogen from the air in a very curious and interesting manner. It is done through the aid of bacteria or germs.

Carefully dig up the roots of several legumes and wash the soil from them. On the roots will be found many small enlargements like root galls; these are called nodules or tubercles. On clover roots these nodules are about the size of the head of a pin while on the soybean and cowpea they are nearly as large as a pea (see **Fig. 34**).

These nodules are filled with bacteria or germs and these germs have the power of taking nitrogen from the air that finds its way into the soil. After using the nitrogen the germ gives it to the plant, which then uses it to build stem, leaves and roots. In this way the legumes are able to make use of the nitrogen of the soil air, and these germs which help them to do it by catching the nitrogen are called nitrogen-fixing germs.

The work of these germs makes it possible for the farmer to grow nitrogen, so to speak, on the farm.

By growing crops of legumes and turning them under to decay in the soil, or leaving the roots and stubble to decay after the crop is harvested, he can furnish the following crop with a supply of nitrogen in a very cheap manner and lessen the necessity of buying fertilizer.

NITRIFYING GERMS

Almost all the nitrogen of the soil is locked up in the humus and cannot in that condition is used by the roots of plants. The nitrogen caught by the nitrogen-fixing germs and built into the structure of leguminous plants, which are grown and turned, under to feed other plants cannot be used until the humus, which is produced by their partial decay, is broken down and the nitrogen built into other substances upon which the root can feed. The breaking down of the humus and building of the nitrogen into other substances is the work of another set of bacteria or germs called nitrifying germs.

These nitrifying germs attack the humus, break it down, separate the nitrogen, cause it to unite with the oxygen of the air and thus build it into nitric acid, which can be used by plant roots. This nitric acid if not immediately used will unite with lime or potash or soda or other similar substances and form nitrates, as nitrate of lime, nitrate of potash or common saltpeter. These nitrates are soluble in water and can be easily used by plant roots. If there are no plant roots to use them they are easily lost by being washed out of the soil. The work of the nitrifying germs is called nitrification.

To do their work well the nitrogen-fixing germs and the nitrifying germs require certain conditions.

The soil must be moist.

The soil must be well ventilated to supply nitrogen for the nitrogen-fixing germs and oxygen for the nitrifying germs.

The soil must be warm. Summer temperature is the most favorable. Their work begins and continues slowly at a temperature of about forty-five degrees and increases in rapidity as the temperature rises until it reaches ninety or ninety-five.

The nitrifying germs require phosphoric acid, potash and lime in the soil.

Direct sunlight destroys these bacteria, therefore they cannot work at the surface of the soil unless it is shaded by a crop.

From this we see that these bacteria or germs work best in the soil that has conditions necessary for the growth and development of plant roots.

DENITRIFYING GERMS

These germs live on the coarse organic matter of the soil. Like the nitrifying germs they need oxygen, and when they cannot get it more readily elsewhere they take it from the nitric acid and nitrates. This allows the nitrogen of the nitrates to escape as a free gas into the air again, and the work of the nitrogen-fixing and nitrifying germs is undone and the nitrogen is lost. This loss of nitrogen is most apt to occur when the soil is poorly ventilated, because of its being very compact, or when the soil spaces are filled with water. This loss of nitrogen by denitrification can be checked by keeping the soil well ventilated.

CHEMICAL PROPERTIES OF A FERTILE SOIL

By the term chemical properties we have reference to the chemical composition of the soil, the chemical changes that take place in the soil, and the conditions that influence these changes.

The sand, clay and humus of the soil are made up of a great variety of substances. The larger part of these act simply as a mechanical support for the plants and also serve to bring about certain physical conditions. Only a very small portion of these substances serve as the direct food of plants and the chemical conditions of these substances are of great importance.

In Chapter VIII we learned that plants are composed of several elements and that seven necessary elements are taken from the soil. These seven are nitrogen, phosphorus, potassium, magnesium, calcium, iron and sulfur.

Now a fertile soil must contain these seven elements of plant food and they must be in such form that the plant roots can use them.

Plant roots can generally get from most soils enough of the magnesium, calcium, iron, and sulfur to produce well developed plants. But the nitrogen, phosphorus and potassium, although they exist in sufficient quantities in the soil, are often in such a form or condition that the roots cannot get enough of one or more of them to produce profitable crops. For this reason these three elements are of particular importance to the farmer for, in order to keep his soil fertile, he must so treat it that these elements will be made available or he must add more of them to the soil in the proper form or condition.

Nitrogen in the soil. – Plant roots use nitrogen in the form of nitric acid and salts of nitrogen called nitrates. But the nitrogen of the soil is very largely found in the humus with the roots cannot use. A chemical change must take place in it and the nitrogen be built into nitric acid and nitrates. This, we have learned, is done through the aid of the nitrifying germs.

Phosphoric acid in the soil. – Phosphorus does not exist pure in the soil. The plant finds it as a phosphoric acid united with the other substances forming phosphates. These are often not available to plants, but can to a certain extent be made available through tillage and by adding humus to the soil.

Potash in the soil. – The plant finds potassium in potash that exists in the soil. Potash like phosphoric acid often exists in forms that the plant cannot use but may be made available to a certain extent by tillage, the addition of humus, and the addition of lime to the soil.

Lime in the soil. – Most soils contain the element

calcium or lime, the compound in which it is found, in sufficient quantities for plant food. But lime is also of importance to the farmer and plant grower because it is helpful in causing chemical changes in the soil that tend to prepare the nitrogen, phosphoric acid and potash for plant use. It is also helpful in changing soil texture.

The chemical changes which make the plant foods available are dependent on moisture, heat, and air with its oxygen, and are therefore dependent largely on texture, and therefore on tillage.

When good tillage and the addition of organic matter and lime do not render available sufficient plant food, then the supply of available food may be increased by the application of manure and fertilizers.

It will be seen that all these classes of properties are necessary to furnish all the conditions for root growth.

The proper chemical conditions require the presence of both physical and biological properties and the biological work in the soil requires both chemical and physical conditions.

From the farmer's standpoint the physical properties seem to be most important, for the others are dependent on the proper texture, moisture, heat and ventilation, which are controlled largely by tillage.

Therefore the first effort of the farmer to improve the fertility of his soil should be to improve his methods of working the soil.

Every one of these properties of the fertile soil, and consequently every one of the conditions necessary for the growth and development of plant roots, is influenced in some way by every operation performed on the soil, whether it be plowing, harrowing, cultivating, applying manure, growing crops, harvesting, or anything else, and the thoughtful farmer will frequently ask himself the question: "How is this going to effect the fertility of my soil or the conditions necessary for profitable crop production?"

MAINTENANCE OF FERTILITY

The important factors in maintaining or increasing the fertility of the soil are:

The mechanical operations of tillage, especially with reference to the control of soil water.

The application of manures and fertilizers, especially with reference to maintaining a supply of humus and plant food.

Methods or systems of cropping the soil, with reference to economizing fertility.

CHAPTER XVII

Soil Water

The more important tillage tools and tillage operations we studied in Chapters XI and XII. They will be noticed here only in connection with their influence over soil water, for in the regulation of this important factor in soil fertility the other conditions of fertility are also very largely controlled.

IMPORTANCE OF SOIL WATER

"Of all the factors influencing the growth of plants, water is beyond doubt the most important," and the maintaining of the proper amount of soil water is one of the most important problems of the thinking farmer in controlling the fertility of his soil.

NECESSITY OF SOIL WATER

The decay of mineral and organic matter in the soil, and the consequent setting free of plant food, can take place only in the presence of moisture. The plant food in barn manures and crops plowed under for green moisture, can be made available only when there is sufficient moisture in the soil to permit breaking down and decomposition.

The presence of moisture in the soil is necessary for the process of nitrification to take place.

Soil moisture is necessary to dissolve plant food. Plant roots can absorb food from the soil only when it is in solution, and it seems to be necessary that a large quantity of water pass through the plant tissues to furnish the supply of mineral elements required by growth.

Moisture is necessary to build plant tissues. The quantity of water entering into the structure of growing plants varies from sixty to as high as ninety-five per cent, of their total weight.

During the periods of active growth there is a constant giving off of moisture by the foliage of plants and this must be made good by water taken from the soil by their roots.

In a series of experiments at the University of Wisconsin Agricultural Experiment Station, it was found that in raising oats, every ton of dry matter grown required 522.4 tons of water to produce it; for every ton of dry matter of corn there were required 309.8 tons of water; a ton of dry red clover requires 452.8 tons of water to grow it. At the Cornell University Agricultural Experiment Station, a yield of potatoes at the rate of 450 bushels per acre represented a water requirement of 1310.75 tons of water.

SOURCES AND FORMS OF SOIL WATER

The soil which is occupied by the roots of plants receives moisture in the form of rain, snow and dew from above and free and capillary water rising from below.

"Free water is that form of water which fills our wells, is found in the bottom of holes dug in the ground during wet seasons, and is often found standing on the surface of the soil after heavy or long continued rains. It is sometimes called 'ground water' or 'standing water,' and flows under the influence of gravity." Free water is not used directly by plants unless they are swamp plants, and its presence within eighteen inches of the surface is injurious to most farm plants. Free water serves as the main source of supply for capillary water.

"Capillary water is water which is drawn by capillary force or soaks into the spaces between the soil particles and covers these particles with a thin film of moisture." It is a direct source of water to plants. Capillary water will flow in any direction in the soil, the direction of flow being determined by texture and dryness, the flow being stronger toward the more compact and drier parts. If the soil is left lumpy and cloddy then capillary water cannot rise readily from below to take the place of that which is lost by evaporation. If, however, the soil is fine and well pulverized, the water rises freely and continuously to supply the place of that taken by plant roots or evaporation from the surface.

TOO MUCH WATER

Some farm lands contain too much water for the growth of farm crops; for example, bottom lands which are so low that water falling on the surface cannot run off or soak down into the lower soil. The result is that the spaces between the soil particles are most of the time filled with water, and this checks ventilation, which is a necessary factor in soil fertility. This state of affairs occurs also on sloping uplands, which are kept wet by spring water or by seepage water from higher lands. Some soils are so close and compact that water falling on the surface finds great difficulty in percolating through them, and therefore renders them too wet for profitable cropping during longer or shorter periods of the year. Nearly all such lands can be improved by removing the surplus water through drains. (See Chapter XXV.)

Percolation and ventilation of close compact soils can be improved by mixing lime and organic matter with them.

NOT ENOUGH WATER

In some sections of the country, particularly the arid and semi-arid sections of the West, the soil does not receive a sufficient supply of rain water for the production of profitable yearly crops. These soils are rendered unfertile by the lack of this one all important factor of fertility. They can be made fertile and productive by supplying them with sufficient water through irrigation.

The crop-producing power of some lands is lowered even in regions where the rainfall is sufficient, because these lands are not properly prepared by tillage and the addition of organic matter to absorb and hold the water that comes to them, or part of the water may be lost or wasted by lack of proper after-tillage or after-cultivation. This state of affairs is of course improved by better preparation to receive water before planting the crop and better methods of after-cultivation to save the water for the use of the crop.

LOSS OF SOIL WATER

Aside from what is used by the crops the soil may lose its water in the following ways:

Rain water, which comes to the soil, may be lost by running off over the surface of the land. This occurs especially on hilly farms and in the case of close, compact soils.

Water may be lost from the soil by leaching through the lower soil.

Water may be lost from the soil by evaporation from the surface.

The soil may lose water by the growth of weeds that are continually pumping water up by their roots and transpiring it from their leaves into the air.

HOW SOME FARM OPERATIONS INFLUENCE SOIL WATER

Plowing and soil water. One of the first effects of deeply and thoroughly plowing a close, compact soil, is that rain will sink into it readily and not be lost by surface wash. In many parts of the country, especially the South, great damage is done by the surface washing and gullying of sloping fields.

The shallow layer of soil stirred up by small plows and practice of shallow plowing so prevalent in the South takes in the rain readily, but as the harder soil beneath does not easily absorb the water the shallow layer of plowed soil soon fills, then becomes mud, and the whole mass goes down the slope. Where the land is plowed deep there is prepared a deep reservoir of loose soil that is able to hold a large amount of water till the harder lower soil can gradually absorb it.

The soil stirred and thoroughly broken by the plow serves not only as a reservoir for the rainfall, but also acts as a mulch over the more compact soil below it, thus checking the rapid use of capillary water to the surface and its consequent loss by evaporation. The plow that breaks and pulverizes the soil most thoroughly is the one best adapted to fit the soil for receiving and holding moisture.

If the plowing is not well done or if the land is too dry when plowed and the soil is left in great coarse lumps and clods, the air circulates readily among the clods and takes from them what little moisture they may have had and generally the soil is left in a worse condition than if it had not been plowed at all.

Fall plowing on rolling land and heavy soil leaving the surface rough helps to hold winter snows and rains when they fall, giving to such fields a more even distribution of soil water in the spring.

Spring plowing should be done early, before there is much loss of water from the surface by evaporation.

Professor King, of the University of Wisconsin Agricultural Experiment Station, carried on an experiment to see how much soil water could be saved by early plowing. He selected two similar pieces of ground near each other and tested them for water April 29th. Immediately after testing one piece was plowed. Seven days later, May 6th, he tested them for water again and found that both had lost some water, but that the piece that was not plowed had lost 9.13 pounds more water per square foot of surface than the plowed piece. This means that by plowing one part a week earlier than the other he saved in it water equal to a rainfall of nearly two inches or at the rate of nearly 200 tons of water per acre.

HOEING, RAKING, HARROWING, AND CULTIVATING

These operations when properly and thoroughly done tend to supplement the work of the plow in fitting the soil to absorb rain and in making a mulch to check loss by surface evaporation. The entire surface should be worked and the soil should be left smooth and not in ridges. Rolling cutters and spring-toothed harrows are apt to leave ridges and should have an attachment for smoothing the surface or be followed by a smoothing harrow. Cultivators used to make mulches to save water should have many narrow teeth rather than few broad ones. If a large broad-toothed tool is used to destroy grass and large weeds it should be followed by a smoother to level the ridges and thus lessen the evaporating surface. The soil should be cultivated as soon after a rain as it can be safely worked.

Rolling compacts the soil and starts a quicker capillary movement of water toward the surface and a consequent loss by evaporation. When circumstances will permit, the roller should be followed by a light harrow to restore the mulch.

Ridging the land tends to lessen the amount of moisture in the soil because it increases the evaporating surface. It should be practiced only on wet land or in early spring to secure greater heat.

Drains placed in wet land remove free water to a lower depth and increase the depth of soil occupied by capillary water and therefore increase the body of soil available to plant roots.

MANURES AND SOIL WATER

Humus, as we learned in Chapter IV, has a very great and therefore important influence over the water-absorbing and water-holding powers of soils. Therefore, any of the farm practices that tend to increase or diminish the amount of humus in the soil are to be seriously considered because of the effect on the water content of the soil. For this reason the application of barn manures and green crops turned under tend to improve the water conditions of most soils.

The mixing of heavy applications of coarse manures or organic matter with light sandy soils may make them so loose and open that they will lose moisture rapidly. When this practice is necessary the land should be rolled after the application of the manure.

METHODS OF CROPPING AND SOIL WATER

Constant tillage hastens the decay of organic matter in the soil. Hence any method or system of cropping which does not occasionally return to the soil a new supply of humus tends to weaken the powers of the soil toward water.

All of the operations and practices which influence soil water also affect the other conditions necessary to root growth; namely, texture, ventilation, heat, and plant food, and those operations and practices which properly control and regulate soil water to a large degree control and regulate soil fertility.

SELECTION OF CROPS WITH REFERENCE TO SOIL WATER

While climatic conditions determine the general distribution of plants, the amount of water which a soil holds and can give up to plants during the growing season determines very largely the crops to which it is locally best adapted.

With crops that can be grown on a wide range of soils the water which the soil can furnish largely determines the time of maturing, the yield, and often the quality of the crop. With such a crop a small supply of water tends to hasten maturity at the expense of yield.

The sweet potato, when wanted for early market and high prices, is grown on the light sandy soils called early truck soils. These soils hold from five to seven per cent, of water. That is, the texture is such that during the early part of the growing season one hundred pounds of this soil is found to hold an average of from five to seven pounds of water under field conditions. This soil, holding little water, warms up early and thus hastens growth. Then as the warmer summer weather advances, the water supply diminishes, growth is checked, and the crop matures rapidly. On account of the small amount of water and the early checking of growth, the yield of the crop is less than if grown on a soil holding more water, but the earlier maturity makes it possible to realize a much higher price per bushel for the crop. A sweet potato grown on such a light soil is dry and starchy, a quality which brings a higher price in the northern markets than does the moist, soggy potato grown on heavier soils that contain more water and produce larger yields.

Early white potatoes, early cabbage, water melons, musk-melons, tomatoes and other early truck and market garden crops are also grown on light soil holding from five to seven per cent of water. The main crop of potatoes and cabbage and the canning crop of tomatoes are grown on the loam soils holding from ten to eighteen per cent of water. Such soils produce a later though much larger yield.

Upland cotton produces best on a deep loam that is capable of furnishing a uniform supply of about ten or twelve per cent of water during the growing season.

Sea Island Cotton grows best on a light, sandy soil holding only five per cent of water.

On light, sandy soils the Upland Cotton produces small plants with small yield of lint, while on clay and bottom land, which are apt to have large amounts of water, the plants grow very large and produce fewer bolls, which are very late in maturing.

Corn, while it will grow on a wide range of soils, produces best on loam or moist bottomlands holding about fifteen per cent of water during the growing season.

The grasses and small grains do best on cool, firm soils holding eighteen to twenty-two per cent of water.

Sorghum or "Molasses Cane" grows best on good corn soil, while the sugar cane of the Gulf States requires a soil with twenty-five per cent of water for best growth.

While the amount of water which a soil will hold is determined largely by texture, it is also considerably influenced by the amount and frequency of rainfall and the location of the soil as to whether it be upland or bottom land.

The average percentage of water held by a soil during the growing season may be approximately determined in the following manner:

Sample the soil in one of the following methods:

Take to the field a spade, a box that will hold about half a bushel, and a pint or quart glass jar with a tight cover. If a cultivated field, select a place free from grass and weeds. Dig a hole one foot deep and about eighteen inches square. Trim one side of the hole square. Now from this side cut a slice about three inches thick and one foot deep, quickly place this in the box and thoroughly break lumps and mix together, then fill jar and cork tightly.

Another method is to take a common half-inch or two-inch carpenter's auger and bore into the soil with it. Pull it out frequently and put the soil that comes up with it into the jar until you have a sample a foot deep. If one boring twelve inches deep does not give sufficient soil make another boring or two close by and put all into the jar.

Take the sample, by whatever method obtained, weigh out ten or twenty ounces of the moist soil and dry it at a temperature just below 212 degrees. When it is thoroughly dry weigh again. The difference between the two weights will be the amount of water held by the sample. Now divide this by the weight of the dry sample and the result will be the percent of water held by the soil.

Several samples taken from different parts of the field will give an average for the field. Repeat this every week or oftener through the season and an approximate estimate of the water-holding capacity of the soil will be obtained and consequently an indication of the crops to which the soil is best adapted.

Example.

Weight of a soil sample, 20 ounces.

When dried this sample weighs $17\frac{3}{4}$ ounces.

$20 - 17\frac{3}{4} = 2\frac{1}{4}$, the water held by the soil.

$2.25 \div 17.75 = .12$ plus.

This soil held a little over twelve per cent of water. If this soil continues to give about the same result for successive tests during the growing season, the results would indicate a soil adapted to cotton, late truck or corn.

CHAPTER XVIII

The After-Cultivation Of Crops

The term "after-cultivation" is here used in referring to those tillage operations, which are performed after the crop is planted. Synonymous terms are "cultivation," "inter-tillage," "working the crop."

After-cultivation influences the texture, ventilation, heat, plant food and moisture factors of fertility, but most particularly the moisture factor.

Under ordinary circumstances the greatest benefit derived from after-cultivation when properly performed is the saving of soil water for the use of the crop.

LOSS OF WATER BY EVAPORATION

Soil water is seldom at rest unless the soil be frozen solid. When rain falls on a fertile soil there is a downward movement of water. When the rain ceases, water begins to evaporate from the surface of the soil. Its place is taken by water brought from below by capillarity. This is in turn evaporated and replaced by more from below. This process continues with greater or less rapidity according to the dryness of the air and the compactness of the soil.

LOSS OF WATER THROUGH WEEDS

We learned in a former chapter that during their growth farm plants require an amount of water equal to from 300 to 500 times their dry weight. Weeds require just as much water and some of them probably more than the cultivated plants. This water is largely absorbed by the roots and sent up to the leaves where it is transpired into the air and is lost from the soil, and therefore is unavailable to the growing crop until it again falls onto the soil.

In some parts of the country, particularly the semi-arid West, the rainfall is not sufficient to supply the soil with enough water to grow such crops as it could otherwise produce. In the moister regions the rainfall is not evenly distributed throughout the growing season, and there are longer or shorter intervals between rains when the loss of water through evaporation and weeds is apt to be greater than the rainfall. For these reasons it is best to check these losses and save the water in the soil for the use of the crops.

SAVING THE WATER

This can be done by:

Preventing the growth of weeds and by checking losses by evaporation with a soil mulch.

TIME TO CULTIVATE

A seedling plant is easiest killed just as it has started into growth. The best time to kill a plant starting from an underground stem or a root is just as soon as it appears above the surface in active growth.

The best time to cultivate, then, to kill weeds is as soon as the weeds appear. At this time large numbers can be killed with the least of effort. Do not let them get to be a week or two old before getting after them.

In planting some crops the ground between the rows becomes trampled and compact. This results in active capillarity which brings water to the surface and it is lost by evaporation.

Every rainfall tends to beat the soil particles together and form a crust, which enables the capillary water to climb to the surface and escape into the air. This loss by evaporation should be constantly watched for and the soil should be stirred and a mulch formed whenever it becomes compact or a crust is formed.

The proper time to cultivate, then, to save water is as soon as weeds appear or as soon as the surface of the soil becomes compact or crusted by trampling, by the beating of rain or from any other cause, whether the crop is up or not. The cultivation should start as soon after a rain as the soil is dry enough to work safely.

The surface soil should always be kept loose and open. The efficacy of the soil mulch depends on the thoroughness and frequency of the operation. It is particularly beneficial during long, dry periods. During such times it is not necessary to wait for a rain to compact the soil; keep the cultivators going, rain or no rain.

TOOLS FOR AFTER-CULTIVATION

The main objects of after-cultivation are to destroy weeds and to form a soil mulch for the purpose of controlling soil moisture. These ends are secured by shallow surface work. It is not necessary to go more than two or three inches deep. Deeper work will injure the roots of the crop. Therefore the proper tools for after-cultivation in the garden are the hoe and rake and for field work narrow-toothed harrows and cultivators or horse-hoes that stir the whole surface thoroughly to a moderate depth.

These field tools are supplemented in some cases by the hand hoe, but over wide areas of country the hoe never enters the field.

A light spike-toothed harrow can be used on corn, potatoes, and similar crops, and accomplish the work of cultivation rapidly until they get to be from four to six inches high; after that cultivators which work between the rows should be used.

A very useful class of tools for destroying weeds in the earlier stages are the so-called "weeders." They somewhat resemble a horse hay rake and have a number of flexible wire teeth which destroy shallow rooted weeds but slip around the more firmly rooted plants of the crop. These weeders must be used frequently to be of much value, for after a weed is well rooted the weeder cannot destroy it.

There is a larger class of hand wheel hoes that are very useful in working close planted garden and truck crops. They either straddle the row, working the soil on both sides at the same time, or, running between the rows, work the soil to a width of from six to eighteen inches.

For best results with the weeder and hand wheel hoes the soil should be thoroughly prepared before planting by burying all trash with the plow and breaking all clods with harrow and roller.

The objection made to the deep-working implements, like the plow, is that they injure the crop by cutting its feeding roots, and this has been found by careful experiment and observation to diminish the crop.

Some farmers object to using a light harrow for cultivation in the early stages of the crop because they say the harrow will destroy the crop as well as the weeds. This danger is not so great as it seems. The seeds of the crop are deeper in the soil than the seeds of the weeds that germinate and appear so quickly. The soil has also been firmed about them. Hence they have a firmer hold on the soil and but few of them are destroyed if the work is carefully done.

In working crops not only should weeds be destroyed but also surplus plants of the crop, as these have the same effect as weeds; namely, they occupy the soil and take plant food and moisture that if left to fewer plants would produce a larger harvest.

HILLING AND RIDGING

Except in low, wet ground, the practice of hilling or ridging up crops is now considered by those who have given the matter thorough study, to be unnecessary, flat and shallow culture being cheaper. It saves more moisture, and for this reason, in the majority of cases, produces larger crops.

Sometimes during very long-continued periods of wet weather weeds and grass become firmly established among the plants of the crop. Under such circumstances it is necessary to use on the cultivator teeth having long, narrow sweeps that will cut the weeds just beneath the surface of the soil. Sometimes a broad-toothed tool is used that will throw sufficient soil over the large weeds near the rows to smother them.

The condition to be met and the effect of the operation should always be given serious thought.

We have considered after-cultivation as influencing soil fertility by checking a loss of water by evaporation and weed transpiration, and this is its main influence but other benefits follow.

Keeping the surface soil loose and open benefits fertility because it directly aids the absorption of rain, favors ventilation, and has a beneficial influence over soil temperature. Indirectly through these factors it aids the work of the beneficial soil bacteria and the chemical changes in the process of preparing plant food for crop use.

CHAPTER XIX

Farm Manures

In Chapter II we learned that the roots of plants for their growth and development need a soil that is firm yet mellow, moist, warm, ventilated and supplied with plant food. We also learned that of the plant foods there is often not enough available nitrogen, phosphoric acid, potash and lime for the needs of the growing plants.

Manures and fertilizers are applied to the soil for their beneficial effects on these necessary conditions for root growth and therefore to assist in maintaining soil fertility.

CLASSIFICATION OF MANURES AND FERTILIZERS

Manures may be classified as follows:

Farm manures.	{ Barn or stable manures, Green-crop manures, Composts.
Commercial fertilizers or artificial manures.	Materials furnishing nitrogen, Materials furnishing phosphoric acid, Materials furnishing potash, Materials furnishing lime.

IMPORTANCE OF FARM MANURES

Of these two classes of manures the farmer should rely chiefly on the farm manures letting the commercial fertilizers take a secondary place because:

Farm manures are complete manures; that is they contain all the necessary elements of plant food.

Farm manures add to the soil large amounts of organic matter or humus.

The decay of organic matter produces carbonic acid that hastens the decay of mineral matter in the soil and so increases the amount of available plant food.

The organic matter changes the texture of the soil.

It makes sandy soils more compact and therefore more powerful to hold water and plant food.

It makes heavy clay soils more open and porous, giving them greater power to absorb moisture and plant food. This admits also of better circulation of the air in the soil, and prevents baking in dry weather.

Farm manures influence all of the conditions necessary for root growth while the commercial fertilizers influence mainly the plant food conditions.

The farm manures are good for all soils and crops.

They are lasting in their effects on the soil.

BARN OR STABLE MANURE

Barn or stable manure consists of the solid and liquid excrement of any of the farm animals mixed with the straw or other materials used as bedding for the comfort of the animals and to absorb the liquid parts.

The liquid parts should be saved, as they contain more than half of the nitrogen and potash in the manure.

The value of barn manure for improving the soil conditions necessary for root growth depends in a measure upon the plant food in it, but chiefly upon the very large proportion of organic matter that it contains when it is applied to the soil.

These factors are influenced somewhat: by the kind of animal that produces the manure; by the kind of food the animal receives; by the kind and amount of litter or bedding used; but they depend particularly on the way the manure is cared for after it is produced.

LOSS OF VALUE

Improper care of the manure may cause it to diminish in value very much.

Loss by leaching.

If the manure is piled against the side of the stable where water from the roof can drip on it, as is often the case, or if it is piled in an exposed place where heavy rain can beat on it, the rain water in leaching through the manure washes out of it nitrogen and potash, which pass off in the dark brown liquid that oozes from the base of the pile.

Loss by heating or fermenting.

When barn manure is thrown into piles it soon heats and throws off more or less steam and gas. This heating of the manure is caused by fermentation or the breaking down of the materials composing the manure and the forming of new compounds. This fermentation is produced by very small or microscopic plants called bacteria.

The fermentation of the manure is influenced by the following conditions:

A certain amount of heat is necessary to start the work of the bacteria. After they have once started they keep up and increase the temperature of the pile until it gets so hot that sometimes a part of the manure is reduced to ashes. The higher the temperature the more rapid the fermentation. This can be seen particularly in piles of horse manure.

The bacteria that produce the most rapid fermentation in manure need plenty of air with its oxygen. Therefore fermentation will be more or less rapid according as the manure is piled loosely or in a close compact mass.

A certain amount of moisture is necessary for the fermentation to take place, but if the manure is made quite wet the temperature is lowered and the fermentation is checked. The water also checks the fermentation by limiting the supply of air that can enter the pile.

The composition of the manure influences the fermentation. The presence of considerable amounts of soluble nitrogen hastens the rapidity of the fermentation.

Now when the manure ferments a large part of the organic matter in it is broken down and changed into gases. The gas formed most abundantly by the fermentation is carbonic acid gas, which is produced by the union of oxygen with carbon of the organic matter. The formation of this gas means a loss of humus. This loss can be noticed by the fact that the pile gradually becomes smaller.

The next most abundant product of the fermentation is water vapor that can often be seen passing off in clouds of steam.

When manure ferments rapidly the nitrogen in it is changed largely into ammonia. This ammonia combines with part of the carbonic acid gas and forms carbonate of ammonia, a very volatile salt that rapidly changes to a vapor and is lost in the atmosphere. This causes a great loss of nitrogen during the rapid decomposition of the manure. This loss can be detected by the well known odor of the ammonia, which is particularly noticeable about horse stables and piles of horse manure.

Besides these gases a number of compounds of nitrogen, potash, etc., are formed which are soluble in water. It is these that form the dark brown liquid that sometimes oozes out from the base of the manure heap.

At the Cornell University Agricultural Experiment Station, the following experiment was carried out to find out how much loss would take place from a pile of manure:

Four thousand pounds of manure from the horse stable were placed out of doors in a compact pile and left exposed from April 25th to September 22d. The results were as follows:

	April 25	Sept. 22	Loss per cent
Gross weight	4,000 lbs.	1,730 lbs.	57%
Nitrogen	19.6 lbs.	7.79 lbs.	60%
Phos. acid	14.8 lbs.	7.79 lbs.	47%
Potash	36 lbs.	8.65 lbs.	76

This shows a loss of more than half the bulk of the manure and more than half the plant food contained in it.

CHECKING THE LOSSES

The first step to be taken in preserving the manure or in checking losses is to provide sufficient bedding or litter in the stable to absorb and save all the liquid parts.

The losses from fermentation of hot manures like horse manure may be largely checked by mixing with the colder manure from the cow stable.

Losses from fermentation may also be checked.

By piling compactly, which keeps the air out.

By moistening the pile, which lowers the temperature and checks the access of oxygen.

The manure may be hauled directly to the field each day and spread on the surface or plowed in. This method is the best when practicable because fermentation of the manure will take place slowly in the soil and the gases produced will be absorbed and retained by the soil.

Gypsum or land plaster is often sprinkled on stable floors and about manure heaps to prevent the loss of ammonia.

Copperas or blue stone, kainite and superphosphate are sometimes used for the same purpose. There is, however, nothing better nor so good for this purpose as dry earth containing a large percentage of humus.

Losses from washing or leaching by rain may be prevented by piling the manure under cover or by hauling it to the field as soon as produced and spreading it on the surface or plowing it under.

APPLYING THE MANURE TO THE SOIL

From ten to twenty tons per acre is considered a sufficient application of barn manure for most farm crops. Larger amounts are sometimes applied to the soil for truck and market garden crops.

Barn manures are applied to the soil by these methods:

The manure is sometimes hauled out from the barn and placed in a large pile in the field or in many small piles where it remains for some time before being spread and plowed or harrowed in.

Some farmers spread it on the field and allow it to lie some time before plowing it in.

It is sometimes spread as soon as hauled to the field and is immediately plowed in or mixed with the soil. This last is the safest and most economical method so far as the manure alone is concerned.

When the manure is left in a large pile it suffers losses due to fermentation and leaching.

At the Cornell University Agricultural Experiment Station, five tons of manure from the cow stable, including three hundred pounds of gypsum that was mixed with it, were exposed in a compact pile out of doors from April 25th to September 22d. The result was as follows:

	April 25	Sept. 22	Loss per cent
Gross weight	10,000 lbs.	5,125 lbs.	49%
Nitrogen	47 lbs.	28 lbs.	41%
Phos. acid	32 lbs.	26 lbs.	19%
Potash	48 lbs.	44 lbs.	8%

When distributed over the field in small piles and allowed to remain so for some time, losses from fermentation take place, and the rain washes plant food from the pile into the soil under and immediately about it. This results in an uneven distribution of plant food over the field, for when the manure is finally scattered and plowed in, part of the field is fertilized with washed out manure while the soil under and immediately about the location of the various piles is often so strongly fertilized that nothing can grow there unless it be rank, coarse weeds.

When the manure is spread on the surface and allowed to lie for some time it is apt to become dry and hard, and when finally plowed in, decays very slowly.

When the manure is plowed in or mixed with the soil as soon as applied to the field there results an even distribution of plant food in the soil, fermentation takes place gradually and all gases formed are absorbed by the soil, there is very little loss of valuable nitrogen and organic matter, and the fermentation taking place in the soil also aids in breaking down the mineral constituents of the soil and making available the plant food held by them.

Fig. 79. – A CROP OF COWPEAS.

Fig. 80. – RED CLOVER.

Therefore it seems best to spread the manure and plow it in or mix it with the soil as soon as it is hauled to the field, when not prevented by bad weather and other more pressing work.

PROPER CONDITION OF MANURE WHEN APPLIED

A large part of the value of barn manure lies in the fact that it consists largely of organic matter, and therefore has an important influence on soil texture, and during its decay in the soil produces favorable chemical changes in the soil constituents.

Therefore it will produce its greatest effect on the soil when applied fresh. For this reason it is generally best to haul the manure to the field and mix it with the soil as soon after it is produced as possible.

If coarse manures are mixed with light, sandy soils it is best to follow with the roller, otherwise the coarse manure may cause the soil to lie so loose and open that both soil and manure will lose moisture so rapidly that fermentation of the manure will be stopped and the soil will be unfit for planting.

If it is desired to apply manure directly to delicate rooted truck and vegetable crops it is best to let it stand for some time until the first rank fermentation has taken place and the manure has become rotten.

A good practice is to apply the manure in its fresh condition to coarse feeding crops like corn, and then follow the corn by a more delicate rooted crop that requires the manure to be in a more decomposed condition than is necessary for the corn.

In this case the corn is satisfied and the remaining manure is in proper condition for the following crop when it is planted.

Another practice is to broadcast the coarse manure on grass land and then when the hay is harvested the sod and remaining manure are plowed under for the following crop.

A study of root development in Chapter II. tells us that most of the manure used for cultivated crops should be broadcasted and thoroughly mixed with the soil. A small amount may be placed in the drill or hill and thoroughly mixed with the soil for crops that are planted in rows or furrows in order to give the young plant a rapid start.

For the vegetable garden and flower garden and lawns, it is best to apply only manure that has been piled for some time and has been turned over several times so that it is well rotted and broken up.

There may not be a single farm where it will be possible to carry out to the letter these principles applying to the treatment and application of barn manures.

This is because climate, crops and conditions vary in different parts of the country and on different farms.

Therefore we should study carefully our conditions and the principles and make our practice so combine the two as to produce the best and most economical results under the circumstances.

If we can get manure out in the winter it will very much lessen the rush of spring work.

In some parts of the country on account of deep snows, heavy rainfall and hilly fields, it is not advisable to apply manure in the winter. This will necessitate storing the manure.

If conditions are such that we can get the manure on to the land as soon as it is made, it should be applied to land on which a crop is growing or land which is soon to be planted. If land is not intended for an immediate crop, put a cover crop on it.

COMPOSTS

Composts are collections of farm trash or rubbish, as leaves, potato tops, weeds, road and ditch scrapings, fish, slaughter-house refuse, etc., mixed in piles with lime, barn manure, woods-earth, swamp muck, peat and soil.

The object of composting these materials is to hasten their decay and render available the plant food in them.

There are certain disadvantages in composting, namely:

Expense of handling and carting on account of bulk.

Low composition.

Loss of organic matter by fermentation.

Compost heaps serve as homes for weed seeds, insects and plant diseases.

Nevertheless, all waste organic matter on the farm should be saved and made use of as manure.

These materials when not too coarse may be spread on the surface of the soil and plowed under; they should never be burned unless too coarse and woody or foul with weed seeds, insects and disease.

Fig. 81. – SOY BEANS IN YOUNG ORCHARD.

Fig. 82. – A YOUNG ALFALFA PLANT JUST COMING INTO FLOWER.

CHAPTER XX

Farm Manures – concluded

Green-crop manures are crops grown and plowed under for the purpose of improving the fertility of the soil.

The main object of turning these crops under is to furnish the soil with humus. Any crop may be used for this purpose.

By growing any of the class of crops called Legumes we may add to the soil not only humus but also nitrogen. Cowpeas, beans, clover, vetch and plants having foliage, flowers, seed pods and seeds like them are called Legumes.

Most of the farm plants take their nitrogen from the soil. This nitrogen is taken in the form of nitric acid and nitrogen salts dissolved in soil water. The legumes, however, are able to use the free nitrogen that forms four-fifths of the atmosphere. This they do not of their own power but through the aid of very minute plants called bacteria or nitrogen-fixing germs. These germs are so small that they cannot be seen without the use of a powerful microscope. It would take ten thousand average sized bacteria placed side by side to measure one inch.

These little germs make their homes in the roots of the legumes, causing the root to enlarge at certain points and form tubercles or nodules (**Figs. 34 and 35**).

Carefully dig up a root of clover, cowpea, soy bean or other legume and wash the soil from it. You will find numbers of the little tubercles or nodules. On the clover they will be about the size of a pin head or a little larger.

On the soy bean they will be nearly as large as the beans. These nodules are filled with colonies or families of bacteria that take the free nitrogen from the air that penetrates the soil and give it over to the plant in return for house rent and starch or other food they may have taken from the plant.

In an experiment at Cornell University Agricultural Experiment Station, in 1896, clover seeds were sown August 1st, and the plants were dug November 4th, three months and four days after the seeds were sown. The clovers were then weighed and tested and the following results were obtained:

	Nitrogen in an Acre of Clovers		
	Lbs. in tops.	Lbs. in roots.	Lbs. total.
Crimson Clover	125.28	30.66	155.94
Mammoth Clover	67.57	78.39	145.96
Red Clover	63.11	40.25	103.36

A large part of the nitrogen found in these plants was undoubtedly taken by the roots from the soil air.

Besides adding humus and nitrogen to the soil the legumes, being mostly deep-rooted plants, are able to take from the subsoil food that is out of reach of other plants. This food is distributed throughout the plant and when the plant is plowed under the food is deposited in the upper soil for the use of shallow-rooted plants.

BENEFITS

The benefits derived from green crop manuring then are as follows:

We add to the soil organic matter or humus, which is so helpful in bringing about the conditions necessary for root growth.

By using the legumes for our green manure crops we may supply the soil with nitrogen taken from the air.

We return to the surface soil not only the plant food taken from it but also plant food brought from the subsoil by the roots of the green manure plants.

CHARACTER OF BEST PLANTS FOR GREEN CROP MANURING

The plants best adapted to green crop manuring are deep-rooted, heavy-foliaged plants. Of these the legumes are by far the best, as they collect the free nitrogen from the air that other plants cannot do. This enables the farmer to grow nitrogen that is very expensive to buy.

THE TIME FOR GROWING GREEN MANURE CROPS

Green manure crops may be grown at any time that the soil is not occupied by other crops, provided other conditions are suitable. Land which is used for spring and summer crops often lies bare and idle during fall and winter. A hardy green manure crop planted after the summer crop is harvested will make considerable growth during the fall and early spring, and this can be plowed under for the use of the following summer crops. If there is a long interval of time during spring or summer when the land is bare, that is a good time for a green manure crop.

Green manure crops are often planted between the rows of other crops such as corn or cotton at the last working of the crop for the benefit of the crop that is to follow.

It is advisable to arrange for a green manure crop at least once in three or four years.

LEGUMINOUS GREEN MANURE CROPS

Cowpea. (Field pea, stock pea, black pea, black-eyed pea, clay pea, etc.) (**Fig. 79.**)

The cowpea is perhaps the most important leguminous plant grown for soil improvement in the South. It will grow anywhere south of the Ohio River and can be grown with fair success in many localities farther north.

It is a tender annual, that is, it is killed by frost and makes its entire growth from seed to seed in a single season. It should therefore be planted only during the spring and summer. This crop not only has power like the other legumes to take nitrogen from the air, but it is also a strong feeder, that is, it can feed upon mineral plant food in the soil that other plants are unable to make use of. For this reason it will grow on some of the poorest soils, and is a good plant with which to begin the improvement of very poor land. It is a deep-rooted plant. On the farm of the Hampton Normal and Agricultural Institute cowpea roots have been traced to the depth of sixty-one inches.

Cowpeas will grow on almost any land that is not too wet. From one and one-half to three bushels of seed are used per acre. These are sown broadcast and harrowed in or are planted in drills or furrows and cultivated a few times. Aside from its value as a green manure crop the cowpea is useful as food for man and the farm animals. The green pods are used as string beans or snaps. The ripened seeds are used as a food and the vines make good fodder for the farm animals.

"Experiments at the Louisiana Experiment Station show that one acre of cowpeas yielding 3,970.38 pounds of organic matter, turned under, gave to the soil 64.95 pounds of nitrogen, 20.39 pounds of phosphoric acid and 110.56 pounds of potash." – Farmer's Bulletin, 16 U.S. Dept. of Agriculture.

The Clovers. – These are the most extensively grown plants for green manure purposes in the United States. They are deep-rooted, and are able to use mineral food that is too tough for other plants. They furnish large crops of hay or green forage and a good aftermath and sod to turn under as green manure, or the entire crop may be plowed under.

Red Clover is the most widely planted (**Fig. 80**). It is a perennial plant and grows from the most northern States to the northern border of the Gulf States. It grows best on the loams and heavier soils well supplied with water, but not wet. It is sown broadcast at the rate of from ten to twenty pounds of seed per acre. In the North it is generally sown in the spring on fields of winter grain. In the South, September and October are recommended as the proper sowing times. It is the custom to let it grow two years, cutting it for hay and seed, and then to turn the aftermath and sod under.

Mammoth Red Clover, also called sapling clover and pea-vine clover, closely resembles the red clover, but is ranker in growth and matures two or three weeks later. It is better adapted to wet land than the red clover.

Crimson Clover, also called German clover and Italian clover, is a valuable green manure crop in the central and southern States east of the Mississippi. It is a hardy annual in that section and is generally sown from the last of July to the middle of October, either by itself or with cultivated crops at their last working. Fifteen and twenty pounds of seed are used to the acre. It makes a good growth during the fall and early winter and is in blossom and ready to cut or plow under in April or May. It grows at a season when the cowpea will not live. Crimson clover will grow on soils too light for other clovers.

The *Soy Bean*, also called soja bean and Japanese pea, is another leguminous crop used for green manuring (**Fig. 81**). It was introduced into this country from Japan and in some localities is quite extensively planted. It grows more upright than the cowpea and produces a large amount of stem and foliage that may be used for fodder or turned under for green manure The seeds are used for food for man and beast. The soy bean is planted and cared for in the same manner as the cowpea.

The *Canadian Field Pea* is sometimes grown in the north as a green manure crop.

White Sweet Clover, white melitot or Bokhara clover, grows as a weed from New England to the Gulf of Mexico. In the Gulf States it is regarded as a valuable forage and green manure plant. One or two pecks of seed per acre are sown in January or February.

Alfalfa, or lucerne, though grown more for a forage crop than for green manuring, should be mentioned here, for wherever grown and for whatever purpose, its effects on the soil are beneficial (**Fig. 82**). This plant requires a well prepared soil that is free from weeds.

Twenty to twenty-five pounds of seed are planted per acre. In the north the seeding is generally done in the spring after danger of frost is past, as frost kills the young plants. In the South fall seeding is the custom in order to give the young plants a long start ahead of the spring weeds. One seeding if well cared for lasts for many years.

Alfalfa is pastured or cut for hay, four to eight tons being the yield. Many fields run out in five or six years and the sod is plowed under. This plant sends its roots thirteen, sixteen, and even thirty feet into the soil after water and food, and when these roots decay they furnish the lower soil with organic matter and their passages serve as drains and ventilators in the soil. Alfalfa is grown extensively in the semi-arid regions of the country.

NON-LEGUMINOUS GREEN MANURE PLANTS

Among the non-leguminous green manure plants are rye, wheat, oats, mustard, rape, and buckwheat. Of these the rye and buckwheat are most generally used, the rye being a winter crop and the other a warm weather plant. They are both strong feeders and can use tough plant food. They do not add new nitrogen to the soil though they furnish humus and prepare food for the weaker feeders that may follow them.

CHAPTER XXI

Commercial Fertilizers

Next to the soil itself, the farmer's most important sources of plant food are the farm manures. But most farms do not produce these in sufficient quantities to keep up the plant food side of fertility. Therefore the farmer must resort to other sources of plant food to supplement the farm manures.

There is a large class of materials called Commercial Fertilizers, which, if judiciously used, will aid in maintaining the fertility of the farm with economy.

We learned in a previous chapter that the plant foods, nitrogen, phosphoric acid, potash and lime, are apt to be found wanting in sufficient available quantities to supply the needs of profitable crops. We learned also that lime is useful in improving the texture of the soil and in making other plant foods available.

Now the commercial fertilizers are used to supply the soil with these four substances and they may be classified according to the substance furnished as follows:

Sources of nitrogen, Sources of phosphoric acid, Sources of potash, Sources of lime.

SOURCES OF NITROGEN

Nitrogen is the most expensive of plant foods to buy, therefore special attention should be given to producing it on the farm by means of barn manures and legumes plowed under.

The principal commercial sources of nitrogen are:

Nitrate of soda, sulfate of ammonia, dried blood, tankage, dry ground fish, and cotton-seed meal.

Nitrate of Soda, or Chile saltpeter containing 15.5 per cent of nitrogen, is found in large deposits in the rainless regions of western South America. In the crude state as it comes from the mine it contains common salt and earthy matter as impurities. To remove these impurities the crude nitrate is put into tanks of warm water. The nitrate dissolves and the salt and earthy matter settle to the bottom of the tank. The water with the nitrate in solution is then drawn off into other tanks from which the water is evaporated, leaving the nitrate, a coarse, dirty looking salt which is packed in three-hundred-pound bags and shipped.

Plants that take their nitrogen from the soil take it in the form of nitrate. Hence nitrate of soda, which is very soluble in water, is immediately available to plants and is one of the most directly useful nitrogen fertilizers. It is used for quick results and should be applied only to land that has a crop or is to be immediately planted, otherwise it is liable to be lost by leaching.

Sulfate of Ammonia contains 20 per cent of nitrogen. It is a white salt, finer and cleaner looking than the nitrate. It is a by-product of the gas works and coke ovens. The nitrogen in it is quite readily available.

Dried Blood contains 8 to 12 per cent of nitrogen. This is blood collected in slaughter-houses and dried by steam or hot air. It decays rapidly in the soil and is a quick acting nitrogen fertilizer.

Tankage contains 4 to 8 per cent of nitrogen and 7 to 20 per cent of phosphoric acid. Slaughter-house waste, such as meat and bone scrap, are boiled or steamed to extract the fat. The settlings are dried and ground and sold as tankage. It is much slower in its action than dried blood and supplies the crop with both nitrogen and phosphoric acid.

Dried Fish Scrap is a by-product of the fish oil factories and the fish canning factories. It contains 7 to 9 per cent of nitrogen and 6 to 8 per cent of phosphoric acid. It undergoes nitrification readily and is a quick acting organic source of nitrogen and phosphoric acid.

Cotton-seed Meal contains 7 per cent of nitrogen, about 2.5 phosphoric acid, and 1.5 per cent of potash. It is a product of the cotton oil factories and is obtained by grinding the cotton seed cake from which the oil has been pressed. It is a most valuable source of nitrogen for the South.

The nitrogen in the dried blood, tankage, fish scrap and cotton-seed meal, being organic nitrogen, must be changed by the process of nitrification to nitric acid or nitrate before it is available. They are therefore better materials to use for a more gradual and continuous feeding of crops than the nitrate of soda or sulfate of ammonia.

Scrap leather, wool waste, horn and hoof shavings are rich in nitrogen but they decay so slowly that they make poor fertilizers. They are used by fertilizer manufacturers in making cheap mixed fertilizers.

SOURCES OF PHOSPHORIC ACID

The principal commercial sources of phosphoric acid are:

Phosphate Rocks. Bones. Fish scrap. Phosphate slag.

The *Phosphate Rocks* are found in shallow mines in North and South Carolina, Georgia, Florida and Tennessee, and also as pebbles in the river beds. They are the fossil remains of animals. After being dug from the mines the rock is kiln dried and then ground to a very fine powder called "floats" which is used on the soil. The phosphoric acid in the floats is insoluble and becomes available only as the phosphate decays. This is too slow for most plants so it is treated with oil of vitriol or sulfuric acid to make it available. The phosphoric acid in the ground rock is combined with lime, forming a phosphate of lime that is insoluble. When treated with the oil of vitriol or sulfuric acid, the sulfuric acid takes lime from the phosphate and forms sulfate of lime or gypsum. The phosphoric acid is left combined with the smallest possible amount of lime and is soluble in water. It is then called soluble or water soluble phosphoric acid.

Now if this soluble form remains unused it begins to take on lime again and turns back toward its original insoluble form. After a time it gets to such a state that it is no longer soluble in water but is soluble in weak acids. It is then said to be reverted phosphoric acid. Reverted phosphoric acid is also called citrate soluble phosphoric acid, because in testing fertilizers the chemists use ammonium citrate to determine the amount of reverted phosphoric acid.

This form still continues to take on lime and by and by gets back to the original insoluble form called insoluble phosphoric acid.

The soluble phosphoric acid and reverted phosphoric acid are available to plant roots. The insoluble form is not.

The rock phosphates contain from 26 to 35 per cent of insoluble phosphoric acid. The acid phosphates or dissolved rock phosphates contain from 12 to 16 per cent of available phosphoric acid and from 1 to 4 per cent of insoluble.

Bone Fertilizers. Bones have long been a valuable and favored source of phosphoric acid. In addition to phosphoric acid they contain some nitrogen, which adds to their value. They are organic phosphates and are quite lasting in their effect on the soil as they decay slowly.

The terms "Raw Bone," "Steamed Bone," "Ground Bone," "Bone Meal," "Bone Dust," "Bone Black," "Dissolved Bone," indicate the processes through which the bone has passed in preparation, or the condition of the material as put on the market and used on the soil.

Ground bone, bone meal, bone dust, indicate the mechanical conditions of the bones.

The bones are sometimes ground "raw" just as they come from the slaughterhouse or kitchen, or they are sometimes first "steamed" to extract the fat for soap, and the nitrogenous matter for glue.

Raw Bone. Analysis: Nitrogen, 2.5 to 4.5 per cent Available phosphoric acid, 5 to 8 per cent Insoluble phosphoric acid 15 to 17 per cent.

Steamed Bone contains 1.5 to 2.5 per cent of nitrogen, 6 to 9 per cent of available phosphoric acid and 16 to 20 per cent of insoluble phosphoric acid.

Steamed bone pulverizes much finer than raw bone and decays more rapidly in the soil because the fat has been extracted from it.

Dissolved Bone. Ground bone is sometimes treated

with sulfuric acid to render the phosphoric acid in it more available. It is then called dissolved bone and contains thirteen to fifteen per cent of available phosphoric acid and two to three per cent of nitrogen.

Dissolved Bone Black. Bone charcoal is used for refining sugar. It is then turned over to the fertilizer manufacturers who sell it as “Bone Black” or treat it with sulfuric acid and then put it on the market as dissolved bone black.

The bone black contains thirty to thirty-six per cent of insoluble phosphoric acid.

The dissolved bone black contains 15 to 17 per cent of available phosphoric acid and 1 to 2 per cent insoluble.

“Thomas Slag,” “Phosphate Slag,” “Odorless Phosphate.” Phosphorous is an impurity in certain iron ores. In the manufacture of Bessemer steel this is extracted by the use of lime that melts in the furnace, unites with the phosphorous and brings it away in the slag. This slag is ground to a fine powder and used as a fertilizer. It contains 11 to 23 per cent of phosphoric acid, most of which is available.

Superphosphate. The term superphosphate is applied to the phosphates that have been treated with sulfuric acid to make the phosphoric acid available. Dissolved bone, dissolved bone black, and the dissolved phosphate rocks are superphosphates.

Fish Scrap, mentioned as a source of nitrogen, is also a valuable source of phosphoric acid, containing 6 to 8 per cent, which is quite readily available owing to the rapid decay of the scrap.

SOURCES OF POTASH

The chief sources of potash used for fertilizers are the potash salts from the potash mines at Stassfurt, Germany, where there is an immense deposit of rock salt and potash salts.

The principal products of these mines used in this country are the crude salts:

Kainite, containing 12 per cent of potash.

Sylvinite, containing 16 to 20 per cent of potash, and the higher-grade salts manufactured from the crude salts:

Muriate of Potash, containing 50 per cent potash.

High grade Sulfate of Potash, containing 50 per cent potash.

Low grade Sulfate of Potash, containing 25 per cent potash.

Wood Ashes, if well kept and not allowed to get wet and leach, contain 4 to 9 per cent of potash.

Cotton Hull Ashes contain 20 to 30 per cent, of potash and 7 to 9 per cent of phosphoric acid.

The potash in all these forms is soluble in water and equally available to plants. The crude salts, kainite and sylvinite, and the muriate contain chlorine and are not considered good for potatoes and tobacco as the chlorine lowers the quality of these products.

In tobacco regions tobacco refuse is a valuable source of potash, the stems are about five per cent potash.

LIME

Lime is generally supplied to the soil in the form of

quicklime made by burning lime stone or shells. Other forms are gypsum or land plaster, gas lime (a refuse from gas works) and marl. Most soils contain sufficient lime for the food requirements of most plants. Some soils, however, are deficient in lime and some crops, particularly the legumes, are benefitted by direct feeding with lime.

Lime is valuable for its effect on the soil properties that constitute fertility.

Physically lime acts on the texture of the soil making clay soils mealy and crumbly, and causing the lighter soils to adhere or stick together more closely.

Chemically, lime decomposes minerals containing potash and other plant foods, thus rendering them available for the use of plants. It also aids the decay of organic matter and sweetens sour soils.

Biologically lime aids the process of nitrification.

The action of lime is greatest in its caustic or unslacked form.

Too much or too frequent liming may injure the soil. It should be carefully tried in a small way, and its action noted, before using it extensively.

A common way of using lime is to place twenty to forty bushels on an acre in heaps of three to five bushels, covering them with soil until the lime slacks to a fine powder. The lime is then spread and harrowed in. Lime tends to hasten the decay of humus. It should not be applied oftener than once in four or five years.

Gypsum, a sulfate of lime, is similar to lime in its action on the soil. Its most important effect is the setting free of potash from its compounds.

Gas lime should be used with great care as it contains

substances that are poisonous to plant roots. It is best to let it lie exposed to the weather several months before using.

Marl is simply soil containing an amount of lime varying from five to fifty per cent. It has value in the vicinity of marl beds but does not pay to haul very far.

CHAPTER XXII

Commercial Fertilizers – continued

Mixed fertilizers. What they are?

There are a large number of business concerns in the country that buy the raw materials described in Chapter XXI, mix them in various proportions, and sell the product as mixed or manufactured fertilizers. If these mixtures contain the three important plant foods: nitrogen, phosphoric acid and potash. They are sometimes called "complete" manures or fertilizers.

MANY BRANDS

These raw materials are mixed in many different proportions and many dealers have special brands for special crops. There are consequently large numbers of brands of fertilizers that vary in the amounts, proportions and availability of the plant foods they contain. For instance, a recent check in the State of Rhode Island showed that twenty-three fertilizer manufacturers offered for sale ninety-six different brands. In Missouri, one hundred and ten brands, made by sixteen different manufacturers, were offered for sale. Eighty-three manufacturers placed six hundred and forty-four brands on the market in New York State.

The result of this is more or less confusion on the part of the farmer in purchasing fertilizers, and with many a farmer it is a lottery as to whether or not he is buying what his crop or his soil needs.

Some of the manufacturers are not above using low-grade raw materials in making these mixtures. This means that the farmer should make himself familiar with the subject of fertilizers if he desires to use them intelligently and economically.

SAFEGUARD FOR THE FARMER

As a safeguard to the buyer of fertilizers State laws require that every brand put on the market shall be registered and that every bag or package sold shall have stated on it an analysis showing the amounts of nitrogen, or its equivalent in ammonia, the soluble phosphoric acid, the reverted phosphoric acid, the insoluble phosphoric acid, and the potash.

The manufacturers of fertilizers comply with the law by printing on the bag or package the per cents of plant food in the fertilizers, and these statements in the great majority of cases agree favorably with the analyses of the experiment stations, but they do not in all cases state what materials were used to furnish the different kinds of plant food.

For instance in mixing a fertilizer one manufacturer may use dried blood to furnish nitrogen and another may use leather waste or horn shavings. The latter contains more nitrogen than the dried blood, but they are so tough and decay so slowly that they are of little benefit to a quick growing plant.

INFLATING THE GUARANTEE

Although the dealer states correctly the percent of plant food in the fertilizer, he is quite frequently inclined to repeat this in a different form, and thus give the impression that the mixture contains more than it really does.

The dealers also give the nitrogen as ammonia because it makes a larger showing.

Phosphoric acid is often stated as "bone phosphate" because in this the amount appears to be greater.

Fertilizers are generally mixed and sold to the farmer on the ton basis.

LOW-GRADE MIXTURES

Many dealers, to meet a certain demand, furnish mixtures that are necessarily low-grade and sometimes are more expensive than the higher-priced high-grade mixtures.

BUY ON THE PLANT FOOD BASIS

The farmer generally buys his fertilizer on the ton basis. A better method is to buy just as the fertilizer manufacturers buy the raw materials they use for mixing, namely, on the basis of actual plant food in the fertilizer. The dealers have what they call the "unit basis," a "unit" meaning one per cent of a ton or twenty pounds of plant food. A ton of nitrate of soda, for instance, contains 310 pounds or 15½ units of nitrogen.

Buy your mixture of a reliable firm, find out the actual amounts of the plant foods in the mixture and pay a fair market price for them.

CHAPTER XXIII

Commercial Fertilizers – Concluded

When a considerable amount of fertilizer is used a better plan than buying mixed fertilizer is to buy the raw materials and mix them yourself. For example, a farmer is about to plant five acres of cabbages for the market. He finds that a certain successful cabbage grower recommends the use of fifty pounds nitrogen, fifty pounds phosphoric acid and seventy pounds potash per acre. For the five acres this will mean 250 pounds nitrogen, 250 pounds phosphoric acid and 350 pounds potash. To furnish the nitrogen he can buy 1,613 pounds of nitrate of soda or 2,500 pounds dried blood or 1,250 pounds sulfate of ammonia, or a part of each. To furnish the phosphoric acid he can buy 1,786 pounds acid phosphate. Seven hundred pounds of either sulfate or muriate of potash will furnish the potash.

These materials can be easily mixed by spreading in alternate layers on a smooth floor and then shoveling over the entire mass several times. The mixture can be further improved by passing it through a sand or coal screen or sieve.

By following this method of buying the raw materials and mixing them on the farm, the farmer can reduce his fertilizer bill by quite a considerable amount and at the same time can obtain just the kinds and proper amounts of plant foods needed by his crops.

KIND AND AMOUNT TO BUY

The farmer should make the best use of farm manures and through tillage to render plant food available for his crops before turning to commercial fertilizer for additional plant food.

If he grows leguminous crops for green manuring, for feeding stock or for cover crops, he can in many cases secure, chiefly through them, sufficient high priced nitrogen for the needs of his crops, and it is necessary only occasionally to purchase moderate amounts of phosphoric acid, potash and lime.

For special farming and special crops it may be necessary to use the commercial fertilizer more freely.

It is impossible to say here just what amounts or what kinds of fertilizer should be purchased, because no two farms are exactly alike as to soil, methods of cropping or methods of tillage.

There are certain factors, however, which will serve as a general guide and which should be considered in determining the kind and amount of fertilizer to buy.

These factors are:

- The crop.
- The soil.
- The system of farming.

THE CROP

Crop roots differ in their powers of feeding, or their powers of securing plant foods. Some roots can use very tough plant foods, while others require it in the most available form. Some roots secure nitrogen from the air.

The cowpea roots, for example, can take nitrogen from the air and they can use such tough phosphoric acid and potash that it seldom pays to feed them directly with fertilizers.

A bale per acre crop of cotton requires for the building of roots, stems, leaves, bolls, lint and seed:

103 pounds of Nitrogen.
41 pounds of Phosphoric Acid.
65 pounds of Potash.

And yet experiment and experience have proved that the best fertilizer for such a crop contains the following amounts of plant food:

Nitrogen	20 pounds
Phosphoric Acid	70 pounds
Potash	20 pounds

This means that cotton roots are fairly strong feeders of nitrogen and potash, but are weak on the phosphoric acid side.

The small grains, wheat, oats, barley and rye, can use tough phosphoric acid and potash, but are weak on nitrogen, and as they make the greater part of their growth in the cool spring before nitrification is rapid, they are benefitted by the application of nitrogen, particularly in the form of nitrate, which is quickly available.

Clover, peas, beans, etc., have the power of drawing nitrogen from the air, but draw from the soil lime, phosphoric acid and potash. Hence the phosphates, potash manures and lime are desirable for these crops.

Root and tuber crops are unable to use the insoluble

mineral elements in the soil, hence they require application of all the important plant foods in readily available form. Nitrogen is especially beneficial to beets. Turnips are benefitted by liberal applications of soluble phosphoric acid. White and sweet potatoes require an abundance of potash.

If we are growing tender, succulent market garden crops, we need nitrogenous manures, which increase the growth of stem and foliage.

Fruit trees are slow growing plants and do not need quick acting fertilizers.

The small fruits, being more rapid in growth, require more of the soluble materials.

A dark, healthy green foliage indicates a good supply of nitrogen, while a pale yellowish green may indicate a need of nitrogen.

A well developed head of grain, seed pod or fruit indicates liberal supplies of phosphoric acid and potash.

THE SOIL

Soils that are poor in humus are generally in need of nitrogen.

Heavy soils are generally supplied with potash but lack phosphoric acid.

Sandy soils are apt to be poor in potash and nitrogen.

SYSTEM OF FARMING

A system of general or diversified farming embracing crop products and stock raising, requires much less artificial manuring than does a system which raises special crops or quick growing crops in rapid succession, as in the case of truck farming or market gardening.

TESTING THE SOIL

Every farmer should be more or less of an investigator and experimenter.

The factors mentioned previously as indicating the presence or absence of sufficient quantities of certain plant foods serve as a general guide, but are not absolute. The best method of determining what plant foods are lacking in the soil is to carry on some simple experiments.

The following plan for soil testing with plant foods is suggestive: To test the soil for a possible need of the single plant foods, a series of five plots may be laid off.

These plots should be long and narrow and may be one-twentieth, one-sixteenth, one-tenth, one-eighth acre or larger. A plot one rod wide and eight rods long will contain one-twentieth acre. The width of the plot may be adjusted to accommodate a certain number of rows of crop and the length made proper to include an even fraction of an acre. A strip three or four feet in width should be left between each two plots. These strips are to be left unfertilized and are for the purpose of preventing one plot being affected by the plant food of another.

The plots are all plowed, planted and cared for alike, the only difference in treatment being in the application of plant food.

If the plots are one-twentieth acre in size, plant foods may be applied as follows:

Plot 1.	Nitrate of Soda 8 lbs.

Plot 2.	Acid Phosphate 16 lbs.
Plot 3.	Nothing.
Plot 4.	Muriate of Potash 8 lbs.
Plot 5.	Lime 1 bushel.

Plot 3 is a check plot for comparison.

The measuring of the plots, weighing and application of the fertilizers, planting and care of the crops, weighing and measuring at harvest, should be carefully and accurately done.

A number of additional plots may be added if desired to test the effect of plant foods in combination. For instance:

Plot 6.	Nitrate of Soda 8 lbs. Acid Phosphate 16 lbs.
Plot 7.	Nitrate of Soda 8 lbs. Muriate of Potash 8 lbs.
Plot 8.	Nothing.

Plot 9.	Muriate of Potash 8 lbs. Acid Phosphate 16 lbs.
Plot 10.	Nitrate of Soda 8 lbs. Acid Phosphate 16 lbs. Muriate of Potash 8 lbs.

If the amount of fertilizer is too small to distribute evenly over the plot, mix it thoroughly with a few quarts of dry earth or sand to give it more bulk and then apply it.

In the use of fertilizers it should always be remembered that small crops are not always due to lack of plant food, but may be caused by an absence of the other conditions necessary for root growth and development. The soil may not be sufficiently moist to properly supply the plants with water. Too much water may check ventilation. Poor tillage may check root development. Unless the physical conditions are right the possible effects of additional plant food in the form of fertilizers are greatly diminished. The farmer who gets the largest return from fertilizers is the one who gives greatest attention to the physical properties of the soil. He makes use of organic matter and is very thorough in his methods of tillage.

CHAPTER XXIV

The Rotation of Crops

There are two methods or systems of cropping the soil: The One Crop System, or the continuous cropping of the soil year after year with one kind of crop.

The Rotation of Crops or the selection of a given number of different crops and growing them in regular order.

The purpose of this chapter is to inquire into the effect of these two systems of cropping:

On the soil conditions necessary for the best growth and development of the crops.

- On the market value of the crops.
- On the increase of or the protection from injurious diseases and insects.
- On the distribution of labor throughout the year.
- On the caring for farm stock.
- On the providing for home supplies.

This inquiry and the conclusion will be based on the following facts learned in the foregoing chapters.

Plant roots need for their growth and development (see Chapter II):

A mellow yet firm soil.

- A moist soil.
- A ventilated soil.
- A warm soil.
- A soil supplied with plant food.

Decaying organic matter or humus is one of the most

important ingredients of our soils. Because:

It greatly influences soil texture and therefore the conditions necessary for root growth.

Its presence or absence greatly influences the attitude of soils toward water, the most important factor in plant growth. Its presence helps light, sandy soils to hold more water and to better pump water from below, while it helps close, heavy soils to better take in the water that falls on their surface. Its absence causes an opposite state of affairs.

The presence of organic matter checks excessive ventilation in too open, sandy soil by filling the pores, and improves poor ventilation in heavy clay soils by making them more open.

Humus, on account of its color, influences the heat absorbing powers of soils.

The organic matter is constantly undergoing more or less rapid decay unless the soil be perfectly dry or frozen solid. Stirring and cultivating the soil hasten this decay.

As the organic matter decays it adds available plant food to the soil, particularly nitrogen.

As it decays, it produces carbonic acid and other acids that are able to dissolve mineral plant food not soluble in pure water and thus render it available to plants.

Plants, although they require the same elements of plant food, take them in different amounts and different proportions.

Plants differ in the extent and depth of root growth and therefore take food from different parts of the soil. Some are surface feeders while others feed on the deeper soil.

Plants differ in their power to take plant food from the

soil; some are weak feeders, and can use only the most available food; others are strong feeders, and can use tougher plant food.

Plants vary in the amount of heat they require to carry on their growth and development.

THE ONE-CROP SYSTEM

We are now ready for the question. What effect has the continuous cultivation, year after year, of the same kind of crop on the soil conditions necessary to the best growth and development of that crop or any other crop? Suppose we take cotton for example.

How does cotton growing affect soil humus?

During the cultivation of cotton, the organic matter or humus of the soil decays in greater quantities than are added by the stalks and leaves of the crop. Therefore, cotton is a humus wasting crop, and the continuous cultivation of this crop tends to exhaust the supply of organic matter in the soil.

How does cotton growing affect soil texture?

Cotton growing wastes soil humus and therefore injures soil texture by making the lighter soils more loose and open, and the heavier soils more dense and compact.

How does cotton growing affect soil water?

By wasting humus cotton growing injures soil texture and so weakens the water holding and water pumping power of light soils and weakens the water absorbing power of heavy soils. Therefore the continuous cultivation of cotton weakens the power of the soil over water, that most important factor in crop growth.

How does cotton growing affect soil ventilation?

Continuous cotton culture, by wasting humus, injures texture and therefore injures soil ventilation, causing too much ventilation in the lighter soils and too little in heavier soils.

How does cotton culture affect plant food in the soil?

Continuous cotton growing wastes plant food:

- Because it wastes organic matter which contains valuable plant food, particularly nitrogen.
- Because by wasting organic matter it increases the leaching of the lighter soils and the surface washing of the heavier soils.
- Because its roots occupy largely the upper soil and do not make use of much food from the lower soil.
- Because it grows only during the warm part of the year and there is no crop on the land to check loss of plant food from leaching and surface wash during the winter.
- Because it is a weak feeder of phosphoric acid, and can use only that which is in the most available form. In applying fertilizer to cotton it is necessary for best results to apply at least twice as much phosphoric acid as the crop can use, because it can use only that which is in the most available form and the remainder is left in the soil unused.

Continuous cotton culture then has an injurious effect on all the important soil conditions necessary to its best growth and development, and the result is a diminishing yield or an increasing cost in maintaining fertility by the use of fertilizer.

How does continuous cotton culture affect the economics of the farm?

- The injury to the soil conditions necessary to root

growth diminishes the yield and therefore increases the cost of production.

- The poor soil conditions tend not only to diminish yield but also to diminish the quality of the crop, which tends to lower the price received for the cotton.
- Keeping the land constantly in cotton tends to increase the insect enemies and the diseases of the crop.
- The continuous growing of cotton does not permit the constant employment of one set of laborers throughout the year.
- The continuous growing of cotton generally means that most of the farm goes into cotton. A small patch of corn is planted for the stock, which are apt to suffer from a lack of variety in food.

The same is true with reference to home supplies. Very few vegetables are grown for the table and there is little milk, butter or eggs for home use or exchange for groceries or dry goods at the store.

Thus we see that the continuous growing of cotton on the soil, year after year, has a bad effect on conditions necessary to its best growth and development and also on the economics of the farm.

These facts are true to a greater or less degree in the case of nearly all of the farm crops. The grain crops are often considered as humus makers because of the stubble turned under, but Professor Snyder, of Minnesota, found that five years' continuous culture of wheat resulted in an annual loss of 171 pounds of nitrogen per acre, of which only 24.5 was taken by the crop, the remaining 146.5 pounds were lost through a waste of organic matter.

THE ROTATION OF CROPS

Now, suppose that instead of growing cotton on the same soil year after year, we select four crops – cotton, corn, oats and cowpea – and grow them in regular order, a rotation practiced in some parts of the South.

We will divide the farm into three fields and number them 1, 2 and 3, and will plant these crops as indicated by the following diagrams:

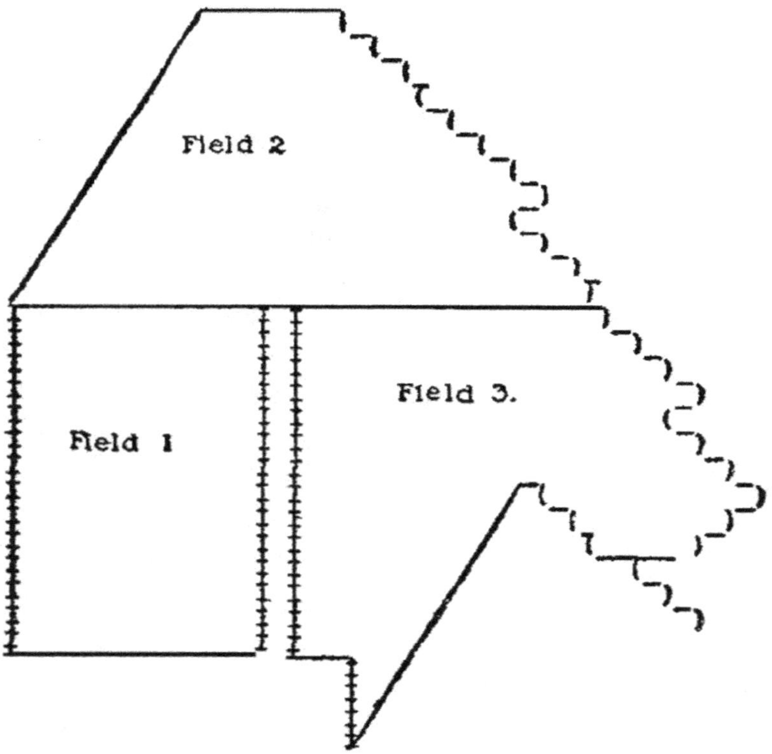

Plan of farm.

Plan for planting.

	Field 1.	Field 2.	Field 3.
1st year	Cotton	Oats, harvested in spring, followed by Cowpeas	Corn, followed by oats, planted in fall
2d year	Corn, followed by oats, planted in fall	Cotton	Oats, harvested in spring, followed by Cowpeas
3d year	Oats, harvested in spring, followed by Cowpeas	Corn, followed by oats, planted in fall	Cotton

Each of these crops occupies one-third of the farm each year, and yet the crop on each field changes each year so that no one kind of crop is grown on any field oftener than once in three years. The cotton is grown for market, the corn partly to sell, partly to feed, the oats to feed and the cowpeas to plow under. All cotton and corn refuse is plowed under.

What effect will such a system have on the conditions necessary for plant growth? Suppose we follow the crops on Field 1. Cotton, corn, and oats are humus wasting crops but the pea crop which is grown the third year is plowed under, and largely, if not entirely, remedies the loss by furnishing a new supply of organic matter, and the ill effects which we noticed would follow the loss of organic matter due to the continuous growing of cotton are avoided, soil texture is preserved, soil ventilation is not injured, and the power of the soil over water is preserved.

What is the effect on plant food in the soil?

Before answering this question let us see what amounts of plant foods these crops take out of the soil.

We will assume that the soil is a good loam at the start and will produce:

One bale of five hundred pounds of lint cotton per acre, sixty bushels shelled corn per acre, thirty bushels oats per acre, or two tons cowpea hay per acre.

Such a yield of crop would take from the soil the following amounts of plant food per acre:

	Nitrogen, pounds	Phosphoric Acid, pounds	Potash, pounds
Cotton (whole plant)	103	41	65
Corn (whole plant)	84	26	61
Oats (whole plant)	32	13	27
Cowpea	78	23	66

Now suppose we sell the lint of the cotton, keeping all the rest of the plant, including the seed, on the farm and turning it back into the soil.

Of the corn suppose we sell one-half the grain and

keep the other half and the fodder for use on the farm. Suppose the oats be made into oat hay and be fed on the farm and the cowpeas be turned under. Assuming that the cowpeas take half their nitrogen from the air. This will mean that in the course of three years we take out of the soil of each acre in the crops:

Nitrogen.	Phosphoric Acid.
258 pounds.	103 pounds.

but we return to the soil in crop refuse and manure from the stock:

Nitrogen.	Phosphoric Acid.
256 pounds.	87 pounds.

This assumes that we have taken from the farm in products sold:

	Nitrogen, pounds.	Phosphoric Acid, pounds.	Potash, pounds .
Cotton Lint	2	1	2
Corn	28	12	10
Animal products	11	3	10
Totals	41	16	22

The plant food charged to animal products is twenty per cent of that in the grain and forage fed to the stock.

At the end of the three years the plant food account

will balance up with:

Nitrogen	a gain of 2 pounds.
Phosphoric Acid	a loss of 16 pounds.
Potash	a loss of 22 pounds.

This result is of course approximate. There will be some loss of nitrogen through leaching and denitrification. Some of the potash and phosphoric acid will be converted into unavailable forms. This can be made good by applying to the cotton a fertilizer containing twenty pounds of nitrogen, sixty pounds of phosphoric acid and twenty pounds of potash.

Additional nitrogen and organic matter can be grown to turn under by planting crimson clover in the cotton at the last working for a winter cover crop to be turned under for the corn, and by planting cowpeas or soy beans between the rows of corn.

If this is done it may not be necessary to add any nitrogen in the fertilizer, letting that supply only phosphoric acid and potash.

If commercial fertilizer is used on the cotton, it would be a good plan to apply the manure from the stock to the corn.

To follow our crop on Field 1 through the three years we will have, first, cotton drawing large amounts of plant food from the soil and diminishing the humus of the soil.

Growing a winter crop of crimson clover, turning back all the cotton refuse except the lint and oil, and applying the barn manure will furnish ample plant food for the corn and replenish the organic matter.

The corn is a rather stronger feeder of phosphoric acid than cotton and will be able to get sufficient from that left by the cotton.

The oats will be able to get a full ration after the corn, and the cowpeas will readily take care of themselves on the score of plant food and will put the soil in fine condition for cotton again.

The peas may be left on the ground to turn under in the spring at cotton planting time, or they may be plowed under in the early fall and a crimson clover or vetch cover crop planted, which will be plowed under for the cotton.

These same facts will be true of each of the three fields. The humus and, therefore, texture will be taken care of; ventilation, soil temperature and plant food will be controlled to advantage.

Each of the crops will be represented on the farm each year and the yields of each crop will be better than if grown continuously alone.

The quality and therefore the market value will be greater. Insects and disease will be easier kept in control, and stock will be more economically furnished with a variety of foods.

BENEFITS DERIVED FROM ROTATION OF CROPS

Rotation of crops economizes the natural plant food of the soil and also that which is applied in the form of manure and fertilizer. This is because:

Crops take food from the soil in different amounts and different proportions.

Crops differ in their feeding powers.

Crops differ in the extent and depth to which they send their roots into the soil in search of food and water.

Crops differ in the time of year at which they make their best growths.

Rotation helps to maintain or improve the texture of the soil because the amount of humus in the soil is maintained or increased by turning under green manure and cover crops that should occur in every well-planned rotation.

Rotation helps to maintain or increase the plant food in the surface soil. When crops like cowpeas or clover which take mineral food from the subsoil and nitrogen from the air, are plowed under, they give up the plant food in their leaves, stems and upper roots to the surface soil, and thus help to maintain or increase fertility.

Rotation tends to protect crops from injurious insects and diseases. If one kind of crop is grown continuously on one piece of land the soil becomes infested with the insects and diseases that injure that particular crop. If the crop is changed, the insects and diseases find difficulty in adapting themselves to the change and consequently diminish in numbers.

Rotation helps to keep the soil free from weeds. "If the same kind of crop were grown year after year on the same field, the weeds which grow most readily along with that crop would soon take possession of the soil." For example, chick weed, dock, thistle, weeds peculiar to grain and grain crops tend to increase if the land is long occupied by these crops.

Rotation helps the farmer to make a more even distribution of labor throughout the year. This is because crops differ as to the time of year at which they are planted and harvested.

Rotation of crops enables the farmer to provide for his stock more economically. Live stock fares better on a variety of food, which is more cheaply secured by a system of rotation than otherwise.

THE TYPICAL ROTATION

A typical rotation for general farming should contain at least:

- One money crop that is necessarily an exhaustive crop.
- One manurial crop that is a soil enricher.
- One feeding crop which diminishes fertility only a little.
- One cleansing crop, a hoed or cultivated crop.

CONDITIONS THAT MODIFY THE ROTATION

There are certain conditions that tend to modify the rotation or to influence the farmer in his choice of crops. They are as follows:

- First of all the climate will set a limit on the number and varieties of crops from which a choice can be made for a given locality.
- The kind of farming which he chooses to carry on, whether stock raising, grain farming, truck farming, or a combination of two or more of these, or others.
- Kind of soil. Certain soils are best adapted to particular crops. For example, heavy soils are best suited to wheat, grass, clover, cabbages, etc. Light, sandy soils to

early truck, certain grades of tobacco, etc.

- The demand for crops and their market value.
- Facilities for getting crops to market, good or bad country roads, railroads and water transportation.
- The state of the land with respect to weeds, insect pests and plant diseases.

GENERAL RULES

A few general rules may be made use of in arranging the order of the crops in the rotation though they cannot always be strictly followed.

- Crops that require the elements of plant food in the same proportion should not follow each other.
- Deep-rooted crops should alternate with shallow-rooted crops.
- Humus makers should alternate with humus wasters.
- Every well-arranged rotation should have at least one crop grown for its manurial effect on the soil, as a crop of cowpeas, or one of clover, to be turned under.

The objection often made to this last rule is that, aside from the increase in fertility, there is no direct return for the time, labor and seed, and the land brings no crop for a year. It is not necessary to use the entire crop for green manuring – a part of it may be used for hay or for pasture with little loss of the manurial value of the crop, provided the manure from that part of the crop taken off is returned and the part of the crop not removed is turned under.

LENGTH OF THE ROTATION

The length of the rotation may vary from a two-course or two crop rotation to one of several courses. Crimson clover may be alternated with corn, both crops being grown within a year.

A three-course rotation, popular in some parts of the country, is wheat, clover, and potatoes; potatoes being the money crop and cleansing crop, wheat a secondary money crop or feeding crop, and clover the manurial and feeding crop.

A popular four-course rotation is corn, potatoes or truck, small grain, clover; the potatoes being the chief money crop, corn the feeding crop, the small grain the secondary money or feeding crop, and clover the manurial and feeding crop.

On many New England farms near towns, hay and straw are the chief money crops. Here the rotation is grass two or more years, then a cleansing crop and a grain crop. A Canadian rotation is wheat, hay, pasture, oats, and peas. A rotation for the South might be corn, crimson clover, cotton, crimson clover; this rotation covering a period of two years. A South Carolina rotation is oats, peas, cotton, and corn – a three-year rotation. It might be improved as follows: Oats, peas, crimson clover, cotton, crimson clover, corn.

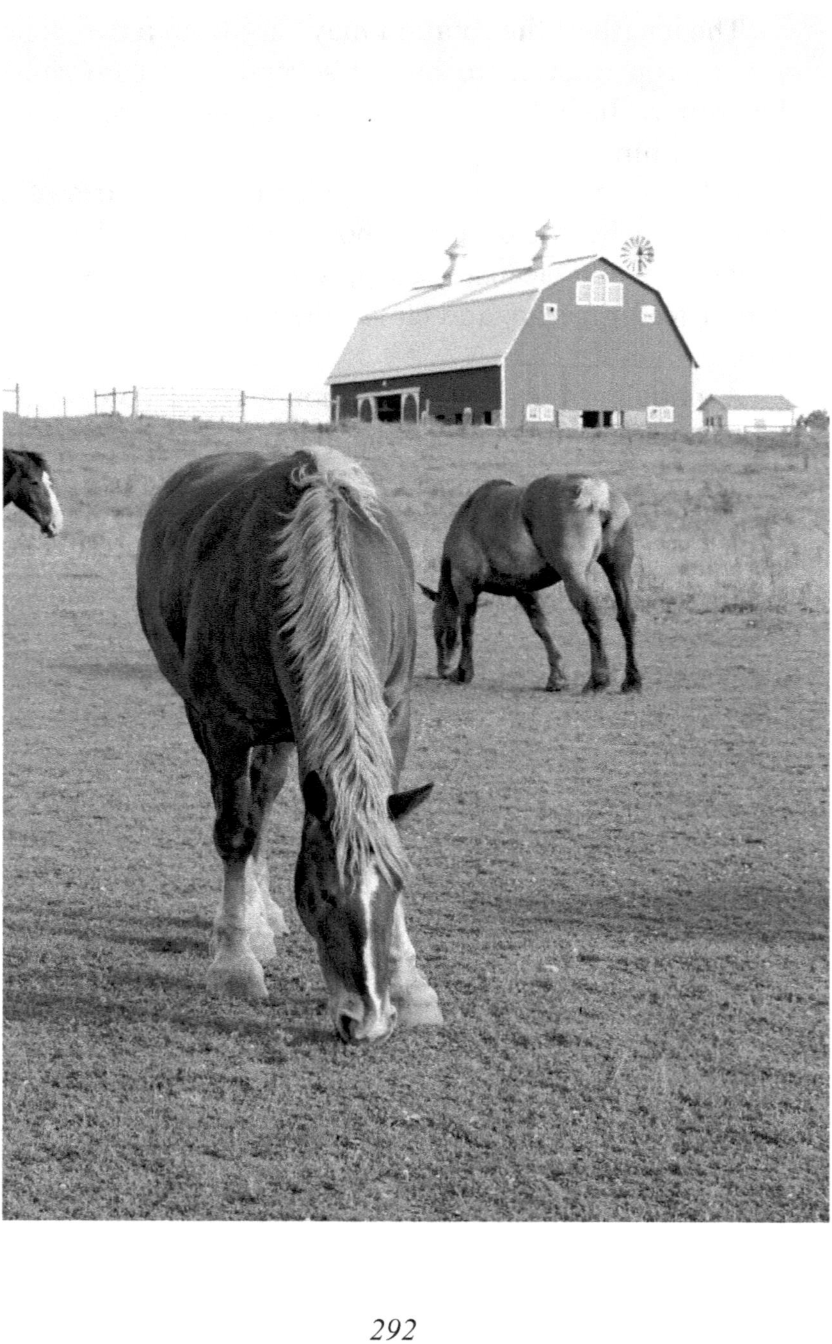

CHAPTER XXV

Farm Drainage

Some farm lands contain so much water that the conditions of fertility are interfered with and therefore the crop producing power of these lands is lowered.

HOW SURPLUS WATER AFFECTS FERTILITY

This surplus water diminishes fertility by reducing the area of film water in the soil.

- It checks soil ventilation.
- It tends to keep the soil cold.
- It dilutes plant food in the soil.
- It interferes with proper tillage.

INDICATIONS OF A NEED OF DRAINAGE

The above-mentioned state of affairs occurs sometimes in fields at the foot of hills, or on sloping uplands that receive spring water or seepage water from higher lands.

Some fields are underlaid by a close, compact subsoil which so checks percolation that the surface soil is too wet for tillage operations the greater part of the year. In such cases:

A need of drainage is generally indicated by the presence of more or less free water standing on the surface.

In some lands the surface water does not appear as free water standing on the surface. In such cases:

A need of drainage is indicated by the curling and

wilting of the leaves of corn and other crops during dry, hot weather. This curling and wilting is due to the fact that during the early growth of the crop free water stands so high in the soil that the crop roots are confined to a shallow layer of soil. When dry, hot weather comes, the free water recedes, the upper soil dries out, and the roots cannot get sufficient water to supply the demands of transpiration, hence the curling and wilting of the leaves.

If drains are placed in this soil, the free water will be kept at a lower level in the spring and the plant roots will develop deeper in the soil, where there will be constant supply of film water during the dryer and warmer summer weather.

The wiry and spindling growth of grass and grain crops may indicate too much water.

The growth of moss on the surface of the ground and the cracking of the soil in dry weather are also indications of too much water.

DRAINS

How can we get rid of this surplus free water?

We can make passageways through the soil to a lower level and then let gravity pull the water through them to lower ground below. These passageways are called drains.

Drains may be classed as:

Surface drains which are shallow, open channels made in the soil with a plow, hoe or other tool, to carry off surface water. They are temporary and need frequent renewing.

Open-ditch drains are deeper, more permanent water passageways around or across the fields.

Surface and open-ditch drains take only surface water. They also carry off surface soil and manures washed into them. They frequently become choked or stopped by trash and soil, and are in the way of cultivation and harvesting operations.

Covered drains, under drains or blind ditches are water passageways made of brush, poles, stones, tiles, etc. (**Figs. 80-81**), placed in the bottoms of ditches and then covered with soil.

INFLUENCE OF COVERED OR UNDER DRAINS ON FERTILITY

Influence on soil water.

Covered or under drains take not only surface water, but also remove free water from the soil beneath down to nearly the level of the bottom of the drains, and thus increase the area of film water. Removing the free water enables the soil to absorb more readily rain water falling on the surface and therefore checks surface wash and the gullying of fields.

Influence on soil ventilation.

Lowering the free water allows a deeper penetration of air and, therefore, a deeper root development and enables crops to better resist dry periods.

Influence on soil temperature.

Lowering the free water in the soil influences soil temperature:

By diminishing the amount of water to be heated.

By checking evaporation.

By letting warm showers sink down into the soil.

By increasing ventilation and therefore permitting the

circulation of warm air in the soil.

The cropping season is lengthened by causing the soil to be warmer and drier earlier in the spring and later in the fall.

Influence on plant food in the soil.

Covered or under drains check losses of plant food that occur with surface and open ditch drains. They render available more plant food, for lowering free water and increasing ventilation:

Deepen the feeding area of the roots.

Aid the process of nitrification.

Aid chemical changes that make plant food available.

Check denitrification.

LOCATION OF DRAINS

As gravity is the force that is to take the surplus water from the soil, the outlet of the drainage system should be at the lowest part of the area to be drained.

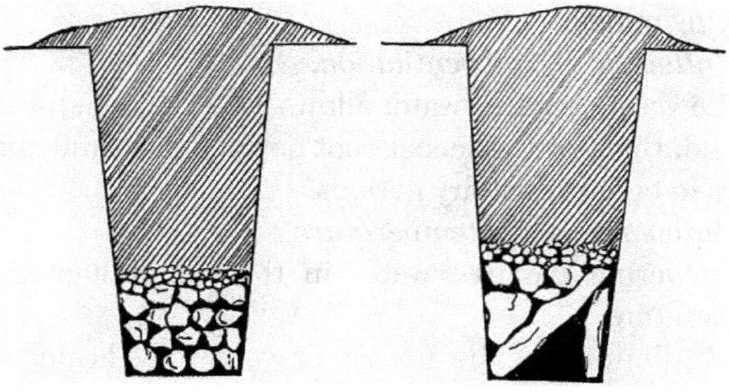

Fig. 83. – CROSS-SECTIONS OF STONE-DRAINS.

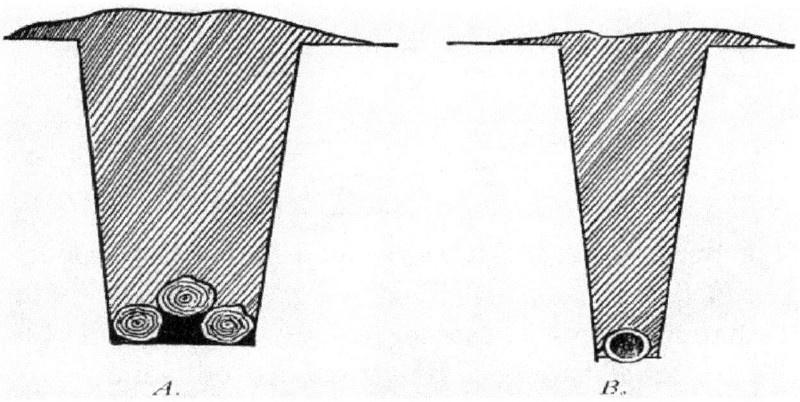

Fig. 84. *A*. Cross-section of a pole-drain. *B*. Cross-section of a tile-drain.

Fig. 85. – A COLLECTION OF DRAINAGE TOOLS.

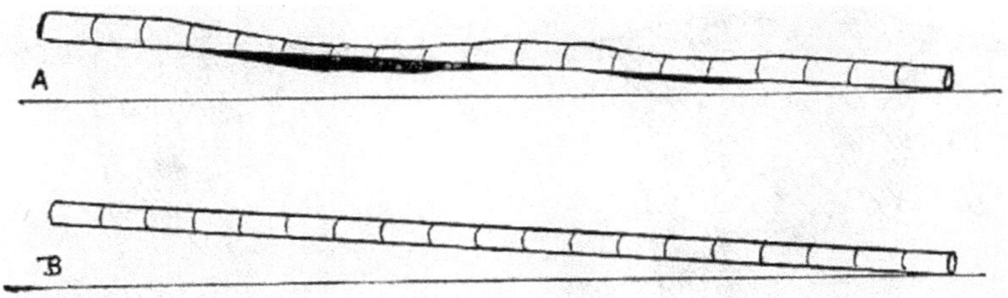

Fig. 86. *A* represents a poorly laid tile-drain. It is poorly graded, and has partly filled with soil. It has lost more than half its water carrying capacity. *B* was properly graded, and has kept free from sediment.

The main drains should be located in the lowest parts of the fields, indicated by courses taken by water after a rain or by small streams running through the farm.

The lateral drains, if surface or open ditch drains, should run across the slopes; if under drains, they should run up and down the slopes.

Grade or slope of the drain.

The grade of the drain should be sufficient to cause a flow of the water. In the case of open ditches it should not be steep enough to cause too rapid a current and a consequent serious washing of the banks of the ditch. Large, deep ditches will carry water with a grade of one inch to a hundred feet.

Tile drains.

Covered or under drains are made of brush, poles, planks, stones, tiles, etc. (**Figs. 83-84**). Where tiles can be obtained at reasonable prices they are considered best. Tiles are made of clay and are burnt like brick. They are more lasting than wood and are easier and cheaper to lay than stone, unless the stone must be gotten rid of.

The most approved form of drain tile is the round or circular form. These are made in sizes ranging from two and one-half to six and eight inches in diameter, and in pieces one foot in length.

The size used depends on the length of the drain, the amount of water to carry, the frequency of heavy rainfalls and the character of the soil.

The distance apart varies from twenty-five feet in heavy soils to over two hundred feet in light soils. The usual depth is about three feet, though the farther apart the deeper they are put.

A lateral tile drain should enter a main at an acute angle to prevent too great a check in the current.

In putting in a drainage system the first thing to be done is to make a plan of the ground and determine the slope of the land and the grade of the drain. The ditches are then staked out and the digging proceeds. In digging the ditches plows are sometimes used to throw out the top soil, then the work is finished with spades and shovels.

Professional ditchers use special tools and they take out only sufficient earth to make room for the tiles (**Fig. 85**). The tiles are then laid end to end, the joints covered with a piece of sod, some grass, straw, paper or clay, to prevent loose soil sifting in. As the tiles are laid, enough soil is placed on them to hold them in place until the ditch is filled.

In laying the tiles an even grade should be maintained (**Fig. 86**). A lessening of the grade checks the current of water and tends to cause a stoppage of the drain.

The water gets into the drain through the joints where the tiles come together.

The outlet of a tile drain should be protected by brick work or should be of glazed tile such as the so-called terra-cotta tile, to prevent injury by frost.

The mouth of the drain should be protected by a screen of wire to prevent the entrance of rats and other small animals.

CHAPTER XXVI

Vegetables Suited To Farm Culture Everywhere

In this chapter are grouped a number of vegetables of easy culture. They may be grown with success almost anywhere. Some of them are produced by market gardeners, but by reason of the amount of ground that they occupy they are more particularly adapted to horse culture by farmers.

The chapter will treat briefly of asparagus, beans, beets, cabbage, carrots, sweet corn, horseradish, parsnip, potato, pumpkin and squash, salsify, tomato, turnip, etc.

ASPARAGUS

Asparagus demands a deep, rich, well-drained soil. Its culture is profitable, and it yields ready cash at an early season of the year, when other sales are limited. The cutting term covers six weeks, beginning (at Philadelphia) in the middle or latter part of April. Cutting must here cease in June, in order to give the roots ample time to regain strength and make vigorous tops.

In selecting a situation for a bed, a warm spot should be chosen, having a deep and mellow soil, and with good natural or artificial drainage. A small area is better than a large one, as being more likely to receive sufficient manure; and it is desirable that the land should have been tilled for a year or two before the planting of the roots, and a heavy coat of manure incorporated with the soil – the more manure the better.

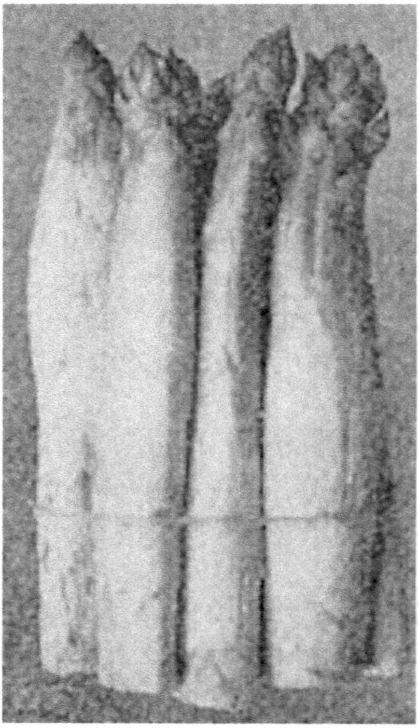

Fig. 87. Donald's Elmira

Roots – The roots are set in early spring, in deep trenches, 5 or 6 feet apart, made with a plow. If the plow be run both ways and the loose dirt shoveled out, it is quite easy to reach a depth of 15 or more inches. It is not material whether strong one-year-old roots or two-year-old roots be used.

Varieties – As to varieties, it is almost as much a matter of culture as of name; still, there are better and worse kinds. Asparagus varies in color from purple to green, and even to white. There are certain so-called mammoth sorts, whose shoots are larger, but less numerous than the old-fashioned kinds. There is a slight difference in flavor, also, but the preference of the local market must determine the farmer in making a choice of roots. If a green "grass" be preferred, that kind can be had from seedsmen; but, no matter how carefully the roots may be grown, there will be some slight variations in the color of the shoots, for asparagus does not always come true from seed. Market gardeners usually sort their asparagus shoots at bunching time; always for size, and sometimes for color, especially when supplying a fancy trade.

As a rule, it is wise to select a variety that will produce a good number of large-sized shoots, such as Donald's Elmira or Barr's Mammoth, and trust to manure and culture for the best results. Quality of shoots depends on quick growth, and size depends somewhat on distance of the root under ground. The deeper the asparagus root under the surface, the larger in diameter will be the shoot, provided the plants are not crowded; a fact of which gardeners often take advantage by heaping soil up over the crowns of the plants during the growing season.

Setting out – The young roots should be set carefully, crowns up, at intervals of 1½ to 2 feet, in the deep furrows or trenches heretofore mentioned. A few inches of manure can be put in the bottom, covering slightly with soil and about 6 inches of soil put upon them. The spaces between the rows may be cultivated during the first year, and some quick crop grown there. The working of this crop will gradually fill up the furrows about the stems of the young asparagus, which, during the first year, is quite small and insignificant in appearance. By fall, the furrows will be entirely filled and the surface of the patch level. The asparagus slug, the larva of the well-known beetle, may be kept down by occasionally dusting with slacked lime containing Paris green. The following year the asparagus will show up to some advantage, but should not be cut. The third year (second after planting) will yield some marketable shoots; but cutting should not continue more than two or three weeks. The fourth year the bed may be said to be in full bearing.

Treatment – The spring treatment of an asparagus bed in profit begins with a light plowing parallel with the rows, great care being observed to use a wheel on the plow so that not more than a few inches of soil may be turned, lest the crowns be cut and injured. The bed then lies until the cutting season is well advanced, when the plow may be again used.

The first plowing was merely to break the surface of the ground and turn under the winter coat of manure, leaving the land level. The second plowing (if given) is to be toward the rows, for the purpose of throwing them further under the surface, so as to get larger shoots as warm weather advances.

Another plowing, very shallow, followed by harrow or cultivator, should be given at the end of the cutting season, in June, to destroy all weeds and to encourage summer growth of the asparagus.

The patch should be kept clear of weeds during the summer, and growth encouraged by cultivation. In the late autumn the tops are mowed off and burned, as there seems to be no economic way of composting them, for, if moved to the compost heap or barnyard, they will seed the whole farm with asparagus. There should be a good coat of manure for winter protection, to be turned under in early spring, as already mentioned.

Marketing – The preparation of the crop for market involves some time and trouble. The shoots are cut every day. Some growers do the work early in the morning, and carry the bunches to market the same day. Others cut and bunch one day, put in water over night and carry to market the following day. Circumstances must decide which is best.

If asparagus is to be shipped long distances, it must either be packed in open crates (like strawberry crates), or else thoroughly chilled by ice before starting. Otherwise, it will heat and spoil. The usual asparagus bunch is just about the size of a dry-measure quart in diameter, and from 6 to 9 inches in length.

Fig. 88. Acme Asparagus Buncher, with Knife Guard.

In fact, a quart cup or tin fruit can is frequently used in shaping the bunch. Home-made wooden bunchers are also in common use. The Acme asparagus buncher is the best, coming in two sizes. The asparagus is tied in two places with raphia or soft string, and thus makes a neat and attractive package. The butts are cut off square with a knife after the bunch is finished, and in this shape asparagus will remain fresh for a long time, if kept standing in shallow water.

In tying up the bunches the shoots are separated into two or three sizes. The small shoots are quite as good for food as the larger ones, but the latter always bring more money in market, which warrants the additional trouble involved.

Salt – Salt is frequently used on asparagus beds, but not always. Salt is sometimes an indirect fertilizer, acting upon fertility already in the soil, and having a distinct tendency to attract and hold moisture, but it has no direct fertilizing influence. It is beneficial in helping check the growth of weeds.

Fertilizers – Kainite is an excellent thing for asparagus beds, as it contains a considerable percentage of sulfate of potash, which is a direct fertilizer. It also contains a fourth of its bulk of salt. Ground bone, which contains nitrogen (ammonia) and phosphoric acid, is also a good thing to use on asparagus. It is very lasting in its action, and with the kainite makes a complete manure, especially in connection with the winter coat of stable manure.

Asparagus is a gross feeder, and will take almost any amount of fertilizer. Market gardeners, who raise the most and best asparagus, depend mainly on enormous quantities of first-class stable manure; and this is probably the best fertilizer of all for this succulent and valuable vegetable.

Tools – No special tools are demanded in asparagus culture, though such tools are on the market. Any long knife will do for cutting the shoots, although a very good knife is especially made of solid steel, and can be bought for 25 cents. The cut should be made just below the surface of the ground, care being taken not to injure other shoots just coming up. Crooked shoots often make their appearance, resulting from injury done by the cutting knife. Other causes, such as insects, hard soil, etc., produce crooked or deformed shoots. Asparagus bunchers, made of wood and metal, mentioned in the seed catalogues, are sometimes used, the Acme, heretofore referred to, being the best and cheapest.

Fig. 89. Solid Steel Asparagus Knife.

Any light plow with a wheel will answer for the asparagus bed. A light-weight harrow is also desirable. Where asparagus trenches are laid out and dug by hand of course a garden line must be used, in order to have them straight and uniform. The practice of digging deep trenches for asparagus still prevails to some extent in private gardens, but the farm gardener must use cheaper methods.

Roots per Acre – With rows 5 feet apart and plants

2 feet apart in the rows, it is evident that each plant represents just 10 square feet of space. Hence, about 5,000 asparagus plants would be required for an acre of land set at these distances; they are, however, often set closer than this, sometimes at the rate of 7,000 roots and over per acre. An asparagus bed containing 100 roots will supply an ordinary family.

Fig.90. Improved Round Green Pod Extra Early Valentine Bean.

BEANS

Bean-growing in a small way is fully warranted in every garden, but on a large scale it is a different question, being somewhat a matter of soil and location.

Food Value – The bean is one of the most excellent of human foods. Its botanical kinship is close to the pea, and both are legumes. The leguminous plants, it will be remembered, have the rare ability of obtaining nitrogen through the tubercles on their roots, taking this expensive element partly from the air, and not greatly impoverishing the soil by their growth.

Something of the food value of the bean may be learned by comparing its chemical analysis with that of beef. In 100 pounds of beans there are 23 pounds of protein (nitrogenous matter), while in 100 pounds of beef there are but about 15 to 20 pounds of protein. Peas are almost as rich as beans in protein, which is the tissue-building element of all foods, and, hence, it is easy to realize the fact that both beans and peas are foods of the highest economic value. They are standard foods of the world, entering into the diet of soldiers, laborers and persons needing physical strength.

It is generally safe to grow beans for the retail market of any town or center of population, but to compete in the open wholesale market demands experience and good equipment on the part of the grower to insure profits.

Varieties and Types – The varieties of beans are well nigh endless. Some demand poles, while some are dwarf, being called bush beans. The influence of man has developed the bean into a vast number of different forms, which frequently show a disposition to revert or go back to some ancestral type, no matter how carefully the seeds may be kept.

The pole beans, in general terms, yield larger crops and bear through a longer season than the bush beans. The green-podded beans, as a rule, are more prolific and more hardy than the yellow-podded or wax beans. The climbers demand a whole season, and bear until frost. The bush beans are mostly employed where two or more crops are demanded per year from the ground.

The so-called cut-short or snap-short beans are those in which the whole pod, in its green state, is used for food. They are of both types, climbing and bush. The Lima forms include a number of distinct beans, differing greatly in size and shape and also in habit of growth.

Bush Beans (green pod) – We recommend Improved Round Pod Extra Early Valentine; also, New Giant Stringless Valentine.

Bush Beans (yellow pod) – Wardwell's Kidney Wax and Davis' White Wax are largely grown in the South for shipment North. Valentine Wax is recommended for the North.

White Field or Soup Beans – We recommend Day's Leafless Medium and New Snowflake Field.

Pole Lima Beans – We especially recommend Ford's Mammoth Podded Lima and Siebert's Early Lima.

Pole Snap Beans – Golden Andalusia Wax is one of the best yellow-pod pole beans, and Lazy Wife's one of the best green-pod sorts.

Dwarf Lima – Dreer's, Burpee's and Henderson's represent three distinct types.

Location – In choosing a spot for bean culture the

farm gardener should select good mellow soil that has been manured the previous year. Fresh manure produces an excessive growth of vine at the expense of pods.

Making Ready – Much stable manure, which is rich in nitrogen, should be avoided. In good ordinary soil, with some rotted manure from the previous crop, the bean plant will do well. It will obtain nitrogen, in great part, from the air, as already explained. Old manure is very favorable as a starter, as it contains the minute organisms mentioned in the preceding pages. Complete fertilizers or those containing phosphoric acid and potash must be supplied. Only nitrogen is derived from the air.

Soil Inoculation – The soil of a new bean patch is sometimes inoculated with soil from an old patch, to get quick action of the bacteria (little organisms), which form the lumps or tubercles on the roots. The scattering of a little soil over the surface is all that is required.

Care should be taken to avoid the transfer of soil for this purpose from a patch affected with rust or blight, as diseases are carried from place to place with only too much ease.

When to Plant – Beans may safely be planted when the apple is in bloom, in May; not so early as peas, as beans are less hardy. The ground should be dry and warm. Beans of all kinds demand shallow planting, as the seeds must be lifted from the ground in the earliest process of growth. The seed swells, bursts, sends a shoot (radicle) downward, and the two parts of the seed, called the seed-leaves, are pushed up into the daylight. Small round beans can take care of themselves, as they turn easily in the soil, but lima beans often perish in the effort to get above ground. This is why lima beans should always be planted eye down, and less than an inch deep. A half inch is deep enough for most beans. If lima beans are wanted extra early, they should be started on small squares of inverted sod, under glass.

The earliest bush beans yield marketable pods within forty to fifty days from planting; the pole beans in from seventy to ninety days from planting. There should be successional plantings made of the bush beans from the first date to within fifty days of frost. The different types of beans are fully and carefully described in the seed catalogues.

Fig. 91. Plant of the New Valentine Wax Bean.
The Earliest Wax or Yellow Podded Snap Short.

Distances – Poles for beans should be set about 4 feet apart each way; or, in single rows, about 3 feet apart. Not more than three or four plants should be allowed to a hill. Wires stretched between posts, with strings down to the ground, are sometimes used. The bush beans are planted in rows 3 feet apart for horse culture, or half that distance where a hoe or hand cultivator is to be used. The plants in the rows should stand 3 or 4 inches apart for best yield.

On a Large Scale – In large field operations, where the dried bean is the object in view, a clover sod is a favorite location. The ground is enriched by 400 or 500 pounds of complete fertilizer, and the beans are planted with a grain drill, using every fourth tube. The culture is by horse-power, and the vines are pulled by hand or by means of a bean-harvester, and threshed with a flail or grain thresher. These white grocery beans are sold everywhere in large quantities.

Cultivation – All bean cultivation should be shallow. Nothing is gained by cutting the feeding roots. The climbing sorts twine "against the sun;" that is, in a contrary direction to the apparent motion of the sun. The shoots must be tied up several times, to keep them on their own poles.

Diseases – The worst bean enemies are rust and blight. In new soil, with good weather, these troubles seldom appear. During prolonged wet weather there seems to be no help for them. Spraying with Bordeaux mixture is a preventive. The spraying should be done in advance of blossoming. The seed is sometimes soaked in Bordeaux mixture for an hour where rust is anticipated. Prevention is better than cure, and new soil and fresh seed are the best precautions. Diseased vines should be burned.

Insects – The weevil that attacks the bean is closely allied to the pea weevil. Some practical people say there is no remedy known; others recommend heating the beans to 145° for an hour; others use bisulfide of carbon in a closed vessel, along with the beans.

Profits – By far the largest cash receipts per acre are obtained by selling beans in their fresh state; preferably in the pods. The production of bush beans (pods) may run up to 75 or 80 bushels per acre, or even more. Lima beans are more profitably sold in the pods than shelled, though some markets demand the shelled article. The consumer gets a fresher and better article in the pods, and the producer is saved much trouble, and this method should be encouraged. Beans should be cooled, if possible, before shipment in bulk to distant markets, thus avoiding danger from heating, moulding and spotting.

BEETS

Beets are produced in enormous quantities by market gardeners near all large cities, both under glass and in the open ground. They also have a place in the farm garden, as they are of easy culture.

Excellence in the table beet depends partly on variety, but mainly on the quickness of growth. Sweetness and succulence result from high culture in rich, mellow soil.

Mangels and sugar beets, of course, have a place on every farm, for stock-feeding purposes, and table beets may also be grown, if good soil is available, for market purposes.

Fig. 92. Crosby's Improved Egyptian,
the Earliest Blood Turnip Beet.

The winter-keeping sorts are frequently in demand, and may be included among the farmer's cash crops.

No amount of stable manure is excessive in beet-growing. Partially rotted manure is best. For horse culture the rows should be 3 feet apart. Five to six pounds of seed will plant an acre.

Planting – Planting may be done as soon as the ground can be worked in the spring, as the beet is hardy, and not injured by a little frost; and successional plantings may be made until June. The June sowing will produce autumn beets, which can be stored for winter use or sale.

It is well to soak the seed in tepid water before planting; it should be scattered thinly in the rows and lightly covered. In dry weather the soil must be pressed firmly on the seed, to insure sufficient moisture for germination. The plants in the rows should be thinned out to 3 or 4 inches.

It is very important to remember that the more space each plant has about it the sooner will it reach a marketable size. Beet plants standing 5 inches apart in the row will be ready long before plants standing only 2 inches apart.

Fig.93. Ford's Perfected Half-long Beet.
The Best Winter Keeper.

Beets vary in shape very considerably. Some are round and some are long, with intermediate grades. The turnip-shaped beets are the earliest, while the half-longs and longs are the heaviest. For market purposes, if sold in bunches, the round ones are the most profitable.

The color of the foliage varies greatly; but the color of the leaf is not always typical of the root. Some of the blood beets have green leaves. There are many shades and colors of the roots, from deepest blood red to white, with zones of pink. The beet is an excellent and highly esteemed article of food, and is always in demand.

Varieties – For earliest, we especially recommend Crosby's Improved Egyptian and Surprise; for winter, Ford's Perfected Half-Long.

Marketing and Storing – A bunch contains five, six or seven beets, with tops tied together and superfluous leaves cut off. The bunching and topping may be done in the field, and the bunches afterward washed in a tub of water, by means of a scrubbing brush. It always pays to send roots to market in a clean and attractive condition.

Winter storage in cellars, under sand, is often practiced; or the beets may be kept in pits in the open ground, covered with straw and earth.

Enemies – The beet is remarkably free from enemies of any kind. The root sometimes cracks, and is occasionally attacked by insects, but the farmer or gardener has little to fear if soil be good and weather be favorable. All farmers attending market should have a few beets to help make up the weekly load for the wagon.

Fig. 94. Early Jersey Wakefield Cabbage.

CABBAGE

Early cabbage is not a farm gardener's crop at the North, though in the Southern States the early varieties can be grown by farmers for shipment to the great Northern markets. The Northern farmer, unless provided with glass, usually finds more profit in the later and larger sorts, which mature in autumn.

Soil – Rich, loamy soil, containing much clay, is best for this vegetable, which is a rank feeder. Large amounts of manure are demanded.

The manure is best applied in a partially rotted form, as fresh manure of any kind (especially hog manure) is liable to produce the disease or deformity known as club-root, the spores of the disease apparently being in the fresh manure; though land too long cropped with cabbage is likely to produce the same disease without the application of fresh manure of any kind.

Seed – It is of especial importance that good seed be planted, as cabbage varies so much and shows such a disposition to go back to undesirable types that great dissatisfaction and loss attend all experiments with poorly-selected seed. The choice of seed not infrequently determines the size and success of the crop. Expert cabbage growers are well aware of this fact.

Planting – The manure should be broadcasted, and an ample amount used, with a high-grade fertilizer in the row. The young plants, previously started in a seed-bed, should (at the North) be set out in July. The seed for late cabbage is planted in May. A quarter pound of seed will give enough plants for an acre.

The rows should be 4 feet apart, and the plants 2½ feet apart in the rows. These distances favor good cultivation and quick growth. In some parts of New England the seed is sown in the open field, in rows where the cabbage is to grow, but the practice of transplanting from seedbeds is found most satisfactory.

The rainfall here usually insures a fair crop of cabbage, but any crop that requires transplanting in midsummer is liable to delay or injury in case of protracted dry weather. Hence, irrigation is desirable. At the distances just recommended for planting (4 × 2½ feet) there would be 4,356 plants to the acre. In the case of such varieties as Johnson & Stokes' Earliest and Jersey Wakefield cabbage, where the number of plants per acre would be perhaps 10,000, the Michigan Experiment Station obtained 5,000 more marketable heads per acre under irrigation than where water was not used upon the growing crop. (This fact is mentioned in a book on irrigation just issued by the publishers of this book).

Varieties – The earliest varieties of cabbage have small, conical heads; the midsummer sorts mostly round heads; and the late or drumhead sorts have large, flat heads. There are cabbages which never head; as, for instance, the collards of the South; and there are varieties of crinkled-leaf cabbages, known as the Savoy types. The kales are closely related to the cabbages. Both cabbages and kales have purple-colored forms, sometimes called red forms.

Cultivation – Thorough horse cultivation between the rows should be supplemented by a hand-hoe between the plants in the rows. The cultivation must be good and continuous until the heads begin to form.

Diseases and Insects Enemies – Club root has been mentioned. It is a fungous trouble. The best remedy is new ground. The black flea on very young plants can be conquered with air-slacked lime or wood ashes. The cutworm is troublesome only in spring; not with late cabbage. The root maggot is sometimes very destructive, both with cabbage and cauliflower. New ground is the most satisfactory remedy. Green aphides or lice often follow lack of strength in the cabbage. Pyrethrum powder, air-slacked lime, kerosene emulsion, etc., are used as remedies for lice. The pyrethrum may be used dry or in water, at the rate of a tablespoonful to two gallons. The green cabbage worm, one of the worst of all enemies, can be pretty effectually checked by means of air-slaked lime dusted over the leaves. Other caterpillars yield to the same treatment.

Bursting – Bursting of cabbage heads is caused by a second growth, the result perhaps of continued wet weather, or warm weather following cold weather. The best remedy is to cut part of the feeding roots, either by close cultivation or with a hoe.

Selling – Cabbage prices vary between extremes that are far separated. Early cabbage usually sells at a good profit. Summer and autumn prices may be low. Winter and spring prices are almost always fair, and occasionally extra. Pennsylvania farmers sometimes ship to wholesalers in the cities and sometimes sell at public sale in the open field, in the autumn, just as the crop stands. The latter plan is an excellent one, where auction prices warrant it. It avoids the cost and risk of storage, as each buyer removes and stores his purchase.

Storage – Cabbage will bear much freezing without injury. The art of winter storage is to put it where it will have the fewest changes of temperature, and where it will be cool and damp without being wet.

Fig. 95. Cutting J & S Earliest Cabbage for Market.

The most common practice is to cover two or three rows of inverted heads, with roots attached, with from 6 to 12 inches of soil, making provision for good drainage by ditches on both sides of the wedge-shaped heap.

This system may be modified so as to include six or more rows of inverted cabbage, the heap being flat instead of wedge-shaped on top. It does not turn water so well, but in practice is usually satisfactory. A good plan is to use about 6 inches of soil, and to add straw or litter as the cold increases.

Under a steady low temperature it is no trouble to keep cabbage through the winter, but it is hard to provide against the many changes of our variable climate.

Fig. 96. Matchless Late Flat Dutch Cabbage.

Where heads are to be carried over for seed, or where it is intended to head up soft cabbages during the winter (a feasible thing) the roots are set downward instead of upward. If care be taken to remove the roots without much injury, they may be set in furrows or trenches, and the earth heaped over the cabbages just as in the several ways above mentioned, and they will make decided growth during their life under ground. In fact, a cabbage with any sort of immature head in November will, under proper management, be in good marketable condition in March or April.

Solid freezing in the trenches is not necessarily destructive, but if the temperature falls much below 15° (at the point occupied by the heads), there is danger that they will perish. They may be in good edible condition after such severe freezing, but the chances are that they will fail to grow if set out for seed. The cabbage decays with a strong, offensive smell when its tissues finally break down after repeated changes of temperature and moisture. A uniform temperature is favored by the use of earth in storage, and though storage in buildings and cellars is quite feasible, there is nothing better or cheaper than the soil of the open field.

If the crop is not all to be marketed at one time, it is well to make a number of separate trenches, so that each can be wholly cleared of its contents at a single opening. These trenches and ridges must be made upon dry ground, where there is no standing water.

For Stock – Cabbages make good food for cows, but should be fed after milking; and frozen cabbages should never be fed in any considerable quantity, as they are liable to cause hoven or bloat.

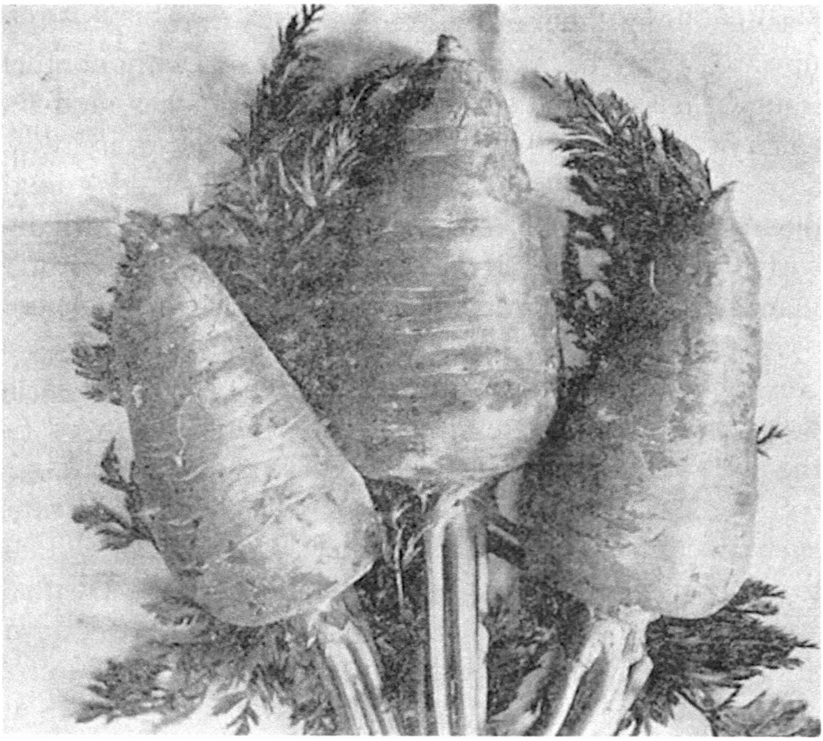

Fig. 97. Average Specimens of Rubicon Half-Long Carrots.

CARROTS

A sandy soil or light loam is best for carrots, but they will grow anywhere under good culture. Enormous quantities are grown by the market gardeners, both under glass and in the open ground, for use in soups and for seasoning purposes. The short or half-long varieties are demanded by this trade.

Farm gardeners will do best with half-long and long

kinds, unless a special demand calls for the smaller carrots. The large half-long and long ones are suited to both culinary and stock-feeding purposes.

It requires from three to four pounds of seed to the acre, depending on the distance between the rows. The plants should be from 3 to 5 inches apart in the rows, and the rows as near together as is feasible for horse work. Clean culture is demanded. The seed must be planted shallow, and may go into the ground as early as it can be worked in the spring, and from that time until the middle of June. The only danger about late planting is the possibility of dry weather.

The carrot is quite free from insect or other enemies, as a rule, and its culture is not difficult. It demands thinning and hoeing after the plants are well above ground, but no extra attention of any kind.

The winter storage is the same as for beets or turnips, either to be put away in earth-covered heaps or preserved in a cool, non-freezing root cellar.

The so-called Belgian carrots (both yellow and white) are used only as stock food; though the other sorts, such as Rubicon, Danvers and Long Orange, if in excess of market demands, are equally good for stock. Cows and horses are fond of them, and they are most wholesome. The farm gardener should raise them, however, for their cash value in the produce markets. The carrot is in high favor with good cooks everywhere.

The carrot does not demand excessively rich ground; in fact, too much manure tends to stimulate the growth of the top at the expense of the root, and fresh manure makes the root rough.

SWEET CORN

There is no money crop more available to the farm gardener than sweet corn. It will grow anywhere, and the young ears are always in demand. Any sod land plowed shallow will yield a crop of sweet corn. It is easy in this latitude to have an unbroken succession of marketable ears from July 1st to October 1st, or even somewhat earlier and later.

Shallow plowing and the use of a little fertilizer or compost in the hills will put the ground in order. A complete fertilizer is best. A compost containing hen manure is excellent.

Planting – Eight or ten quarts of seed are required to plant an acre of corn in hills, allowing for replanting of what is injured by grubs or other causes. The larger varieties should be planted 4 feet by 3; the rows 4 feet apart and the hills 3 feet apart, with not more than three stalks in a hill. The smaller varieties may be grown much closer – 3 feet by 2. Any method may be used in laying out a corn field that will give each stalk (of the large kinds) the equivalent of 4 square feet of ground space. The dwarf sweet corns demand about half that space.

Varieties – The sweet corns require from sixty to eighty days to produce ears fit for boiling. The earliest varieties are small, and are lacking in sweetness as compared to the best intermediate types. Still, the early prices are so much better than midsummer prices, that the early varieties will always be grown for market. Indeed, the best profits of the business are from the extra early and extra late sales.

Sweet corn should not be grown by shippers who are

distant more than twenty-four hours from market, as the ears lose quality and flavor soon after being pulled from the stalks. Forty-eight hours from market is an extreme distance, but is feasible if the ears can be chilled in a cold storage house previous to shipment; otherwise, they will heat and spoil. Even when designed for a near-by market a load of sweet corn ears may heat and spoil during a single night. It is best to scatter them upon the grass, if pulled during the afternoon for shipment the following morning.

The most profit to the grower will be found in ears, which are not too large, as corn is often sold by the dozen, the large sorts being too weighty.

The early kinds, though small, can be planted closely, and a large number of ears secured; and they are out of the way so soon that the ground can be used for celery or other late crop. Celery can be set out between the rows of corn, and thus be shaded to some extent during the critical period following transplanting.

The Evergreens, Early and Late, and the shoe-peg types, such as Country Gentleman and Zig Zag Evergreen, are among the sweetest of all. The grains are of irregular shape and arrangement, and the appearance of the ears is not altogether prepossessing. When once known, however, they are in demand by consumers.

The red-cob corns should be cooked by dropping into boiling water. If cooked slowly, the red color of the cob affects the appearance of the grains.

For first early, we recommend Burlington Hybrid and Mammoth White Cory. The former closely resembles a true sugar corn in appearance. For second early, Early Champion and New Early Evergreen; for late, original

Stowell's Evergreen, Country Gentleman, Zig Zag Evergreen.

Cultivation, Enemies, etc. – Shallow culture, frequently repeated, is demanded by sweet corn. The growth at first is timid and slow; afterward, if well cultivated, the stalks grow with great rapidity and vigor.

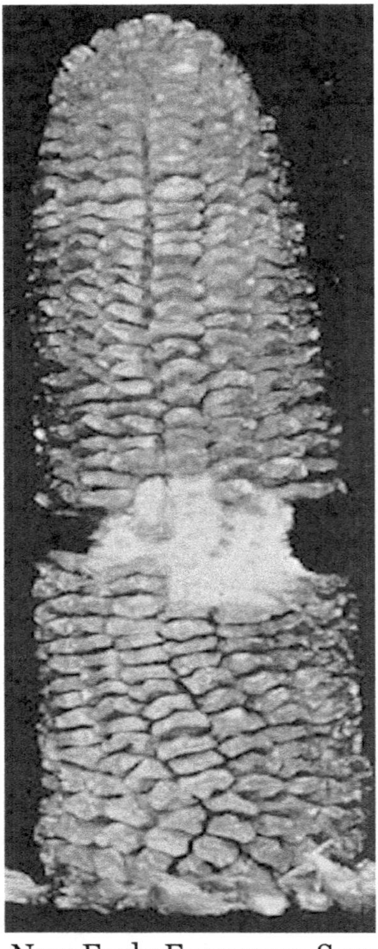

Fig. 98. New Early Evergreen Sweet Corn.

To make the most of the stalks, they should be cut as soon as possible after the last ears have gone to market and fed to stock. Sweet corn stalks when dry make excellent fodder.

The main enemies of corn are the cut worm, which is only troublesome in spring; a fungus which attacks the ears and which is always most prevalent on the small, early sorts; and a worm which cuts and injures the grain while the corn is in milk. Crows sometimes pull up the seeds, but can be disposed of by scattering a little yellow corn on the surface of the ground around the edges of the field. As the crow destroys many cut worms, it is better to feed him with corn than to shoot him.

The prevalence of fungus-troubled or smutty corn is probably a symptom of weakness, the result of planting too early, or of too much wet weather. All plants that are weak are liable to fungus attacks, and it is the early corn that suffers most. This corn is often planted before the ground is sufficiently warm, and there is a consequent weakness of growth. Indian corn, at Philadelphia, should not be planted before May 10th, and yet it is not uncommon to see gardeners planting sweet corn two weeks earlier. They say they are "going to risk it." The result may be a good crop of corn, or it may be a crop of worms and fungus. Of course, the high price of the first corn in market is the excuse for the unseasonable date of planting. But it is not quite fair to blame the seed or the variety of corn for what is partly the result of the gardener's impatience. All traces of smut on corn stalks should be burned, and not allowed to be fed to cattle.

The Corn Worm – Far more destructive and

disastrous than smut is the corn worm (Heliothis armiger). This is the cotton worm of the South, there called boll worm. It is also sometimes called the tomato worm. It is the larva of a day-flying moth.

The difficulty in dealing with it is that when in the corn ear it is out of the reach of poisonous applications of any kind. Its depredations are extensive, especially in early corn. It prefers corn to all other foods, and cotton planters protect their crops by planting early corn in the cotton fields and then destroying the corn and the worms within the ears.

The best remedy at the North is to feed all wormy ears to pigs; and to plow the corn land in autumn, when the insects are in the pupa or chrysalis state. If turned up by the plow, it is believed that they mostly perish. The worms are said to be cannibals, eating each other to a great extent.

This worm is, perhaps, the greatest enemy with which the grower of sweet corn has to contend. The plan of feeding wormy ears to pigs offers the double advantage of destroying the enclosed pests, while at the same time fattening the pigs.

Successional Planting – The skillful farmer will arrange successional plantings of corn, beginning (at Philadelphia)

May 10th and ending about July 10th. The first and last plantings should be of the early sorts; the intermediate plantings of the full-sized varieties.

Suckering – Time is often spent in pulling the suckers from the stalks of sweet corn. Such time is wasted. If the suckers are let alone they will not reduce the number or quality of the marketable ears.

HORSERADISH

Farmers who have soil that is both rich and deep can find profit in growing horseradish on a large scale, in connection with early peas, beans or sweet corn. The sets are planted in May, in the rows between crops, and after the crops are removed the horseradish makes its main growth. It is perfectly hardy, and comes on rapidly during the late summer and autumn months. Where the ground is not strong enough to produce large roots the first year, the business will not prove very remunerative.

The Sets – Horseradish sets are made by cutting small roots (¼ to ½ inch in thickness) into pieces 6 or 8 inches long. The upper end is cut square off; the lower end with a slope. This is to get them right end up at planting time. The small roots are available in quantities in the autumn, when the large roots are trimmed for market. The sets are kept in sand during the winter, or buried in the open ground, in a carefully-marked spot, where they can be easily found in the spring.

If planted 2 feet apart in rows 3 feet apart, each plant will represent 6 square feet of space, and, hence, about 7,300 sets will be needed for an acre. The method of planting is to strike out rows, and with a long dibber or crowbar make holes 8 or 10 inches deep. A set is dropped into each hole and the earth pressed about it.

Shoots will soon appear above the surface, and when the early crop has been removed from the land, the horseradish should be well cultivated once or twice. Little further attention is needed.

The roots should be lifted the same year, in December, and stored in an earth-covered heap or pit, or else in sand in a root cellar. The small lateral roots should be saved for the next year's sets. There is a good demand for horseradish, both wholesale and retail; but prices should be ascertained before going into the business in a large way.

Good roots, after trimming and washing, should weigh half a pound or more each.

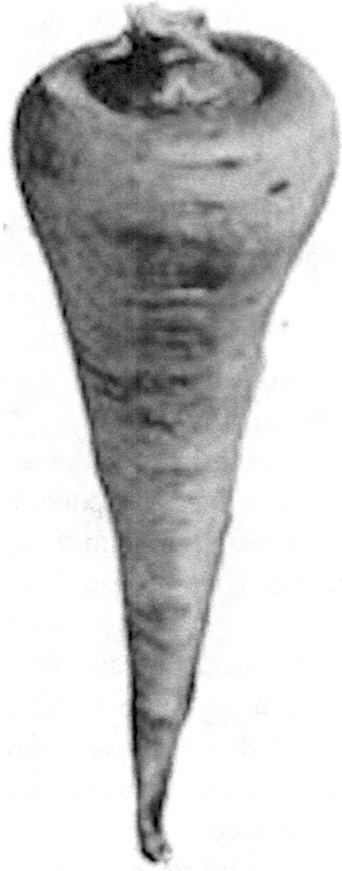

Fig. 99. Ideal Hollow Crown Parsnip.

PARSNIP

The cultural requirements of the parsnip are quite similar to those of the carrot. Any soil that is deep mellow and moderately rich may be used for parsnips.

Fresh manure is to be avoided, as it makes the roots rough.

The seed should be planted in early spring, while the ground is moist, as it germinates very slowly. It should be covered to a depth of half an inch, and the soil pressed down firmly. The plants must be thinned out to stand 3 or 4 inches apart.

The parsnip is a vegetable of a perfectly hardy character. It may remain in the ground, just where it grows, all winter. The flavor is said to be improved by hard freezing, and no amount of freezing will hurt it.

It has a high value as human food, and is demanded in large quantities in some markets. It also has a high value as a stock food, especially for cows. It should be fed after milking, in quantities not sufficient to taint the milk. The price is variable, but about the same as the carrot.

We recommend Ideal Hollow Crown.

THE POTATO

The cultivation of the potato is so well understood by every American farmer and gardener that it seems unnecessary to discuss the details of cutting the tubers, planting, cultivating, harvesting, etc. The weak points of potato culture are most commonly the fertilizing and the treatment of diseases. These will be briefly discussed. As to lack of moisture, to be remedied by artificial watering, the reader is referred to our new book, entitled, "Irrigation by

Cheap Modern Methods," in which a case is mentioned where water alone made a difference of 129 bushels per acre in the crop.

Potatoes – Best for the South, Bliss Triumph, Pride of the South, Crown Jewel, Early Thoroughbred. General crop in the North – Houlton Early Rose, Table King, Late Puritan, Rural New-Yorker No. 2.

Fig. 100. An Average Tuber of Table King, One of the Best All Around Potatoes.

Fertilizing – A ton of potatoes (33-1/3 bushels) contains 4·2 pounds of nitrogen (equal to 5·1 pounds of ammonia), 1·5 pounds of phosphoric acid and 10 pounds of potash. This shows that nitrogen and potash are the elements mainly abstracted from the soil by a crop of potatoes.

An analysis is not an infallible index of what must be applied to any soil, for that soil may be naturally rich in some one fertilizing element and deficient in the others. Only experiment will determine what is best. But a knowledge of the analysis of the crop is necessary to intelligent experimentation.

Nitrogen and potash will evidently be demanded in most cases, yet the Ohio Station recently reports that "phosphoric acid has been the controlling factor in the increase of the potato yields" in the trials made there. This shows how greatly soils vary in their requirements.

Barnyard manure would answer all purposes and would be an ideal potato fertilizer, except for the fact that it so often carries with it the spores of such diseases as blight, scab and rot. Still, barnyard manure in a partly rotted condition is very widely used by potato growers.

Clover sod is an excellent source of nitrogen, as heretofore explained. The clover is, perhaps, the best of the leguminous crops for green manuring purposes. Many successful potato farmers depend largely upon clover, supplementing it with a small amount of high-grade complete fertilizer in the rows.

Where phosphoric acid is necessary, it can be had in the form of ground bone or acidulated rock, and potash can be had in the form of sulfate or as kainite. Where the scab is prevalent, it may prove better to use kainite, on account of the salt that it contains, as will be presently explained.

Planting – It requires from seven to ten bushels of

tubers to plant an acre. Some growers use as much as fifteen bushels. The date of planting, depth, distance between rows, etc., are details for individual determination. Flat culture is better than ridge culture, so far as conservation of moisture is concerned.

Fig. 101. Harvesting Seed Potatoes
near Houlton, Maine.

It is important that good Northern-grown seed be planted; tubers which have not lost their strength by excessive sprouting. Storage in a cool, dark, dry place is best for potatoes. Whether planted early or late, or at successional dates, must be determined by the market requirements of the grower.

Varieties – The varieties of potatoes are many, and while it is wise to experiment in a small way on new kinds, it is best to depend for business purposes on standard sorts that have been fully tested.

Irrigation – After the farmer has exhausted his best efforts in the preparation and fertilization of the soil, and after good seed has been planted and the best possible culture given, there may come a season of prolonged drought that will defeat his purpose of securing a large crop. This result is not common, but neither is it rare; and where farmers are looking toward the high culture of certain special crops, it would be well for them to consider the matter of artificially watering their potato fields.

Diseases and Enemies – Not counting dry weather, which sometimes robs the farmer of two-thirds of his crop, there are four diseases which exert a disastrous influence on the potato, and which are liable to occur any season. Two of these diseases are of the leaf and stem and two of the tubers.

The two leaf troubles are respectively known as blight or downy mildew and the Macrosporium disease. The two tuber troubles are scab and rot.

Leaf Blights – No attempt will be made here to separately describe the two leaf diseases. Both destroy the foliage and check the further growth of both vine and tuber. The leaves turn brown or black, and the stem quickly wilts and falls. There can be no growth of tuber without vigorous health of vine. Spraying with Bordeaux mixture, in advance of the occurrence of any disease, is recommended.

Bordeaux mixture for this purpose is made by using six pounds of copper sulfate and four pounds of quick lime, dissolved in separate wooden vessels, and the lime water poured into the dissolved blue stone. This should be diluted with water sufficient to fill a forty-five gallon barrel. Paris green to the amount of from one-quarter to three-quarters of a pound to the barrel should be added, to destroy beetles and other insects.

The vines should be sprayed five or six times, beginning when they are 6 inches high, at intervals of ten days or two weeks. During rainy weather the spraying should be more frequent than during clear weather. The object is to prolong the life and vigor of the vines.

Scab and Rot – The evidence about scab and rot is still contradictory, but it is likely that these diseases will presently be under control. At the New Jersey Station, Professor Halsted completely conquered scab with an application of 300 pounds of flowers of sulfur per acre scattered in the rows, while the same treatment at the Ohio Station was less successful. At the latter station benefit was found in the use of salt, kainite, sulfate of potash, etc.

The various experiments and observations on potato scab and rot seem to indicate that scab flourishes best on a soil inclined to be alkaline, while rot is most prevalent on a soil inclined to be acid. The use of lime increases scab, while the use of kainite diminishes it.

The best practice, therefore, under present knowledge, would be to use clean seed on new ground, avoiding fresh stable manure. Clean seed can be had by treating tubers with corrosive sublimate. This substance is dissolved to the amount of 2¼ ounces, in two gallons of hot water, and (after standing a day) diluted with water so as to make fifteen gallons. In this solution the uncut seed potatoes should be soaked for an hour and a half. All unplanted seed potatoes should be destroyed, as the corrosive sublimate is highly poisonous.

The use of sulfur, as recommended by Professor Halsted, will prove entirely satisfactory in some soils. In others, the use of kainite or sulfate of potash or acid phosphate would no doubt be found preferable.

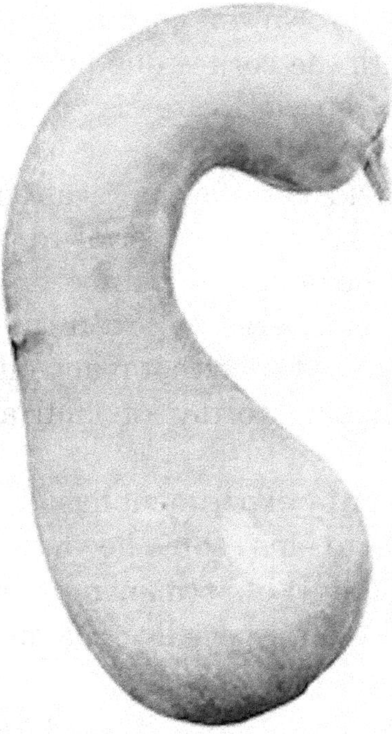

Fig. 102. Mammoth Golden Cashaw Pumpkin,
One of the Best for Market or Stock Feeding.

PUMPKINS AND SQUASHES

There is no clear dividing line between pumpkins and squashes, as they belong to the same botanic family – the Cucurbita. Some members of the group are clearly pumpkins, and others just as clearly squashes, but when an attempt is made to draw a sharp line between them, we get into difficulty. In general terms the pumpkin has a soft rind or shell and the squash a hard rind. But even this thumbnail test is not infallible.

These vegetables belong on the farm, on account of the large ground space occupied by the vines. Pumpkins may be economically grown in cornfields, the seeds being planted along with the corn – one pumpkin seed to every fourth hill. No special care is needed besides the cultivation given the corn.

Farmers should give far more attention to growing squashes, as they are much superior to pumpkins in food quality, both for the table and for stock.

There are numbers of excellent squashes now catalogued by the seedsmen that many farmers have never tried, but which are worthy of cultivation for market purposes.

When a farmer by experiment has found a high quality squash adapted to his soil, he has put himself in possession of a product of permanent market value.

Pumpkin – We especially recommend Mammoth Golden Cashaw and Winter Luxury.

Squash – Early varieties – Mammoth White Bush Scalloped, Giant Summer Crookneck. Winter-keeping varieties – Sweet Nut, Faxon, Chicago Warted, Hubbard, Early Prolific Orange Marrow.

TOMATOES

Tomatoes may justly be rated among the leading crops available to farm gardeners. There is always a brisk market for selected, carefully-washed tomatoes, packed in new baskets. Such produce is seldom offered in excessive quantities.

Any good corn land will produce good tomatoes. Excessive manuring is likely to stimulate the vines at the expense of the fruit. A little complete fertilizer or compost in the hills is desirable.

Tomato seed of early varieties should be started under glass. The seed is sown on heat and the plants once or twice transplanted, and put in the open ground as soon as danger of frost is over. Little is gained by setting out too early, when the ground is cool. The tomato is of tropical origin, and makes rapid growth only at a temperature of 65° or upward. Indeed, it is suspected that one of the worst diseases to which the tomato is liable, the blight, is encouraged, if not wholly caused by too early planting in the open ground.

Varieties and Planting – At 4 feet apart each way, it will require about 2,700 tomato plants for an acre of land. In open field culture the tomato is always allowed to lie upon the ground. In garden culture, it is often tied to stakes or supported on trellises. Three ounces of seed will raise sufficient plants for an acre.

There are many varieties of tomatoes, including the early and late market sorts, the yellow kinds, and the little pear-shaped and plum-shaped tomatoes, both red and yellow, used in pickling. The ideal market tomato is one of medium size and smooth shape. It must have firmness and depth, and the quality of ripening evenly all over. There should be neither greenness nor wrinkles around the calyx, nor should the fruit be of irregular shape. As to color, it is a matter of taste and neighborhood preference. Some markets demand red and some purple fruit.

Tomato – We recommend, for earliest, Atlantic Prize and Money Maker; for second early and main crop, Brinton's Best, New Fortune; for late, Brandywine, Cumberland Red, and Stone.

Successional Planting – If the first tomato plants be set in the open ground (at Philadelphia) May 15th to 20th, there should be at least one and preferably two later crops, because young, vigorous plants yield the most and best fruit. It is good practice to sow tomato seed in the open ground, say about middle of May, and again somewhat later. These out-of-door plants will come forward very rapidly, and will be ready to produce late summer and autumn crops.

Fig. 103. Atlantic Prize Tomatoes, as they Appear for Sale

on Fruit Stands, etc., during the Spring Months.

Cultivation – The tomato is of the easiest cultivation, and will grow even under neglect, but it so abundantly repays attention, that no farmer can afford to be careless about the matter. The nights of May are cool in the North, and the newly-set plant at first makes little growth. Cultivator and hand-hoe should both be kept in motion during this period, and in June also. In the latter month the tomato will make a sudden leap toward maturity, and will yield ripe fruit in July. The out-of-doors cropping season lasts for three full months. The tomato is now grown under glass almost everywhere, and is to be had in the market during all the months of the year.

Fig. 104. The Great B. B. (Brinton's Best) Tomato,

Best for Main Crop.

The out-of-doors season is profitably prolonged by picking all the mature or nearly mature fruit when the first frost comes, in October, and placing these unripe tomatoes on straw in a cold frame. Covered with straw and with the sash to keep out frost, the fruit ripens in a satisfactory manner for several weeks. Such a frame must be well ventilated or the tomatoes will rot rather than ripen.

Fig. 105. New Fortune, one of the Best Second Early Tomatoes.

Diseases and Enemies – Tomato diseases, fortunately, are not numerous. Blight sometimes sweeps off a whole field of early-set tomato plants, on farms where later plantings are quite healthy. This favors the theory that blight results from weakness caused by early planting in cold ground. It is a fungous disease, and may sometimes be prevented by the use of Bordeaux mixture. The same remedy is the best-known preventive of black rot.

Potato bugs may be either handpicked or poisoned with Paris green. The tobacco worm sometimes causes much damage to the tomato. All diseased or blighted tomato vines should be promptly burned, and the crop carried to new soil the following year.

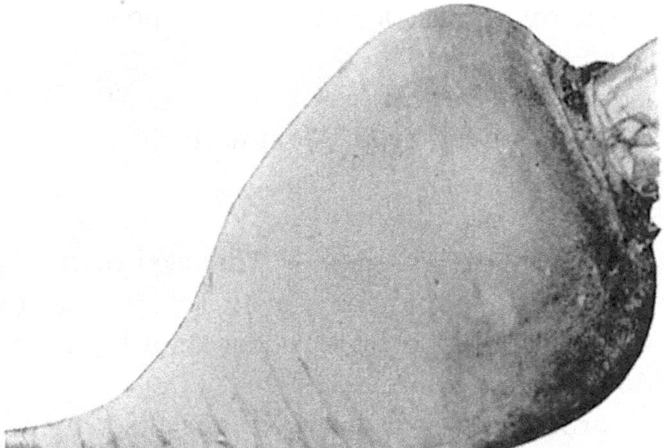

Fig. 106. Budlong or Breadstone Turnip.

TURNIPS AND RUTABAGAS

Turnips and rutabagas are closely related. The latter are turnips in fact, and are frequently called Swedes. The common method on many farms is to sow turnips broadcast, but it is a far better practice to sow both these and the rutabagas in drills, so that they can be kept clear of weeds and worked by horsepower. Not only are these advantages secured, but also the row system makes it possible to take out the superfluous plants, and secure roots of uniform size and shape. Turnips and rutabagas have high economic value as foods, both for humanity and for live stock.

Turnips – Turnips are grown for market purposes both in spring and in fall. In the spring the seed should be sown early, in mellow soil.

For the fall crop the seed may be sown either in July or August. The rows in garden or field may be as close as can be conveniently worked.

Turnip – For earliest, we recommend Purple Top and White Milan. For fall crop, Mammoth Purple Top Globe and Golden Ball.

Rutabagas or Swedes – The seed of rutabaga or Swedish turnip should be sown (in the latitude of Philadelphia) in July, a little earlier than the seed of the common turnip.

The ground should be well enriched with rotted manure, the rows 2½ to 3 feet apart, the seed covered to the depth of half an inch, and the plants afterward thinned out so as to stand 6 or 8 inches apart in the row. The crop is almost always large and satisfactory.

Rutabaga – We recommend Myer's Purple Top Beauty and Budlong.

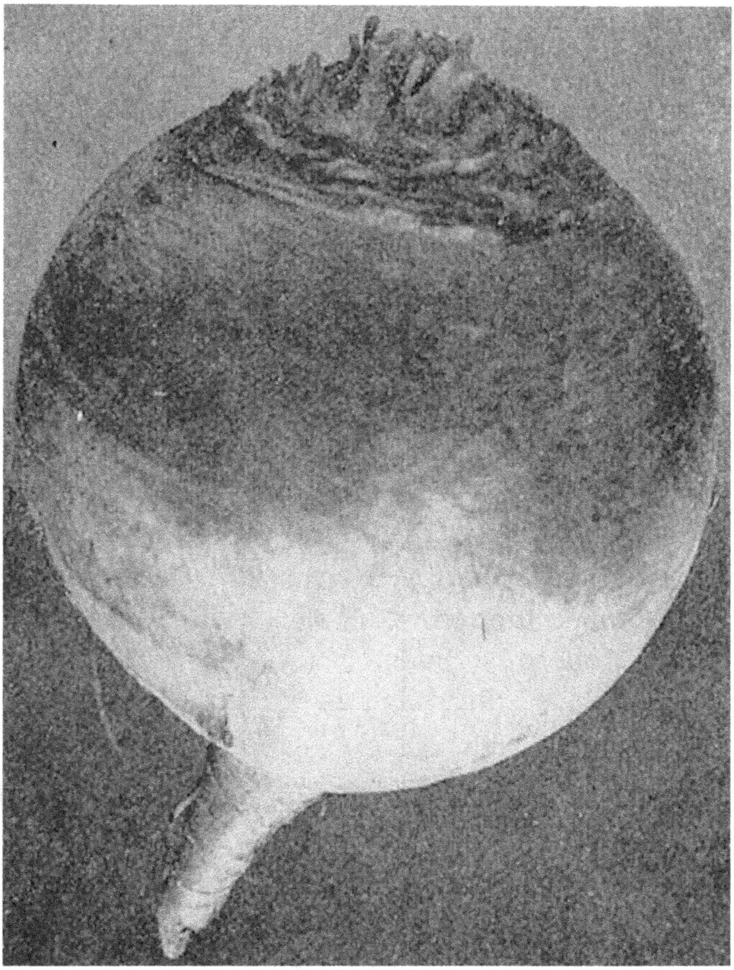

Fig.107. Myer's Purple Top Beauty Rutabaga.

Storage – Turnips of all kinds sell well in the winter markets, to say nothing of their high value as stock foods. They are easily preserved in root cellars, covered with sand, or in pits in dry soil, covered with straw and earth to prevent freezing.

Fig. 108. Distribution of Water through Homemade Hose Pipe. An Illustration from our New Book– "Irrigation by Cheap Modern Methods." No Gardener should miss Reading this Work.

CHAPTER XXVII

Vegetables Suited To Farm Culture In Some Locations

In this portion of the book are grouped a number of vegetables not adapted to every farm or location. The list includes celery, water cress, cucumbers, egg plants, kale, lettuce, melons, mushrooms, onions, peas, radishes, rhubarb, spinach, sweet potato, etc. Where favored locations for their production exist on farms they may be grown with profit, if markets are accessible.

CELERY

On very many farms there are meadows with deep, rich soils that are now lying under grass; or, worse, under tussocks and swamp weeds. Some locations are subject to disastrous overflow during freshets, but innumerable spots exist where such meadows could with safety be converted into celery gardens, capable of easy irrigation, either situated above the level of floods or susceptible of artificial protection by means of cheap embankments. Such situations are entirely too valuable to use for pasturage. They are the truck gardens of the future.

Perfect Celery – The object in celery-growing is to produce thick, robust, tender, solid, crisp, sweet leaf stalks, free from rust or insect attacks. The essentials are rich land and plenty of water, and skill is required in the two points of bleaching and storing. But there are no mysterious processes to be learned. The Kalamazoo growers have, it is true, a rare advantage in their deep muck soil, with a permanent water level only a few inches or feet below the surface, but their success depends on accuracy of working detail almost as much as on perfection of soil. It is not necessary to go to Michigan for good celery ground.

Fertilizers – The best-known fertilizer for celery is thoroughly rotted barnyard manure. Fresh manure is to be avoided for several reasons. It is less available for plant food, more likely to produce rust, and more liable to open the soil and render it too dry. Commercial fertilizers are not infrequently used, but there is a decided preference among many celery growers for the rotted stable product. Shallow plowing (5 inches) is practiced, as celery roots do not go deep.

Planting – It requires from 20,000 to 35,000 celery plants to the acre, according to their distances apart. In the intense culture at the great celery centers two crops (and even three crops) of celery are grown upon the land per year, by a system of planting between rows, but in the operations of farm gardeners not more than one crop per season is grown. This may follow an earlier market crop, such as peas, beans, onions or sweet corn, though where the farmer is hard pushed with other work, the celery may be grown without any other crop preceding it, but not upon newly-turned sod land, as the earth should be loose and mellow.

Seed for early celery must be started under glass, but the farmer will find his best celery market in the autumn. April will, therefore, be ample time for sowing the seed, which should be scattered thinly in rows in finely-raked mellow soil in the open ground, and covered lightly. The seed is very slow to germinate, and the bed should be copiously watered until the plants are well started. In small operations, it is well to transplant at least once. In large operations, the plants are thinned out in the original rows, and carried from thence direct to the field. The upper leaves and the tips of the roots are cut off, and the plants are set firmly in the soil by means of a dibber.

Fig. 109. J. & S. Golder Self-Blanching Celery Prepared for Market.

Dates and Distances – July is a proper time for setting out celery; preferably after a rain or during dull weather. The rows may be from 3 to 5 feet apart, depending on the purpose of the planter, and the plants 5 or 6 inches apart in the rows. If the celery is to be stored for blanching, 3-feet rows may be used. If it is to be blanched in the field, the distance between the rows should be greater, so that more loose soil will be available for hilling.

One ounce of celery seed will furnish 2,500 to 3,000 plants. A half pound is sufficient to furnish plants for an acre.

Even on good ground celery should not be set out later than August 15th (in the latitude of Philadelphia), and preferably earlier.

The system of level planting is practiced by large growers everywhere. Trenching is still followed in some private gardens, but is too expensive for commercial operations.

Varieties – The so-called dwarf and half-dwarf varieties have pushed the larger kinds out of the market almost entirely, though seed of the giant sorts can still be obtained. The dwarf kinds are large enough for all purposes, however, and are in best favor everywhere. They are about 18 inches high, as compared to twice that height in the old-fashioned giant types.

The favorites of late years for early celery are the self-blanching sorts, such as White Plume and Golden Self-Blanching, which are the result of the continued selection of individual plants or sports showing a tendency to blanch easily. For winter keeping, the Perle Le Grand,

Winter Queen and Perfection Heartwell are the best. These varieties are beautiful as well as highly palatable. There are also red or pink sorts, of high table merit and good keeping qualities.

Celery – We recommend Golden Self-Blanching and White Plume for early, Perle Le Grand for both early and late and Winter Queen for late. The latter is the very best keeper.

Cultivation – The proper culture of the celery has already been suggested in the allusion to its need for water and its shallow feeding habits. The surface soil should be highly enriched, the stirring of the soil very shallow, and the water supply copious, either by capillary attraction from below (as at Kalamazoo) or by rainfall or artificial irrigation.

Blanching – The first step in the process of blanching or bleaching is what is known as handling. This operation consists in grasping all the leaves of a celery plant in one hand, while with the other the soil is drawn together and packed so as to hold the stalks in an upright, compact position. This single operation will fit some of the early-planted sorts for market in the course of two weeks; though a second operation, called hilling, is usually considered desirable, even with the self-blanching sorts.

The Kalamazoo growers depend on muck for field blanching, though they also use boards. Muck is merely a dark soil, containing or consisting mainly of vegetable matter. They first "handle," as just described, and about five days later draw 6 inches more of the muck about the celery stalks. Again, three days later, they draw an additional 2 inches about the stalks, and in two weeks from the start the celery is ready for market.

These operations are frequently done by two men working together, one holding the stalks and the other drawing the soil to them. The first operation puts the stalks in an upright, compact position, so that little or no soil can get into the heart of the plant. The second draws about the plant all the soil that will conveniently remain there. The third merely supplements the second, as the hill has had time to become somewhat firm and has settled away a little from the upper leaves.

Boards are used for summer blanching, as they are less heating than soil. Ordinary lumber, free from knot holes, is employed. The boards rest on their edges, one board on each side of the row, the tops being drawn together until within 2½ inches of each other, and the lower edge of the board held in place either by stakes or by soil.

The work of handling or hilling must be done only when the celery is dry and unfrozen. In fact, celery must never be handled when wet (except when preparing it for market), or it will surely be rusted and spoiled.

The same practices of blanching celery as here mentioned in connection with the Kalamazoo operations are in vogue near Philadelphia and other Eastern cities, and are not new. The real reason that Kalamazoo is so celebrated is her possession of that wonderful black muck soil, underlaid with standing water. This has attracted the best celery growers of the country; men who have small places of from one to three acres, and who work out every detail to perfection, employing little labor outside of their own families and concentrating their efforts on the production of perfect celery crops. There are extensive celery growers at Kalamazoo, with tracts of thirty or more acres devoted exclusively to this vegetable, but the majority of the gardens there are small, and much hand-work is done.

Winter Storage – The art of the winter storage of celery, as practiced by large growers, is not hard to learn. Both at Kalamazoo and here in the Eastern States there are two methods in vogue. One is the use of especially built houses, and the other is the open-field plan.

The celery house or "coop" is a low frame structure, half under ground, generally 14 or 16 feet wide, and as long as may be desired. There is a door in one end and a window in the other. The sides, ends and roof are double and filled with sawdust.

There are wooden chimneys or ventilators at intervals of 12 feet along the peak of the roof, and sometimes there are glass windows in the roof, provided with wooden shutters. The celery stands upon the floor, which is of loose soil. There is a narrow walk lengthwise in the middle of the building, and boards extending from the central walk to the sidewalls separate the packed celery into narrow sections.

No earth is placed between the celery stalks as they stand. They are, in fact, rooted in the soil of the floor, and are thus able to make the slight growth demanded for complete blanching. The various doors, windows and ventilators make it possible to keep the air fresh and wholesome, and during cold weather a stove may afford heat to the storage room. Artificial heat is not commonly required.

Fig. 110. Winter Queen, the Best Late Winter Keeping Celery.

Another method, cheaper and quite as satisfactory, especially on farms or in market gardens, is to trench the celery in the open field. The situation of the trench must be a dry one, where there will be no standing water. The trench must be nearly or quite as deep as the height of the celery, with perpendicular sides, and a foot or less in width. The stalks are set upright in the trench, with all decayed or worthless leaves removed, as closely as they will stand, without soil between them. To keep them in that condition is purely a matter of care. If they are buried deeply and the weather proves warm they will rot. But if the covering be decreased in warm weather and increased in cold weather, the celery can be kept in perfect condition. In private gardens celery is often planted in double rows, a foot apart, and wintered where it grows by covering deeply with soil.

An excellent plan is to make an A-shaped trough of two boards to turn the rain, on top of which a greater or less amount of straw, leaves or litter may be piled, if needed.

Mice sometimes do considerable damage to stored celery, but are more easily controlled in short trenches than in long ones.

Small amounts of celery may be stored in cellars, in boxes a foot wide and a foot deep, with damp sand in the bottom. No soil is needed between the plants. The coolest and darkest part of the cellar is best for storage.

Diseases – Celery diseases are preventable and insect attacks are few. For blight, kainite is recommended, both in the seedbed and open field. For rust, the Bordeaux mixture is advised. Hollow-stemmed or pithy celery is the result of poor stock or improper soil, and can be avoided by the use of more manure and more water.

New Process – The method of growing celery in highly enriched soil, with plants set 6 or 8 inches apart both ways, is quite feasible. The plants stand so close as to blanch each other to some extent, but the system has never attracted general favor. A great deal of water is required. Cultivation is possible only when the plants are small.

WATERCRESS

Watercress, a vegetable closely allied to several other edible cresses, is used in very large quantities in all city restaurants. It is a much-esteemed winter relish, and is mostly served with every one of the thousands of beefsteak orders daily filled in the great eating houses and lunch rooms. The demand for it seems to be on the increase.

Fig. 111. Watercress.

Watercress is of the easiest culture. It can be grown in the soil of a forcing house under glass, and is extensively produced in this way by market gardeners.

The cheapest method is to grow it in running water, preferably near a spring head; and many such situations are available to farmers. Flat beds, made of loam, gravel, or sand, covered with 3 or 4 inches of warm, spring water, will yield great quantities of water cress in early spring; and the use of a few sash will keep the cress in growth during the winter. The cress should be cut frequently, as the young shoots are most succulent and tender.

For market purposes the water cress is tied in bunches, and retailed at from 3 to 10 cents per bunch, or packed in pint boxes, leaves uppermost, and retailed for about 10 cents per box. These are winter and early spring prices. Water cress culture is profitable in favored locations.

CUCUMBER

The cucumber market is not easily over-supplied, but the pickling tub should stand ready to receive all cucumbers not sold in a fresh condition.

For field culture, good ground must be selected, and marked out with a plow, 4 × 4 feet; or, a little wider, if the soil is strong. At least one shovelful of well-rotted manure is dropped in every hill, and mixed with the soil, and a dozen seeds planted, to be thinned out finally to three or four plants. It is better to have extra plants, on account of the attacks of the striped beetle.

The cucumber belongs to a botanic family that is naturally tender, and the seeds should not be sown until the soil is quite warm. For farm work, the planting season is the latter part of May and the whole of June; and even July is a suitable month, if the soil can be irrigated. It will require two pounds of seed for an acre.

The variety sown should depend on the purpose in view; but in all commercial operations, well-known and thoroughly tested sorts should be chosen. Shallow cultivation is recommended.

If an early market is to be supplied with cucumbers, the seeds may be started under glass, on bits of inverted sod or in small boxes, and set in the open ground on the arrival of settled warm weather; but the farmer will usually find it most profitable to sow the seeds where the plants are to remain.

The most serious enemy of the cucumber vine is the striped beetle, which attacks the young plant and frequently ruins it. The remedy is air-slaked lime, or soot, or sifted coal ashes, or wood ashes diluted with dry road dust. The best preventive is salt or kainite, used in the hills. The true plan is to have strong, vigorous plants, which, as a rule, will resist and outgrow the striped beetle, and be not greatly injured by its attacks. There is a blight that sometimes destroys the cucumber vine, apparently the result of weakness following a prolonged drought.

The vine of the cucumber must be kept in vigorous growth, not only by cultivation and a sufficient water-supply, but also by care in removing all the fruit as soon as formed, for, if the seeds be permitted to mature, the vine will quickly perish. It is the purpose of the vine's existence to produce ripe seeds, and it will make repeated and long-continued efforts to accomplish this end. In gathering the cucumbers, it is important to avoid injuring the vine. Some growers use a knife; others break the stem by a dexterous twist, without injuring the vine in the least.

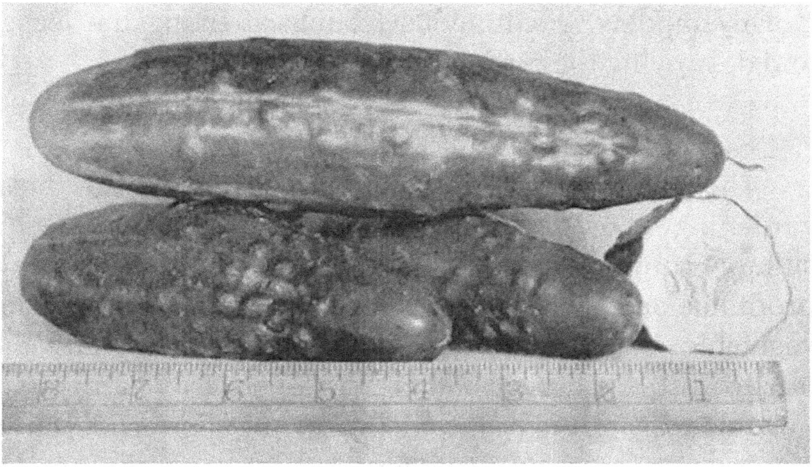

Fig. 112. Perfected Jersey Pickle Cucumber.

It requires 300 cucumbers (more or less) of fair pickling size to make a bushel, and it is estimated that an acre will produce from 100 to 200 bushels, or even more. When the pickles are pulled while quite small, the number runs up to 125,000 per acre; and the pickle factories in some cases make their estimates on a yield of 75,000 per acre. The price is variable, but often quite profitable.

Cucumber – For planting in the South to ship to Northern markets use Improved Arlington White Spine. Giant of Pera is a fine table sort. For pickling, plant the Perfected Jersey Pickle.

Downy Mildew – A disease that lately threatened to destroy the business of growing pickles in New Jersey and elsewhere, the downy mildew of the cucumber, can be fully overcome by spraying the vines with Bordeaux mixture. It requires six or seven applications, at intervals of a week or ten days, to conquer this comparatively new disease. Downy mildew is a fungous trouble affecting the leaves and destroying the further usefulness of the vine.

EGG PLANT

The advisability of growing eggplants in farm gardening operations is a question of location. On a suitable soil, near a good market, the operation will be a profitable one, if rightly managed. The eggplant is a tender vegetable, botanically allied to both the tomato and the potato, but less hardy than either, especially when young. For this reason it is best to delay sowing the seed, even in hot-beds, until cold weather is past, for the tender seedlings never fully recover from a chill or set-back. Indeed, for the farm gardener the month of May is early enough to sow the seed under glass, for this plant grows with great rapidity in a warm soil, and May-sown seed not infrequently yields plants that outstrip those sown a full month earlier.

The eggplant demands a richer soil than either the potato or tomato. It also asks for more water. It is a rank feeder. A good stimulant, if rotted manure cannot be had, is nitrate of soda at the rate of 400 pounds to the acre.

The farm gardener will do well to consider his market before engaging in the production of the eggplant on an extensive scale, for it is a perishable product. It bears shipment well, but its use is mainly limited to consumption while fresh.

Fig. 113. New Jersey Improved Large Purple Smooth Stem Eggplant.

It may command a very high price at some seasons of the year and at other times be practically unsalable at any price, owing to an over-supply.

If egg-plant seed be sown under glass in early May, and carefully protected against cool weather (especially at night), the young plants will be ready to transplant before the end of the month and large enough for the open field in June. They should be set in rows 4 feet apart, and about 3 feet apart in the row. Set at these distances, an acre of ground would accommodate about 3,500 plants.

The enemy of the egg plant, in growth, is the potato bug, which must be hand-picked or poisoned. There is a rot that causes the fruit to drop from the stem before reaching maturity. This rot is a fungus, and the Bordeaux mixture is recommended for it. The blight that sometimes affects the foliage is in part at least caused by cold weather, and for this there is no remedy, except late planting.

Every healthy plant should produce from two to six or more full-sized fruits, and it is therefore easy to calculate that an acre's product under favorable circumstances may be very large.

Egg Plant – There is nothing equal to the New Jersey Improved Large Purple Smooth Stem for the use of farm gardeners.

Fig. 114. New Imperial, or Long Standing Kale.

KALE OR BORECOLE

Kale, of which there are many varieties, is a headless cabbage, closely allied to such vegetables as Brussels sprouts, collards, etc.

It is one of the most hardy of vegetables, and in this latitude it will live over winter in the open ground, with only straw or litter as a protection.

If cut for use when frozen it should be thawed out in cold water.

The kales are among the most delicately flavored cabbages.

Some of them are of such ornamental shape as to be full worthy of cultivation for decorative purposes. The height varies from 1 to 2 feet, and the colors include both greens, dark purples and intermediate shades.

Kale demands a rich, deep soil. The seed should be sown in a border or seed-bed, and transplanted to the open field and set in rows, after the manner of cabbage. It is largely and profitably grown in the South for shipment to the great Northern markets.

Where farmers are situated near centers of population where kale is in demand, its culture will be found profitable, as it requires even less labor than cabbage. It is planted both in spring and autumn. The former crop is for autumn consumption and the latter crop is carried over winter after the manner of spinach, protected by a light covering of some sort of litter.

Kale – For the South, we recommend Extra Dwarf Green Curled Scotch; for the North, New Imperial.

Fig.115. Basket of lettuce.

LETTUCE

In some sections, especially in the South, lettuce can be grown with profit by farm gardeners. Depending on the latitude, the seed may be planted from autumn until spring. The plants are usually sheltered and headed under glass, or under muslin-covered sash, and are sent North in ventilated barrels.

The lettuce is naturally a cool-weather plant, and its culture is easy. The seed is cheap and it germinates quickly. Well-grown lettuce always commands good prices. It is usual to start the seeds in a border or under a frame, and to prick out the plants into more roomy quarters as soon as they are large enough to handle. In a few weeks after transplanting, in good growing weather, they are headed ready for market. Good soil, abundance of moisture and free ventilation are essentials in lettuce production.

In some parts of the North lettuce culture would be found profitable by farmers in the summer season, for there are varieties well adapted to high temperature, provided good soil and sufficient water be furnished. There is not a month in the year when lettuce is not demanded for use in salads, and this demand is likely to increase.

Lettuce – For the South, we especially recommend Reichner's Early White Butter, Big Boston and New Treasure; for the North, New Sensation, Mammoth Salamander and Hornberger's Dutch Butter.

Fig. 116. New Black-eyed Susan Watermelon.

MELONS

Melon culture belongs on the farm rather than in the small market garden, on account of the large space occupied by the growing vines. An acre of ground will accommodate only about 450 watermelon hills (at 10 feet each way) or about 1,200 muskmelon or cantaloupe hills (6 feet each way), and hence the necessity for large areas of ground for the cultivation of these crops.

The requirements of the various melons are quite similar. Broken sod ground or any green crop turned down favors their growth, and well-rotted stable manure in the hill is the best known stimulant. All the melons are tender, and are suited only to warm-weather growth, and this fact must be remembered in sowing the seed. Light alluvial soil near rivers or streams is adapted to melon growth, and many an old meadow now weedy and unprofitable might be used to advantage for one of these crops.

The Watermelon – For cash-producing purposes the best watermelon is a large one, with a hard rind. It must have a dark pink or red center and must be a good shipper. It should weigh thirty to forty pounds, and there should be 900 to 1,000 first-class melons to the acre.

The best melon for family use or for a strictly retail trade is a medium-sized variety, which has a thin rind, pink or red flesh and extra sweetness, weighing from twenty to thirty pounds.

The preparation of the ground has already been suggested. Two shovels of manure should go into each hill. The planting date is May in this latitude; or as soon as the ground is thoroughly warm. Four pounds of seed per acre will be required. But one plant per hill is allowed to grow. The end of the main shoots should be pinched off, to encourage branching and flowering.

Fig. 117. Johnson's Dixie Watermelon.

Cultivation should be thorough. Fungous diseases can be controlled by means of the Bordeaux mixture, except that it is difficult to reach the under side of the leaves. To prevent sunburn on melons, some growers sow buckwheat when the vines are in blossom, and thus secure a partial shade by the time the fruit is large enough to be injured by the sun. Generally, no protection is necessary.

Water Melons – For shipping – Johnson's Dixie, Blue Gem, Duke Jones, Sweet Heart. For home market Black-Eyed Susan, Florida Favorite, Kentucky Wonder, McIver's Wonderful Sugar.

Citron – This small round melon is cultivated in all respects as the watermelon, but being smaller the hills may be closer. It is used in making preserves. The name citron is frequently applied to certain of the cantaloupes.

Fig. 118. McCleary's Improved Early
Jenny Lind Muskmelon.

Cantaloupes or Muskmelons – It is a matter of choice whether the green-fleshed or red-fleshed sorts are grown; or whether the variety be large or small. The sorts covered with strongly webbed or netted markings are in high favor for shipping to distant points, as they carry well. Flavor is in part at least a matter of temperature and sunshine. Cantaloupes may be nicely ripened by removing them from the vines and storing in dry, warm rooms.

The usual planting distance is from 4½ to 6 feet, in hills containing rotted manure. Compost, made of hen manure, is sometimes used in the hill, well mixed with the soil. Good cantaloupes are always in active demand.

Musk Melons – Early sorts for shipping – McCleary's Improved Jenny Lind, Netted Beauty, The Captain, Champion Market, Improved Netted Gem, Anne Arundel. Late sorts – The Princess, Superb, etc.

Enemies – In addition to the fungous diseases of the watermelon and cantaloupe, which are best treated with Bordeaux mixture, all melons are sometimes badly troubled with an aphis called the melon louse. The remedy is whale-oil soap – a pound in six gallons of water; or kerosene emulsion.

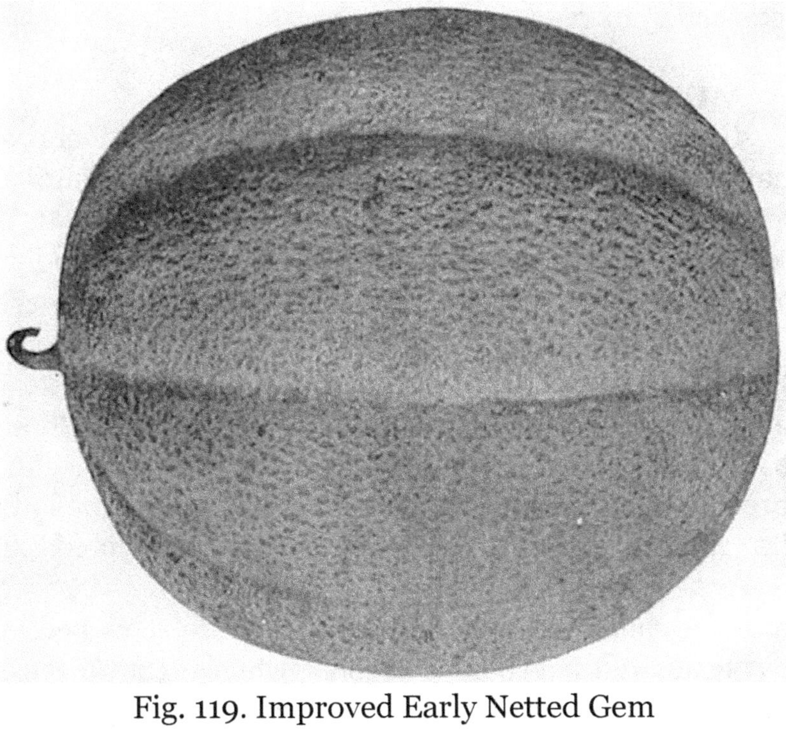

Fig. 119. Improved Early Netted Gem Muskmelon (Rose Gem Strain).

The latter is made by dissolving half a pound of soft soap in one gallon of water; then adding two gallons of kerosene, churning violently; then diluting with ten or twelve gallons of water. This emulsion is put upon the melon vines in the form of a spray, and is one of the best insecticides known. It is to be used on all sucking insects, like lice and squash bugs. Biting insects are easily killed with Paris green – one pound in 100 pounds of flour or plaster, or in 150 gallons of water.

Where the land is suited to melon culture, in any part of the country, the farm gardener will find no more satisfactory or remunerative crop.

MUSHROOMS

Under certain favored circumstances the mushroom may be grown as a farm gardener's crop. The requisites are horse manure and a dark cellar, cave or vault. If the manure be available and a suitable apartment at hand, the growing of mushrooms may be taken up for winter work.

There are many ways of growing mushrooms, and they can be produced in any situation where a steady temperature of 60° can be maintained. A simple method is to prepare a bed consisting of horse manure and loam, three parts by measure of the former and one of the latter, the manure having been somewhat fermented and sweetened by allowing it to heat and turning it several times. A compact bed a foot deep is made. This bed will first heat and then cool. As it cools, when at 80° or 85° an inch below the surface, bits of brick spawn the size of a hen's egg are inserted about 9 inches apart.

Fig. 120. A Bed of Mushrooms from English Milltrack Spawn.

The bed must not be immediately covered, or the temperature will rise sufficiently to kill the spawn. In ten days, more or less, as shown by a thermometer, this danger will be past, and the bed should receive a coating of good loam an inch deep. No water is to be applied until after the bed is in full bearing.

It is assumed that the temperature of the room or cellar has been uniformly 60°, day and night; that the bed has not been made where it could become water-soaked; that it is sufficiently moist, yet not wet; and that no draft of air has passed over the surface in a way either to reduce the temperature of the bed itself or to dry the soil upon the surface. If these conditions cannot be maintained, either by a specially favorable place or by means of covering the bed with litter, it is better to let mushrooms alone.

The crop should appear in six or eight weeks, and should last two months, the total product being from one-half to one pound per square foot. The cash price is from 50 to 75 cents per pound in the large cities; and the crop is sufficiently profitable to warrant the losses that beginners so commonly experience. These losses are the result of carelessness or ignorance in the matter of details.

The usual sources of failure are poorly prepared beds, the medium being either too wet or too dry; frequent changes of temperature; improper use of water; and, lastly, poor or stale spawn.

Mushrooms are packed in small baskets lined with paper, and carefully covered to prevent evaporation. A five-pound package is a favorite shipping size.

Fig. 121. Several of the most Popular American Onions.

ONIONS

The onion is a national crop; as widely though not

quite as extensively grown as the potato. It is available as a money crop for the farm gardener.

Choice of Soil – Heavy, stiff clay land is to be avoided. Sand and gravel dry out too quickly. Stony land renders good culture difficult. The best soil for onions is a deep, rich, mellow loam. Soils that afford natural advantages for irrigation should not be overlooked, as the rainfall is often lacking when greatly needed.

Fertilizers – Onion culture demands high manuring. No amount of rotted stable manure is likely to be excessive. A ton per acre of high-grade, complete fertilizer is not too much, if moisture can be supplied. Hen manure is a good top dressing for onion-beds, furnishing the needed nitrogen. Nitrate of soda is a good source of nitrogen, if nitrogen must be purchased. The clovers and other leguminous crops yield the cheapest nitrogen. Wood ashes, kainite, etc., furnish potash. Either ground bone or acid phosphate will give the needed phosphoric acid. An analysis of the onion shows that it carries away fertility in just about the proportions furnished by stable manure.

It is a singular fact that onions can be grown year after year on the same ground, if well manured. Rotation is necessary only in case of the occurrence of disease or insect attack. The onion loves cool weather.

Planting – To grow onion sets, the seed is sown in close rows, at the rate of from fifty to sixty pounds per acre. To grow large onions direct from seed, five pounds of seed per acre will be required. To plant a field with onion sets will require twelve to fifteen bushels per acre, according to size of the set.

An onion set is merely an immature bulb. Sets vary

from the size of a large pea up to that of a walnut. When the seed is sown thickly the bulbs have no chance to grow, and the summer weather quickly ripens the tops, completely suspending the growth of the bulb. In some parts of the country onion sets cannot be grown with profit, as the tops refuse to die and the bulbs or sets do not ripen properly.

In nearly all parts of the United States onions can be grown direct from the seed the first year; especially from seed grown around Philadelphia, which is earlier than Western-grown. It is quite customary in the South to sow onion seed in late summer or autumn; in August or September. This will give early spring onions of marketable size. In the North, within quite recent years, it has become the practice to sow onion seed in frames, in fall or early spring, and transplant the young onions to the open ground. This is sometimes spoken of as the new onion culture.

Onion sets or young plants should be placed 3 or 4 inches apart, in rows a foot apart, if to be cultivated by hand; the rows farther apart if for horse work.

The onion is hardy. Many varieties will live in the open ground over winter, if covered (at the North) with light litter. It is in this way that shoots for bunching are obtained early in the spring.

The seed should be sown for sets when the apple is in bloom. Sets may be put into the ground earlier; in fact, as soon as the ground can be worked. The set should not produce seed the first year, though it often does so. It should, on the contrary, grow to the size of say 3 inches, and then ripen for winter storage. Excessively large onions are not desirable. To hasten maturity, the tops may be broken down or the roots may be cut by running a knife or sharp plow or cultivator along one side of the row.

The onion, under favorable circumstances, will produce a crop of 800 bushels (fifty-six pounds to the bushel) per acre; though 500 bushels is nearer the average product.

Fig. 122. Weeding a Field of Onion Sets on our Bucks County Seed Farm near Philadelphia.

Storage – The storage of onions and onion sets is simple. The bulbs should first be ripened on the ground, by a brief exposure to wind and sun. This completes the wilting of the tops. They should then be spread out on ventilated trays or racks, or a few inches in depth on a floor, in a dry, shady place, where the air is good, preferably a loft; not a damp cellar. Freezing will not injure them, but they must not be handled when they begin to thaw, or they will rot. They must not be bruised during the operation of gathering or during the process of storage.

A popular and excellent method of wintering onions in cold climates is to spread straw to the depth of 18 inches on a dry floor or scaffold, and put on a layer of onions from 6 inches to a foot deep, and cover with 2 feet of straw. This will not always prevent freezing, but it checks all sudden changes.

Onions not fully cured should never be kept in barrels, but spread out so as to be perfectly ventilated. Onion sets shrink greatly in storage; sometimes as much as one-half between fall and spring.

Varieties – There are many varieties of onions, some of American and some of foreign origin. The former are better keepers, but the latter are of milder flavor. The American sorts (Danvers, Southport Globe varieties, Wethersfield, Extra Early Red, Silver Skin, Strasburg, etc.) are usually considered to be the most profitable; but the foreign kinds (Prize Taker, Prize Winner, Pearl, Bermuda, Giant Rocca, Victoria, etc.) are profitable in those parts of the country where soil and climate warrant their growth from seed in a single season.

The so-called tree onion is a perennial, of American origin, living out over winter. It is sometimes called Egyptian or top onion. It produces bulbs or sets at the top of the seed-stalk.

The potato or multiplier onion divides its large bulb into numerous small ones, which in turn produce large onions the next year.

Onions – For farm gardeners' purposes, we especially

recommend Philadelphia Yellow Globe Danvers, Mammoth Yellow Prizetaker, White Prize Winner. Earliest Onions are – Extra Early Red Globe Danvers, American Extra Early White Pearl, Rhode Island Yellow Cracker. The best for sets – Extra Early Red, Philadelphia Yellow Dutch and White Silver Skin.

Diseases and Enemies – To prevent maggot, the use of kainite is recommended; 600 pounds per acre. For onion smut, which may in part be cured by the kainite, the best-known remedy is a change of soil. Thrip, which causes the cuticle of the leaves to become covered with whitish or yellowish spots, is best treated by means of kerosene emulsion, used as a spray. The onion fly may, in part, at least, be abated by the use of equal parts of wood ashes and land plaster dusted very thoroughly on the young plants. Stiff-necked onions, often called stags, are the result either of improper growth or poor stock. They are sometimes planted in autumn for use as scallions (scullions) the following spring.

Marketing – Onions are sometimes sold in the open field; a good plan when a fair price can be secured. After curing, as already described, they are usually sold by the bushel or barrel. They are always in demand, as the onion is a standard article of human food.

However, in the green state they are sold either by measure, by the bunch, or by the rope. The latter method consists in tying the onions along wisps of straw.

Scallions – No small amount of money is expended by housekeepers in the early spring markets for scallions (scullions), or bunched onion shoots. These tender shoots are washed, tied and sold for 3 to 5 cents per bunch, retail, or half those figures wholesale. Scallions are produced from either sets or large onions planted the preceding autumn, and sheltered either by frames or litter, so as to encourage early spring growth.

PEAS

It will require one and one-half to two bushels of peas to seed an acre, and no crop finds a more ready sale than fresh peas in the summer and autumn markets. Farmers who are near centers of population, or who enjoy good shipping facilities, will find peas a quick money crop.

Any good soil will produce a crop of this excellent vegetable, but it must not be assumed because the pea is a legume, with nitrogen-collecting roots, that it will not well repay the application of manure to the soil. Peas and beans need less assistance than some other things, but they give good returns for the application of rotted manure or artificial fertilizer.

The seed should be put into the ground in early spring, as soon as the soil is dry enough to receive it, beginning with the smooth, extra-early sorts, which are more hardy than the wrinkled varieties. A little subsequent frost will do no harm.

The smooth, early sorts should be sown in rows, about 3 feet apart, the intermediate or half-dwarf sorts in rows 4 feet apart, and the tall, late varieties, in rows 5 feet apart.

In field operations no sticks are used, and large pickings are taken even from the tall-growing vines while sprawling upon the ground; and the labor is vastly less where no sticks are employed.

The early peas should stand closer in the rows than the

later and larger sorts. The Extra Early kinds mature in fifty to fifty-five days from germination; the intermediate kinds in sixty-five to seventy days, and the tall and late kinds in seventy-five to eighty days. For autumn planting, the extra early varieties are used, and are planted until sixty days before frost.

Fig. 123. Plant of New Giant Podded Marrow Pea.

Mildew is a field enemy of the pea, resulting from

unfavorable weather. The weevil often attacks the seed, but does not injure it for market purposes.

The canning of green peas is now an industry of enormous extent in America. The peas are shelled and sorted by machinery, and thousands of bushels are annually disposed of in this manner.

RHUBARB

In some parts of the United States rhubarb or pie plant is grown in very considerable quantities for market purposes, and with profit. Its culture is extremely simple. It is merely necessary to plant seed or roots, and to have the plants about 4 feet apart each way in a permanent bed. The plant is a perennial, lasting for many years. It is a rank feeder, and the more manure given it, the larger and more succulent will be the young shoots. The roots should be divided every five years, as they finally become too large. The demand for rhubarb continues through the spring and into summer, and large quantities are canned for pie-making. Five leaf stalks make a large bunch.

RADISH

Farmers who retail their produce should raise radishes. Rich ground and abundant moisture are the requisites for quick growth, and upon quick growth depends good quality. Slow-growing radishes are hot and pithy. The early sorts are best for spring, but the so-called summer radishes are best for warm weather, as they are not so liable as the early kinds to become pithy. Enormous quantities of winter radishes are grown in autumn, for use and sale during the winter months. They are kept in sand, like other roots.

The early kinds mature in twenty to twenty-five days from sowing. Nitrate of soda in small quantities is one of the best known stimulants. Rotted stable manure is good, but hog manure and night soil are not in favor among radish growers, tending to produce insect attacks. The free use of lime, salt or kainite is recommended as a preventive against insects. Sometimes it is necessary to avoid manure of any kind, on account of maggots, depending wholly on artificial fertilizers. As a last resort the radish-bed must be removed to new ground, as the maggot renders radishes wholly unsalable.

The green seed pods of radishes are sometimes used for pickling. The plant is closely related to the mustard.

It is wrong to wait for radishes to grow large (except the winter sorts), as they are sweetest and most succulent when comparatively small. Crisp, sweet radishes always command ready money.

Fig. 124. Olive Scarlet, the Earliest Radish.

Radish – Early, for the South – Scarlet Turnip White Tipped, Olive Scarlet, Philadelphia Gardeners' Long Scarlet. Summer radishes – Red and White Chartier, White Strasburg, Improved Yellow Summer Turnip. All seasons, radishes that are equally good for summer or winter – New Celestial, New Round Scarlet China. For winter use only – China Rose.

SPINACH

Spinach is grown for its leaves, which are cooked in winter and spring for use as "greens." The leaf is sweet and palatable even when raw, but it is always stewed for table purposes. It is a cool weather plant, almost perfectly hardy. It may be sown in spring, for immediate use, or in the autumn for fall cutting, or for carrying over winter.

Fig. 125. Plants and Roots of Parisian Long Standing Spinach.

It is of the easiest culture, requiring ten or twelve pounds of seed per acre, either broadcasted or sown in rows. In small gardens it is usually grown in rows, but in open field culture it is more commonly broadcasted. Patches of many acres in extent are seen near the large cities.

It is also grown quite extensively in some parts of the South for shipment to Northern markets during January and February.

Blight is the main enemy. The remedy is removal to another soil.

Of spinach there are many types; some smooth and some with savoy or wrinkled leaves. The property of standing a long time before going to seed is desirable, especially when sown in the spring, as it increases the length of the cutting season.

At the North a slight protection of litter or straw is necessary in winter.

South of latitude of Washington no protection is needed. Spinach is cut even when frozen; in fact, at any time when there is no snow on the ground. By throwing it into cold water it quickly thaws, and affords a palatable and healthful food in midwinter.

The dead or yellow leaves should be removed before sending it to market, and if carefully prepared it has an attractive green appearance during cold weather when other vegetables are scarce.

The winter crop is larger than any other, but much is also grown for spring sales. It is admirably adapted to farm culture.

Spinach – For spring planting, we recommend Parisian Long Standing; for autumn, American Savoy or Bloomsdale.

Fig. 126. Plant of New Hardy Bush or Vineless Sweet Potato.

SWEET POTATO

The cultivation of the sweet potato affords profitable employment to thousands of American farmers. It is pre-eminently a farmer's crop, on account of the ground space occupied. It demands a light or sandy soil, well drained and well manured. It has wonderful drought-resisting qualities; though, on the other hand, it is quite unable to withstand continued cold, wet weather. Its territorial range may be said to include nearly the whole of the United States, where the soil is suited to its growth, and it is even cultivated in Canada. It will in all probability increase in favor as it is better known and the manner of preserving or storing it is better understood.

We recommend and endorse the Hardy Bush or Vineless Sweet Potato.

Fertilizers – There is wide diversity of practice in the matter of enriching the land for sweet potatoes, and most of the standard manures are used, either in one place or another. There seems to be an almost universal endorsement of well-rotted stable manure, and next in favor is wood ashes. High-grade fertilizer of any kind, thoroughly incorporated with the soil, may be used.

Young Plants – Sweet potatoes are propagated by sprouts obtained by laying tubers on their sides, not touching each other, covered with soil, in specially prepared heated beds. These sprouts produce abundant rootlets while still attached to the parent tuber, and by pulling them with care, great numbers of young plants can be obtained. A second and even a third crop of young plants may be pulled from the same tubers. In the South no artificial heat is needed.

Growing the Slips or Sprouts as Practiced in New Jersey – The fire-bed, so-called, is quite generally used in Southern New Jersey for obtaining slips or sprouts for spring planting. It is necessary to have bottom heat and a uniform temperature of about 70°.

The fire-bed consists essentially of a pit about 15 by 50 feet in size. It is floored with boards laid upon cross pieces. Beneath the boards there is an air chamber. On top of the boards the bed is made. At one end is a furnace, with flues running out into the air space beneath the bed, but not reaching the chimney or smoke-pipe at the opposite end of the bed. At the hottest end of the bed the soil is over 6 inches deep. At the cool end a depth of 6 inches is quite sufficient. The whole bed is covered either with canvas muslin or with glass sashes, there being a ridge pole above the bed, running lengthwise with it, thus giving a double pitch to muslin or to glass.

After the soil has been heated somewhat, the tubers are laid on the bed, about an inch apart, and covered with about 3 inches of good soil, and the soil, in turn, covered with leaves or hay, to increase the warmth of the bed. In a week, more or less, the sprouts will show above the surface of the soil, when the leaves or hay must be removed.

The object in not connecting the flues from the furnace with the chimney is to economize heat. The air chamber under the entire bed becomes evenly heated, and the smoke escapes finally by the chimney. This chimney may be made of wood, and a height of 8 or 10 feet will afford ample draft. Either wood or coal may be burned, but preferably wood.

The planting distance in the field is about 3 feet by 2, the young plants being set upon ridges. It requires about 9,000 plants to the acre. The work must not be done until the ground is warm. The crop is ready in from sixty to ninety days.

Cultivation – Shallow cultivation is all that is

required. The vines at the North are not permitted to take root along their length, but in the South they are sometimes allowed to do so, and additional tubers thus secured. At the North the vines are lifted and turned, to clear the way for the cultivator and to prevent rooting.

Enemies – Black rot is one of the worst of sweet potato diseases. Stem rot is another serious enemy. The best treatment for these and other fungous troubles is prevention, and the best prevention is a healthy soil. It is, therefore, best to go to new land occasionally.

Harvesting – The common practice is to plow the sweet potatoes out of the ground just after the first frost has touched the vines. The tubers must be exposed to the air for a time, and partially dried. They are prepared for market, if wanted immediately, by rubbing off the soil and sorting into two sizes.

Storage – At the South one of the several methods of winter storage is to build a light wooden flue of lattice work, and pack about it a conical-shaped heap containing about forty or fifty bushels of sweet potatoes. Straw is used as a covering, with earth upon the straw, the earth to be increased as the weather becomes colder. Over the entire heap a rough shed is erected to turn the rain. The top of the flue or ventilator is closed with straw in really cold weather. The spot must be a dry one. The New Jersey sweet potato house is a stone building, say 16 × 18 feet on the inside, with walls 10 feet high, and a good roof. The building is half under ground, and the earth is banked up around it. There is a passage way through the center, and the bins for the sweet potatoes are 6 to 8 feet square and 8 to 10 feet deep. There is a door on the south side, with window above, and a stove is placed inside the building, for use when required. The walls are plastered, and the under side of the roof is also covered with lath and plaster, and the place is thoroughly weather-proof. A house of this kind will afford storage room for 3,000 or more bushels of sweet potatoes, and will keep them in excellent condition, if all details receive proper attention. The requirements for successful storage are that the tubers shall not be too hot, nor too cold, nor too wet, and that sudden changes of temperature shall be avoided. The sweet potato crop may be said to vary from 100 to 150 bushels per acre, under ordinary management, with higher results under good conditions.

CHAPTER XXVIII

Poultry

Hens are the most numerous and profitable, and the most generally useful of the feathered tribe. The hen has the same predisposition for laying eggs that the cow has for secreting milk. Some breeds are better adapted for this object than others: but all, given the proper food and circumstances, will produce a reasonable quantity of eggs.

The *egg* consists of three distinct parts; the shell, the white, and the yolk. A good-sized egg will weigh 1,000 grains, of which about 107 are shell, 604 are white, and 289 are yolk. Of the shell, 97 per cent is carbonate of lime, 1 per cent phosphate of lime and magnesia, and 2 per cent albumen. The white consists of 12 per cent of albumen, 2.7 of mucus, 0.3 of salts, and 85 of water. The yolk has about 17.4 per cent of albumen, 28.6 of yellow oil, 54 of water, with a trace of sulfur and phosphorus.

To produce the largest number of good eggs, several conditions are important; and they must especially have an abundance of the right kind of food. This is the most readily obtained in part from animal food. In warm weather, when they have a free range, they can generally supply their wants in the abundance of insects, earthworms, and other animal matters within their reach. The large proportion of albumen contained in their eggs, requires that much of their food should be highly nitrogenized, and when they cannot procure this in animal matter, it must be given in grains containing it.

If to the usual qualities of hens, a breed of peculiar

elegance, of graceful form, and beautiful plumage, be added, together with entire adaptation to the economical purposes required, good layers and good carcass, we have a combination of utility, luxury, and taste in this bird, which should commend them as general favorites. They can everywhere be kept with advantage, except in dense cities. A hen that costs a shilling or two, if provided with a suitable range, will consume 30 or 40 cents worth of food, and produce from 80 to 150 eggs per annum, worth three or four times the cost of feed and attention.

THE FOOD

Chicken feed may consist of different kinds of grain, either broken, ground, or cooked; roots, and especially boiled potatoes, are nutritious and economical; green herbage as clover and most of the grasses, chickweed, lettuce, cabbage, etc., will supply them with much of their food, if fresh and tender.

Though not absolutely essential to them, yet nothing contributes so much to their laying, as unsalted animal food. This is a natural aliment, as is shown by the avidity with which they pounce on every fly, insect, or earthworm which comes within their reach. It would not of course pay to supply them with valuable flesh, but the blood and offal of the slaughterhouses, refuse meat of all kinds, and especially the scraps or cracklings to be had at the inciters' shops, after soaking for a few hours in warm water, is one of the best and most economical kinds of food. Such with boiled meal is a very fattening food. Grain is at all times best for them when cooked, as they will lay more, fatten quicker, and eat much less when fed to them in this state;

and it may be thus used unground, with the same advantage to the fowls as if first crushed, as their digestive organs are certain to extract the whole nutriment. All grain is good for them, including millet, rice, the oleaginous seeds, as the sun-flower, flax, hemp, etc. It is always better to afford them a variety of grains where they can procure them at their option, and select as their appetite craves.

They are also fond of milk, and especially when it has become curdled; and indeed scarcely any edible escapes their notice. They carefully pick up most of the waste garbage around the premises, and glean much of their subsistence from what would otherwise become offensive; and by their destruction of innumerable insects and worms, they render great assistance to the gardener. Of course their ever-busy propensity for scratching, is indiscriminately indulged just after the seeds have been sown and while the plants are young, which renders it necessary that they be confined in some close yard for a time; yet this should be as capacious as possible.

Water should be supplied at all times within reach of the poultry.

Their food is better when given to them warm, not hot, and there should always be a supply before them to prevent gorging. It is better to be placed on shelves or suspended boxes or hoppers, which are variously and cheaply constructed, to keep it clean and out of the reach of rats. Besides their food, hens ought to be at all times abundantly supplied with clean water, egg or pounded oyster shells, old mortar or slacked lime. If not allowed to run at large, where they can help themselves, they must also be furnished with gravel to assist their digestion; and a box or bed of ashes, sand, and dust, is equally essential to roll in for the purpose of ridding themselves of vermin.

THE HEN HOUSE

Housing for chickens may be constructed in various ways to suit the wishes of the owner, and when tastefully built it is an ornament to the premises, It should be perfectly dry throughout, properly lighted, and capable of being made tight and warm in winter, yet afford all the ventilation desirable at any season. In this, arrange the nests in boxes on the sides, in such a manner as to humor the instinct of the hen for concealment when she resorts to them. When desirable to set the hen, these nests may be so placed as to shut out the others, yet open into another yard or beyond the enclosure, so that they can take an occasional stroll and help themselves to food, &c. This prevents other hens laying in their nests, while setting; and it may be easily managed, by having their boxes placed on the wall of the building, with a moveable door made to open on either side at pleasure. Hens will lay equally well without a nest-egg, but when broken up, they ramble off and form new nests, if they are not confined. They will lay if kept from the cock, but it is doubtful if they will thus yield as many eggs. Hens disposed to set at improper times, should be dismissed from the common yard, so as to be out of reach of the nests, and plentifully fed till weaned from this inclination.

CHAPTER XXIX

Dairying

Quick observation and sound judgment are important qualities in a dairyman. These qualities are not always acquired by long experience, but are oftener the generous gifts of nature. Hence, it frequently happens that men of quick discernment step into a new business and achieve success where others have met only years of failure.

PASTURES

Sweet pastures, with a variety of nutritious grasses growing in them, are essentials to success in dairying – especially in butter making–in summer. Bitter and other bad-flavored weeds must be avoided, as they flavor both the milk and the product manufactured from it. The cows must not be worried, nor overworked in rambling over poor pastures to get sufficient food.

WATER

Plenty of clean water must be conveniently at hand for the cows to drink. The water must be sweet and clean. Abundance of such water is more essential in the pasture – for the cows to drink while secreting milk that contains 87 per cent of water – than it is in the daily barn, where a small amount of water will answer.

FEEDING

There is more to feeding cattle than throwing out coarse fodder and hay. A thorough knowledge of feeding requires a knowledge of physiology and biology, with the chemical composition and nutritive qualities of the different kinds of food. Added to this must be the practical knowledge gained by observation of the effects of the different foods on different animals under various conditions.

It is safe to always feed cotton seed meal, bran, or linseed cake with corn fodder, or fodder corn, or ensilage. And it will always be found to work well if corn meal is fed with clover hay. Corn ensilage with clover hay will constitute a proper feed. To avoid waste, and secure the best results, we must learn to balance the nitrogenous and carbonaceous foods. Our greatest difficulty in feeding, as in manuring the soil, is to secure enough of the nitrogenous elements. These are what we have mainly to look out for, the carbonaceous foods usually being over abundant.

WINTER FOOD

In winter, the food must be in proper condition, properly balanced between the nitrogenous and carbonaceous materials, and in full supply – all the cow can digest and assimilate. At least one ration a day should include sweet ensilage, roots, or other succulent food, to aid in the separation of the butter from the cream by action of the churn, it having been shown that all dry feed not only reduces the flow of milk, but makes churning slow and difficult, leaving a large percentage of fat in the buttermilk.

In a state of nature, roaming free, animals select and balance their rations according to the cravings of appetite.

But when domesticated, they have no such freedom of choice, except perhaps in a few of the summer months. In winter, they must take what is given to them. It is our duty, therefore, to give their food a proper balance of elements as far as possible; and in thus conforming to the laws of nature, we shall find both the greatest economy and the greatest profit.

Summer pasture, composed of mixed grasses, makes the best food for all kinds of stock. Meadow hay, cut at the right time and properly cured – provided there is a mixture of grasses – makes a proper food for winter; but even this needs to be accompanied by roots, ensilage or something of a juicy nature, as a relish, if for nothing else, and as an aid to digestion.

THE STABLE

While in stable, the cow must also have plenty of pure air and sweet water, and not be chilled in obtaining either. Without pure air, the cow becomes debilitated and diseased, and the milk impure and unwholesome. Impure water both taints and corrupts the product. A proper temperature – certainly above freezing – should be kept up. Remember, the cow standing still cannot resist cold as she could if she were free to move about. It is cheaper to build warm stables – always providing for perfect ventilation, the air coming in at the head and passing off in the rear of the cow – and even to resort to artificial heating, than to compel the cow to burn an extra amount of carbonaceous food in her system to keep up the temperature of her body. Not only is fuel cheaper than food, but also the system of the cow cannot devote to producing milk the energy that is expending in consuming fat to maintain a proper amount of vital heat.

SHELTER

Proper shelter in summer, from the scorching rays of the mid-day sun, and from beating storms and winds, is necessary. This should be easily accessible. Especially in early spring and late fall do the animals suffer severely from exposure to the cold winds and storms of all hours in the twenty-four.

DAIRY BARN

Every dairyman should have a good dairy barn. It should be so constructed that the temperature may at all times be kept under perfect control. There should be no surrounding cesspools or other sources of taint, and the ventilation should be free without perceptible drafts or currents of air.

CLEANLINESS

Cleanliness everywhere and at all times is an absolute necessity. There is not the least danger of being too clean. The dairy barn should not only look clean, but also be, as it were, fragrant with neatness and sweetness. And it is all-important that the clothing and person should be clean and neat to a fault. A sweet temper, even is no drawback.

THE HERD

Of course, a thorough knowledge of the business must be had or be acquired. The proper selection or rearing of dairy stock is essential to success. The cow should not only be a good milker, but also give milk suited to the line of dairying pursued.

If cheese making is the object, there must be a large flow of milk rich in casein. In butter making, a large flow of milk is not essential, but there must be a large percentage of fat in it.

And the breeding must be such as to keep up the status of the herd. Some depend on purchasing cows, and exercise great care and judgment in so doing. In exceptional cases, a herd may be kept up in this way. But somebody must breed and rear good cows, or soon none can be had at any price. As a rule, it may be said to be the duty of every dairyman to breed from the best blood obtainable, and to rear the heifer calves from his best cows.

It should be the ambition of every dairyman to constantly improve the value of his herd, and to make progress in every department of his dairy, while improving the quality of his product.

DAIRY STOCK

There is no more important subject connected with the dairy than that of the selection and rearing of stock.

The selection of a herd is a matter of both knowledge and judgment – knowledge of the characteristics of breeds and of the requisites of a good dairy cow, and judgment as to whether the individual cow in question possesses these characteristics and requisites.

We will give some of the generally acknowledged characteristics of the different breeds, first indicating, as far as we can in words, some of the points of a good dairy cow.

POINTS OF A MILKER

The dairy cow should be deep and broad through the flank – deeper and broader than through the shoulders – but must have a comparatively large chest, giving capacity of lungs and stomach, for she must have good digestive powers and inhale plenty of fresh air. Her hips should be broad, setting her thighs well apart, and her thighs should be rather thin. This gives space for a large udder, which is indispensable, for it is unreasonable to expect a large flow of milk from an udder of small capacity.

The udder should be soft and fleshless when empty, and extend high up in the rear. It should also extend well forward, and from it should extend further forward large, protruding milk-veins. If they are double and are crooked and knotty, all the better. These veins carry off the blood after it has passed through the udder and performed its part in elaborating milk, and their size indicates the amount of blood employed, and by inference the amount of milk secreted. So the escutcheon, which should extend out on the thighs and run with even edges and unbroken surface up to or near the vulva, is supposed to be some indication of the extent of the arterial system that contributes blood for the elaboration of milk.

The neck should be slender, taper and thin, the horns small and slender, the face dishing or flat, the eyes wide apart and mild and intelligent in expression, the muzzle broad when viewed from the front but thin when viewed from the side, and the lips thick and strong.

A long, slender tail is indicative of good breeding.

A yellow skin, or one which secretes an oily yellow scurf – especially seen in the ears, along the back and at the end of the tail – is considered a sign of milk rich in fat. The skin should be soft and pliable, the hair fine, and the coat glossy.

Viewed from the front, the general shape of the cow should be a little wedging – thinner in front and thicker in the rear. Viewed from the side, the cow should taper from rear to front, with the upper and lower lines generally straight, with little or no, slope from the rump to the tail.

THE JERSEY

The Jersey is a fawn-like, beautiful animal, with a mild eye and intelligent face, but usually has a quite angular frame, as a consequence of her excessive dairy qualities. She is rather tender, and cannot bear the exposure and harsh treatment that some of the breeds can.

Solid colors and black muzzles are the fashion in Jerseys.

The Jersey gives a small mess of milk, but it is very rich in fat, and the fat readily separates from the milk, leaving the skim milk very poor. But, considering size, the Jersey is conceded to yield more butter than any other breed. The cream globules are very large and very uniform in size. Hence, they not only readily separate from the milk, but churn easily.

The Jersey is out of the question as a beef animal, there is so little of her carcass. But lack of beef qualities we do not consider a very serious objection in a dairy cow. We get our profit from her in the dairy. We cannot reasonably expect all good qualities in one animal or one breed. Nature is nowhere thus partial in her gifts.

THE GUERNSEY

These animals have proved very satisfactory. They are pale red or buff red and white. The colors are about in equal proportions, though the red may predominate. They are considerably larger than the Jersey and possess all the good qualities of the latter. The Guernsey is just as beautiful in face and form as the Jersey, and we think rather hardier and possesses more capacity. For all practical purposes, we should be inclined to give preference to the Guernsey, which has no rival in her line, except the Jersey.

This breed can lay claim to some beef qualities, because of its size. It is a popular favorite in the butter dairy and as a family cow.

HEREFORDS

The Herefords are having quite a boom in the West, but not as dairy stock, but as superior for beef. They have no wide use as dairy purposes.

MILKING

It is a comparatively easy operation to milk, if one knows how. The process is about as simple as that of Columbus in making an egg stand on end, but it requires skill, practice and a muscular hand to do it well.

Grasping the teat so as to fill it with milk, and then tighten the thumb and fore finger so as to prevent a return of the milk to the udder as the rest of the fingers are gently but firmly closed, so as to give a downward pressure and expel the milk, is not likely to be done by the novice the first time trying. But ordinarily, the performance of this operation is soon achieved by any one who wishes to learn.

Still there is a great difference in milkers, as well as in cows, the man or woman with a good grip in the hand having decidedly the advantage, both as regards ease and expedition – and it is quite important that the milk should all be quickly and continuously drawn from the cow after the milking is begun, and while the cow is in the mood of "giving down."

KEEP QUIET

Milking should be done in a quiet and orderly manner. If a cow is suddenly disturbed, so as to get excited, or gets tired and out of patience, the flow of milk may be prematurely stopped. Anything that irritates a cow, while being milked, reduces both quality and quantity.

If this disturbance is continued from time to time, the effect will be to permanently lessen the flow, or "dry up" the cow.

Treat the cow very kindly and gently, so as to gain her confidence, and be as careful as possible not to hurt her teats by unnecessarily tearing open any cracks there may be, or pinching any warts, and be sure to not dig your finger-nails into the teats.

REGULARITY

It is a good plan to milk cows regularly in the same order, taking the same one first, and winding up with the same one every time.

Regularity of hour in commencing the milking of the herd is an advantage, in securing the best results, since animals as well as men are greatly the creatures of habit, and when the time comes around the cow will desire to be milked and all the functions of her system will concur in this desire.

KEEP OUT THE DIRT

Great care should be taken to keep out all hairs, dirt and filth of every kind. The indispensable necessity for clean utensils has already been mentioned. Filth from this source will not only affect odor and flavor, but is quite likely to contain the germs of ferment which will multiply in the milk and cause disastrous results.

With a clean can, clean pails and clean hands, begin the task of milking by brushing off all loose materials from the cow's side that may rattle down into the pail, carefully brush and clean the udder and teats, and then place the pail between your knees in a way to prevent the cow putting her foot into it, or upsetting it, if she should move about nervously, or be suddenly startled – which should not be permitted if it is possible to avoid it.

LET OUT THE COWS

As fast as milked, it is best to let the cows go. This gives more room, reduces the generation of heat in the stable or milking place, and lessens the amount of droppings and consequent bad odors rising from them. Those left will soon understand this and not get uneasy.

A LICK OF MEAL

If the cows have been prepared for milking by giving them a lick of meal, or a little dry hay, when they come into the stable, it will be found to have a good effect. It will also cultivate a willingness to come home at milking time and take their respective places in the stanchions. It pays to please and satisfy a cow.

CARE OF MILK

When the milking is over, the milk should be taken as directly to the place of manufacture as possible. If it must be kept over night, see that it is well stirred and properly cooled to 70 degrees Fahrenheit, before leaving it.

Do not put on a close cover, unless the milk is thoroughly cooled. It is far better to deliver it directly to the cheese or butter maker, who knows how to care for it, and has facilities for doing the work – or, at least, ought to have. Very much depends on having the milk delivered in good condition.

The next object is to preserve the milk in its best condition, all through the handling, in order to reach the best results. Milk is often spoiled in the handling. Hence care and judgment must be exercised to maintain the proper conditions to the end.

COMPOSITION OF MILK

Few understand the delicate and complex nature of milk. It is a compound of many ingredients; and if any one of these is disturbed, it affects the whole. Their union is very weak and unstable, and liable to be broken by many influences. To give a clearer idea of the composition of milk, we copy the following diagram, prepared by Dr. E. Lewis Sturtevant, Director of the New York Agricultural Experiment Station:

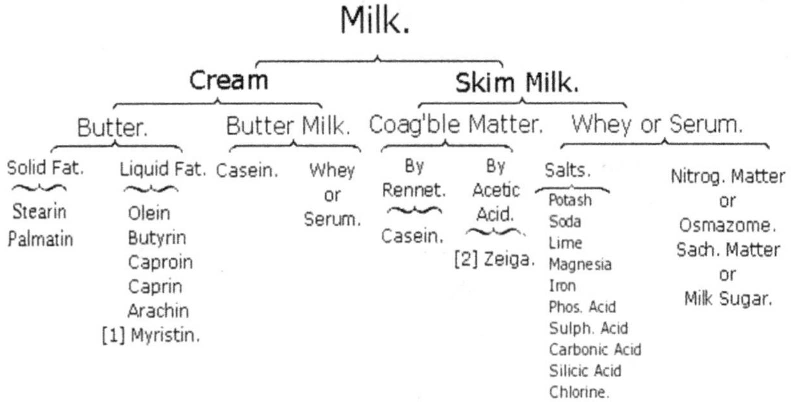
Milk.
Cream
Skim Milk.
Butter.
Butter Milk.
Coag'ble Matter.
Whey or Serum.
Solid Fat.
Stearin
Palmatin
Liquid Fat.
Olein
Butyrin
Caproin
Caprin
Arachin
[1] Myristin.
Casein.
Whey
or
Serum.
By
Rennet.
Casein.
By
Acetic
Acid.
[2] Zeiga.
Salts.
Potash
Soda
Lime
Magnesia
Iron
Phos. Acid
Sulph. Acid
Carbonic Acid
Silicic Acid
Chlorine.
Nitrog. Matter
or
Osmazome.
Sach. Matter
or
Milk Sugar.

[1] Includes, albumen and whatever else is coagulable by acetic acid.

[2] Not found in all milk.

Here are between twenty and thirty different constituents, in various proportions. Their combination is effected through the organism of the cow, the ultimate work being performed by the udder, where it is no sooner completed than reaction begins and change is the result.

❄ ❄ ❄

GLOSSARY

Acid, a chemical name given to many sour substances.

Albumen, a nitrogenous organic compound.

Albuminoid, a nitrogenous substance resembling albumen.

Ammonia, a gas containing nitrogen produced by the decay of organic matter.

Annual, a plant that lives only one year; corn and sunflower are examples.

Anther, the part of a stamen that bears the pollen.

Available, that which can be used.

Bacteria, very small plants, so small that they cannot be seen without the aid of a powerful microscope. They are sometimes called "germs." Some of them are beneficial, some do great harm and some produce disease.

Biennial, a plant that lives two years, usually producing seeds the second year.

Bordeaux mixture, a mixture of copper sulfate, lime and water used to prevent plant diseases. It was invented in Bordeaux, France.

Bud, an undeveloped branch.

Calyx, the outermost part of a flower.

Cambium, the active growing layer between the bark and the wood of a tree.

Capillary, Hair-like. A name given to very small spaces through which water flows by the force of capillary attraction.

Carbohydrate, an organic substance made of oxygen, hydrogen and carbon, but containing no nitrogen; cellulose or woody fiber, sugar, starch are examples.

Carbon, a chemical element. Charcoal is nearly pure carbon.

Carbonic acid gas, a gas consisting of carbon and oxygen. It is produced from the lungs of animals, and by the decay or burning of organic matter.

Catch crop, a crop growing during the interval between regular crops.

Cereal, a name given to the grain crops that are used for food.

Chlorophyll, the green matter in plants.

Commercial fertilizers, materials containing plant food that are bought and sold in the markets to improve the soil.

Compost, a mixture of decaying organic matter used

to enrich the soil.

Cross pollination, the pollination of a flower by pollen brought from some other flower.

Cover crop, a crop to cover the soil during the interval between regular corps.

Cultivator, a farm implement used to loosen the surface of the soil and to kill weeds after a crop has been planted.

Cutting, a part of a plant placed in moist soil, water or other medium with the object of its producing roots and making a new plant.

Dormant, said of plants when they are resting or inactive. Most plants are dormant during the winter season.

Drainage, the method by which surplus water is removed from the land.

Element, a substance that cannot be divided into simpler substances.

Fermentation, the process by which organic substances are broken down or changed and new substances formed.

Fertility, that state or condition of the soil that enables it to produce crops.

Fiber, long thread-like structure.

Flocculate, to make crumbly.

Free water, standing water or water that flows under the influence of gravity.

Function, the particular action of any part of an organism.

Furrow, the trench left by the plow.

Furrow slice, the strip of earth that is turned by the

plow.

Germinate, to sprout.

Grafting, the process of inserting a cion or bud in a stock plant.

Green manure crops, crops intended to be plowed under to improve the soil.

Harrow, an implement used to pulverize the surface of the soil.

Heavy soils, soils that are hard to work; stiff, cloddy soils.

Horticulture, that branch of agriculture that deals with the growing of fruits, vegetables, flowers and ornamental plants.

Humus, partially decayed animal and vegetable matter in the soil.

Hydrogen, a gaseous, chemical element, one of the constituents of water.

Inter-tillage, tillage between plants.

Irrigation, the practice of supplying plants with water by artificial means.

Kainite, a potash salt used in making fertilizer.

Kernel, a single seed or grain.

Leaching, passing through and going off in drainage water.

Legume, a plant belonging to the bean, pea and clover family.

Light soils, soils which are loose and open and easy to work.

Loam, a mixture of sand, clay and organic matter.

Mold board, the curved part of the plow that turns the furrow slice.

Mulch, a covering on the soil. It may be of straw, leaves, pulverized soil or other material.

Nectar, a sweet substance in flowers from which bees make honey.

Nitrate, a soluble form of nitrogen.

Nitrification, the changing of nitrogen into a nitrate.

Nitrogen, a gas forming four-fifths of the air. Nitrogen is a very necessary food of plants.

Organic matter, substances produced by the growth of plants and animals.

Osmosis, the movement of fluids through membranes or thin partitions.

Oxygen, a gas that forms one-fifth of the air. Its presence is necessary to the life of all green plants and all animals.

Ovary, the part of the pistil that bears the developing seeds.

Ovule, an immature seed in the ovary.

Perennial, living through several years.

Phosphoric acid, an important plant food found in phosphates.

Pistil, the part of the flower that produces seeds.

Propagate, to increase in number.

Pollen, the powdery substance produced by stamens.

Pollination, the transfer of pollen from stamens to pistils.

Potash, an important plant food.

Pruning, removing parts of a plant for the good of what remains.

Retentive, holding, retaining, said of soil that holds water.

Reverted, said of phosphoric acid in the process of becoming insoluble.

Rotation of crops, a change of crops in regular order.

Sap, the juice or liquid contents of plants.

Seed bed, the earth in which seeds are sown.

Seedling, a young plant just from the seed. Also a plant raised from a seed in distinction from one produced from a graft or a cutting.

Sepal, one of the parts of the calyx.

Slip, a cutting placed in water or moist soil or other substance to produce roots and form a new plant.

Soil, that part of the earth's crust into which plants send their roots for food and water.

Stamen, that part of a flower that bears the pollen.

Stigma, the part of the pistil that receives the pollen.

Stomata, breathing pores in plants.

Subsoil, that part of the soil that lies beneath the soil that is worked with the tillage tools.

Sap root, a main root that runs straight down into the soil.

Tillage, stirring the soil.

Transpiration, the giving off of water from plants.

Tubercle, a small nodular growth on the roots of plants.

Under drainage, drainage from below.

Vitality of seeds, the ability of seeds to grow.

Basics of ...
A Basic Knowledge Imprint of
ABSOLUTELY AMAZING eBOOKS

AbsolutelyAmazingEbooks.com
or AA-eBooks.com

www.ingramcontent.com/pod-product-compliance
Lightning Source LLC
Chambersburg PA
CBHW071954270326
41928CB00009B/1435
* 9 7 8 0 6 9 2 3 6 1 9 8 6 *